TO PLEASE
THE CARIBOU

TO PLEASE THE CARIBOU

PAINTED CARIBOU-SKIN COATS WORN BY THE NASKAPI, MONTAGNAIS, AND CREE HUNTERS OF THE QUEBEC-LABRADOR PENINSULA

DOROTHY K. BURNHAM

With a foreword by
Adrian Tanner

ROM
ROYAL ONTARIO MUSEUM
TORONTO

Royal Ontario Museum
Publications in Art and Archaeology

The Royal Ontario Museum publishes numbered
series in the fields of art and archaeology, as well as
unnumbered monographs. All manuscripts
considered for publication are subject to the editorial
policies of the Royal Ontario Museum, and to review
by persons outside the Museum staff who are
authorities in the particular field involved.

Art and Archaeology Editorial Board
Editor: B. Stephen
Associate Editor: J. McDonald
Associate Editor: J. Holmes

Manuscript Editor: B. Stephen

The Royal Ontario Museum is an agency of the Ontario
Ministry of Culture and Communications.

Page 103: No. 8. Canadian Ethnology Service,
Canadian Museum of Civilization, Hull-Ottawa (III B
589). See pp. 130–133.

Canadian Cataloguing in Publication Data
Burnham, Dorothy K., 1911–
    To please the caribou

Includes bibliographical references and index.
ISBN 0-88854-399-9 (bound) ISBN 0-88854-396-4 (pbk.)

1. Indians of North America - Quebec (Province) -
Costume and adornment. 2. Indians of North America -
Quebec (Province) - Hunting. 3. Caribou hunting -
Quebec (Province). 4. Coats. I. Royal Ontario
Museum. II. Title.

E78.Q3B87 1992   971.4′1   C91-095593-X

Editing: Andrea Gallagher Ellis, Barbara Ibronyi
Design: Virginia Morin
Production: Lorna Hawrysh

Typesetting by Compeer Typographic Services
Film by Goody Color Separation (Scanner) Ltd.
Printed and bound in Hong Kong by Sheck Wah Tong
Printing Press Ltd.

CONTENTS

This book is dedicated to the memory of two
outstanding scholars who started me on this search
and supported me generously through its
early stages. Sadly, neither has lived to share
the joy of its completion.

Dr. Edward S. Rogers, former curator of
the Department of Ethnology, Royal Ontario Museum

Harold Burnham, former curator of
the Textile Department, Royal Ontario Museum,
my beloved husband and valued research partner

FOREWORD

I first met Dorothy Burnham a couple of years ago, when she came to St. John's to see the painted Naskapi coats in the Newfoundland Museum. She had by then examined most of the coats in museum collections worldwide. When she started talking about her research and her plans for a book, I was immediately captivated by what she had to say.

Although I am not a museum anthropologist, I had for years been aware that, despite the many Naskapi coats in Canadian museums, by far the majority of these amazing works of art were in collections in the United States and in Europe. They were effectively unavailable to most Canadians, including the aboriginal people.

This point was driven home to me when I worked for the Naskapi Band of Schefferville as a land claims negotiator in 1975. A group of elders visited the National Museum of Man in Ottawa (now the Canadian Museum of Civilization, Hull-Ottawa) and were shown the coats and other examples of Naskapi material culture held there. It was clear from their reactions that the coats brought to life for many of them an era that was almost lost. The previous century had been a very hard one for this group. They had suffered starvation due to a combination of the influence of fur traders and a decline in the caribou herds, followed by sickness and the final reluctant acceptance of settlement in a mining town.

By 1975, however, things were looking up; the caribou had returned, and the government was finally about to give the Naskapi of Schefferville not charity, but benefits in recognition of their legal rights. The museum visit contributed to the idea of a revival of self-sufficiency through craft production. No coats had been made for many years, and it was doubtful if anyone in the group who was still active enough to do the demanding work involved also still remembered the skills required. Most of the existing coats, as already noted, were permanently resident in distant museums, and no comprehensive book on the subject was then available.

As Dorothy spoke of her project I knew that here at last was someone, a real museum expert, who was about to produce the kind of illustrated study of the coats that was needed. Actually, as I was to

discover, she had done more. She had used her expertise in clothing and textiles to uncover a previously undiscovered link with European clothing styles, while at the same time confirming the essentially aboriginal cultural significance of the coats.

Dorothy Burnham acknowledges Dr. Edward S. Rogers as an important inspiration for the work, the result of which is the magnificent production now in your hands. Had he lived to see its completion, no doubt it would have been his honour, rather than mine, to write this foreword.

But then, this is not the first time I have followed in the footsteps of Ed Rogers. When I began field-work with the hunting groups of the Mistassini Cree in 1971, my task was made much easier by the fact that Ed had previously spent a year in the bush with a hunting group. Over the years he had maintained contact with his friends there, and my acceptance by the group was in no small measure due to my being able to say that I knew him.

I followed Ed Rogers in another sense, by quickly realizing that, in order to be fully understood, Mistassini culture must be viewed in the context of the whole Quebec-Labrador peninsula. The peninsula is an intriguing area in which to study aboriginal cultures. Looking at the main inhabitants, people of the Northern Algonquian group, one continually encounters important details of cultural variation among sub-regions, even among individuals within a sub-region, but against a background of underlying cultural unity. There are many dimensions to this diversity-within-unity of the East Cree–Montagnais–Naskapi cultural continuum. The archaeological record provides one perspective. The differences of dialect within their common language is another. The variations in ritual, belief, and mythology give us a third. And a fourth aspect, one which has so far been relatively neglected, is that of the material culture.

The material culture was not, I must hasten to add, overlooked by Ed Rogers. His important study of the contacts between the Inuit and the Indians of the Quebec-Labrador peninsula, for example, rests largely on the evidence of material culture (Edward S. Rogers, "The Eskimo and Indian," in *Le Nouveau-Québec: contribution à l'étude de l'occupation humaine,* edited by J. Malaurie and J. J. Rousseau, Bibliothèque arctique et antarctique 2 [Paris: Mouton, 1964]).

Many of the items of material culture — dwellings, clothing, tools — are still in use today and can be studied in the field, as shown, for example, in one of Ed's studies of the Mistassini (Edward S. Rogers, *The Material Culture of the Mistassini*, [Ottawa: National Museum of Canada, 1967]). This study shows that, among the Quebec-Labrador Algonquians, even the most utilitarian objects include an important artistic or decorated component, for which there is usually a particular spiritual association.

This symbolic aspect is important even in the case of an obviously "borrowed" item. For example, many hunters of the Quebec-Labrador peninsula today use a canvas "prospector"-style tent, with a ridge pole and side walls, but for a door they add a flap of canvas, which is usually decorated. The significance of this decoration becomes more clear when we understand that the doorway always faces the rising sun, that several other forms of ritual symbolic display are made in the direction of the rising sun, that a painted "ceremonial hide" is ritually displayed just for the moment the sun breaks the horizon on a clear day, and that the direction of the rising sun is associated with renewal of life.

It would appear that in the past the artistic/spiritual aspect of material culture was even more important than it is today. While the Quebec-Labrador Indians were forced by their nomadic lifestyle to leave their worn-out artifacts behind at their abandoned campsites, where, being made of wood, skin, and bone, they usually quickly disintegrated, a significant number of items have nevertheless accumulated over the historical period in private and museum collections, more by accident than design. Of these, the painted skin coats probably had the greatest importance to the culture. Their universal aesthetic appeal ensured that many were obtained and carefully preserved by visitors. Their importance to us is all the greater today because such coats are now seldom made.

I was once asked to testify at the trial of a member of the Naskapi Band of Schefferville, Quebec, who was charged with hunting geese across the nearby border in Labrador. The border, which was established in 1927, has never been a boundary limiting the hunting activities of the Indians of the Quebec-Labrador peninsula. The accused's basis of defence was that his aboriginal rights in Labrador, including his right to hunt for food, had never been legally extinguished. Previous Canadian court decisions had established that, in order to show that there is an unextinguished aboriginal right, it is necessary to prove, among other things, that there is an "organized society" which has occupied a specific territory since before the establishment of colonial sovereignty.

During cross-examination it became clear that the prosecution wished to show that, since these Naskapi did not live in fixed settlements with permanent housing until 1954, they could not be said to have had an "organized society." This attitude seemed to me to be based on a European cultural perspective, which has difficulty in coming to terms with the reality of a nomadic form of land tenure.

Any organized society is based on a shared set of ideas, beliefs, rules, standards, and values, whether or not these are written down. The social organization of Northern Algonquians is based on an extensive kinship system and includes people who do not always live together, but are nevertheless all part of a vast social network, one which in Quebec-Labrador spans the peninsula. The system had to be flexible, as people continually moved between residential groupings.

The coats in this book show clear evidence of collective artistry and skill, even if they are not the product of a group of artisans in constant contact with one another. The shared values evident in these coats are in no way diminished if part of the inspiration came from the dress of the exotic strangers whom the makers saw when they visited the trading posts. The coats show that, however scattered were the Naskapi, they had, collectively, a shared artistic, religious, and moral tradition. The coats in museum collections are material evidence of this organized tradition, one that spanned at least hundreds of years without decline. They are the expression of the art and the religion of a society, even if it was one whose members travelled constantly and moved residence every few weeks.

The maintenance of their artistic and religious tradition was not without costs for a nomadic people. I recall that when I accompanied a hunting group to the bush, as soon as we set up our first winter camp, we had to make a trip to the place where the group had stored its hunting equipment at the end of the previous winter, to bring some of these items to the new camp. Three of us went on snowshoes, two days there, two days back, hauling loaded toboggans behind us. We had nothing to eat but bannock, as we had not killed any game yet, and we were in too much of a hurry to hunt on the way. On the way there the weather was cold, and the three of us slept under the stars around a fire, sharing a single rabbit-skin blanket. On the return it warmed up, and we slogged and sweated through clinging, wet snow. On the last day I almost passed out with exhaustion.

When we finally arrived in camp, the first thing the hunting group leader wanted from our load was not the traps or the tin stove, but the drum. This instrument, its caribou-skin heads decorated with painted red dots, is used by hunters to accompany the hunting songs, which come to them through spiritual revelation and which they sing in the evening to the spirits, in the belief that this will enable them to have success in the hunt. This religious practice is considered as essential as any other aspect of hunting.

No doubt the making and use of painted coats also involved particular difficulties for a nomadic people: the best caribou skins had to be bleached white, or smoked perfectly evenly; it was sometimes necessary to travel far to gather the various materials needed for the different coloured paints; the cutting and stitching was done with great care; and the coats had to be stored and transported when not in use.

The Naskapi had good reason to consider these efforts worthwhile, and with this book we are finally able to benefit from the trouble that went into maintaining their rich cultural tradition.

Adrian Tanner
Memorial University
St. John's, Newfoundland
March 1990

PREFACE

I begin this preface by saying that I am not an ethnologist. Many years ago I was curator of the Textile Department at the Royal Ontario Museum. The collections of that department cut across curatorial boundaries, embracing not only the usual European silk weaving, lace, embroideries, and fashion costumes, but textiles and costumes of all kinds from all over the world. In the early days of my career, when staff at the museum was very limited, I had to cover all those aspects of the field. As time went on and the staff grew, some specialization was possible, and my interests became centred on North America and more particularly on things Canadian—native Canadian as well as Euro-Canadian.

It was an awareness of my particular background and experience, which combined the history of fashion costume with an abiding interest in native skills, that prompted Dr. Edward S. Rogers, then curator of the Royal Ontario Museum's Department of Ethnology, to ask me a simple question. It concerned a matter that ethnologists had been arguing about for years: Do the Naskapi hunting coats show European influence? That was about thirty years ago, and it is high time that I give my answer. Yes, they definitely do show the influence of the changing fashions in European men's coats. But it is not quite as simple and straightforward a matter as that. The following pages will explain why I think that, although there is strong European influence, it is a surface influence affecting only the visual impact of the coat, not its essence.

This has never been a research project that could take priority over more current concerns. It has been a "fun" project, to be taken up when time was available and reluctantly put aside when time was short, but over the years it has involved much pleasurable reading, seeing, drafting, photography, talking, and thinking!

The Royal Ontario Museum has an excellent Naskapi collection; it comprises fourteen men's coats, plus women's and children's garments and many smaller items, including the tools used for painting the skins. To get some idea of how to answer the question posed by Dr. Rogers, I started by carefully cataloguing the Royal Ontario Museum collection; this included making drawings of the way in which the caribou skins were cut to make the garments. The subject matter fascinated me. My husband, Harold Burnham, also a museum textile person, caught the virus from me, became deeply interested in the research, and took to looking for examples of the coats when he travelled to European museums on other business. The simple question, was there a European influence or not, was leading us into one of those morasses that museum researchers know well—our information was growing in quantity but was far too vague to provide useful conclusions.

These painted caribou-skin hunting coats are rare. Rather surprisingly, in spite of their rarity, they are quite well known. Museums fortunate enough to own one usually display it, for these coats are intriguing to the public and the ethnographic specialist alike. The coats have an arresting shape. On those from the early period, the workmanship is breathtaking, and even in those of later date the painted decoration is often exceptionally skilled, in both design and execution. Sadly, few of the coats that appear to be early in date are accompanied by verifiable histories. It has been necessary, therefore, to go to the coats themselves to see what they could tell—and they have spoken eloquently.

ACKNOWLEDGEMENTS

Firstly, my gratitude must be expressed for the help given by the two men to whose memory this book is dedicated, Dr. Edward S. Rogers and my husband, Harold B. Burnham, both of the Royal Ontario Museum. Then, I give many thanks to the other good friends in that institution who have supported, encouraged, and helped me during many years: in the Department of Ethnology, Dr. Trudy Nicks, Kenneth Lister, Helen Kilgour, Mary Hayes, Valerie Grant, and Arni Brownstone; in the Textile Department, Mary Holford and Judith Cselenyi; in the Department of Mammalogy, the late Dr. Randolph Peterson; in the Department of Botany, Deborah Metsger; in the Department of Vertebrate Palaeontology, Kevin Seymour; in Photography, William Robertson, Brian Boyle, Allan McColl, and Deirdre De Clara; the staff of the Library; and most importantly in Publication Services, to all those who have brought the confusion of my book into order: Hugh Porter and Lorna Hawrysh, who masterminded the production; Virginia Morin, for her sensitive design; Mary Terziano, whose sad death cut short her work on the editing; and Barbara Ibronyi and Andrea Gallagher Ellis, who picked up the editing and carried it through magnificently. A very special thanks must go to Mr. Edwin A. Goodman, former chairman of the Board of Trustees of the Royal Ontario Museum, and to other members of the board who privately funded my research visit to Germany in 1988.

To the staff of the Canadian Ethnology Service of the Canadian Museum of Civilization, Hull-Ottawa, I am most grateful for the warm welcome that always awaited me there and the help given, on more occasions than I can remember, by Judy Hall, Judy Thompson, Dennis Alsford, Ted Brasser, Kitty Glover, Glen Forster, and, in the picture archives, Chris Kirby.

In Ottawa I have also received great assistance at the National Archives, in both the Picture Division and the Archives Library; I am particularly grateful for the special help given by Edward H. Dahl of the Cartographic Division. My thanks go also to Dr. Ruth B. Phillips of Carleton University, for sharing her notes and photographs.

Elsewhere in Canada, much appreciated assistance was provided by Céline Saucier when I examined the coats at the Musée de la civilisation, Québec. Jane Sproull Thomson was most hospitable and helpful during my visits to the Newfoundland Museum in St. John's, and Colleen Lynch, also in St. John's, has helped with information concerning the Grenfell Mission. I would particularly like to thank Alika Podolinsky Webber and Ray Webber of Victoria, British Columbia, for information and photographs shared during our many years of contact.

I am most grateful to have been granted two three-week stays in the seclusion of the Leighton Artists' Colony at the School of Fine Arts in Banff, Alberta. The peace, quiet, and good care that enfolded me in that beautiful environment provided the opportunity to do many of the line drawings that illustrate details of the coats in this book.

In London, June Bedford's enthusiasm lifted my spirits, and Erroll Bedford's photography is much appreciated. In Edinburgh, the warm hospitality of Dale Idiens was a most welcome change for one travelling alone. Another person whose encouragement has meant much is Dr. James VanStone of the Field Museum of Natural History, Chicago.

Since this study has been under way for more than twenty-five years, it is now impossible to name all those who, during that long period, have given much appreciated help in a hundred different ways. But a very important group to whom personal thanks can be expressed are the curators and staff of the various museums that I have visited in Europe and the United States. They opened their display cases and storage cupboards and laid out before me the coats in their collections, making possible the detailed analyses necessary for the catalogue. In Austria: Museum für Völkerkunde, Vienna, Dr. Christian Feest and Dr. Peter. In Denmark: National Museum of Denmark, Copenhagen, Dr. Berete Due and Annie Eriksen. In England: City of Bristol Museum and Art Gallery, Sue Giles; British Museum, London, Jonathan King and Trudy Martin; Horniman Museum, London, Dr. Michael Hitchcock; Royal Artillery Institution, Woolwich, London, Brigadier K. A. Timbers, James Starr, and Alan Pardoe; Pitt Rivers Museum, Oxford, the late Geoffrey Turner and Linda Mowat. In France: Musée de l'Homme, Paris. In Germany: Museum für Völkerkunde, Berlin, Dr. Günther Hartmann and Herr Wedell; Museum für Völkerkunde, Frankfurt am Main, Dr. Mark Münzel and Mona Suhrbier; Deutsches Ledermuseum/Schuhmuseum, Offenbach am Main, Dr. Renate Wente-Lukas and Jutta Göpfrich. In the Netherlands: Rijksmuseum voor Volkenkunde, Leiden, Mr. Gressie. In Scotland: National Museums of Scotland, Edinburgh, Dale Idiens and Maureen Barry; Art Gallery and Museum, Kelvingrove, Glasgow, Helen Adamson; Hunterian Museum, The University, Glasgow, Dr. E. W. MacKie. In Switzerland: Indianer-Museum der Stadt Zürich, Dr. Hans Läng and Frau Christa Läng; Museum für Völkerkunde und Schweizerisches Museum für Volkskunde, Basel, Dr. Gerhard Baer, Dr. Seiler-Baldinger, Mr. Krehl, and Elizabeth Aeschler. In the United States: National Museum of Natural History, Smithsonian Institution, Washington, D.C., Dr. William Sturtevant and Dr. William Fitzhugh.

A very special expression of gratitude goes to Dr. Adrian Tanner of the Department of Anthropology, Memorial University, St. John's, Newfoundland, for writing the foreword to the book, for taking the time from his very busy life to read the manuscript carefully, and, from his knowledge of the native peoples of the Quebec-Labrador peninsula and their environment, for suggesting what he tactfully called minor changes. His recommendations have led to a considerable improvement of the text — but any errors are mine.

This book has been published with the help of a grant from the Social Science Federation of Canada, using funds provided by the Social Sciences and Humanities Research Council of Canada.

INTRODUCTION

Before discussion of the history and the making of these painted caribou-skin coats, their context in time and space should be outlined. The period of their use is quite long, well over two centuries; the earliest coats that have survived probably date from about 1700 and the latest from about 1930. The geographic area within which they were used is less easy to define. The Algonquian-speaking people, who wore the coats, inhabited the Quebec-Labrador peninsula, an enormous area that stretches from the St. Lawrence River north to Ungava Bay and from James Bay and Hudson Bay on the west to the Atlantic Coast on the east (Figure 1).[1] This vast section of northeastern Canada can be roughly divided into two ecological zones: boreal forest to the south and west, and tundra with open woodland to the north and east.[2] Within living memory the painted caribou-skin coats have been found in use only in the latter area where, well into this century, the native people lived a nomadic life, supported by fishing and hunting. Great herds of caribou provided the main source of food and clothing.

A number of apparently early coats have painting that is somewhat different from and much more meticulous than that on the known later northern coats. From this evidence it seems probable that at the end of the 17th century and during much of the 18th, painted caribou-skin coats were not confined to the northeastern part of the peninsula, but were made and worn as far south as the St. Lawrence River, as far west as Quebec City, and at least as far northwest as the Lake Mistassini area.[3] The well-known northern examples may simply be evidence of the survival of a custom that was much more widespread at an earlier date.

During this century the southern limit of the caribou has been from Lake Abitibi to Lac St-Jean and the Saguenay River,[4] but at the time of European contact and for some time afterwards the caribou had a much greater range, which extended well south of the St. Lawrence River.[5] It is therefore not surprising that caribou-skin garments were used in this larger and more southern area. Somewhat of a problem is presented by the fact that because caribou occur only in small groups in the boreal forest zone, not in large herds, they were probably never plentiful

enough to be the mainstay of life in the south and west, as they were in the north. We know that painted coats were used by the northern people to venerate the caribou. We do not know, and probably never will, whether the caribou ever held the same exalted place in the more southerly parts of its range. But the painted caribou-skin coats were, in all probability, made and worn at a comparatively early period in the south, and were cut and painted in much the same ways as the later, more northern examples (see Nos. 1–10).

The native peoples of the Quebec-Labrador peninsula have been recorded as Montagnais, Naskapi, Montagnais-Naskapi, and East Cree. There are varying opinions concerning the validity of these names,[6] but for the purpose of this historical study it seems wise to continue their use. In describing the coats, the term Montagnais has been applied to those that seem to be from the southern part of the area, East Cree to those from farther north and west, and Naskapi to those from the northeast. Montagnais-Naskapi has been used where the origin is probably borderline. Lucien Turner gives an alternative general term, "Nenenot," or "true people,"[7] and the modern name used by the people for themselves is "Innu."

As time went on, contact with Europeans, and especially with the fur traders, generated great and continuing changes, but in the northeast the caribou hunt remained an essential form of life support, and every means of ensuring a successful hunt, both mundane and magical, was undertaken. Hunting had to be approached with careful preparation, part of which was the making and wearing of a painted caribou-skin coat, both for the hunt itself and for a special feast that might be held beforehand.

Dreaming and drumming—reaching out for guidance to the spirit world—were very important in this culture. The men received instructions in their dreams about the motifs that would give them power when put on their hunting equipment, and the women then carried out the work, although it is not known how this partnership, combining the man's dream with the woman's creativity, was worked out. The motifs that were acceptable for use were not many. Twenty-one different elements found on

1

the coats are described in the Design Motifs section. Less than half of these might be considered of significance worthy of a hunter's dream. When the decoration of the coats is carefully analysed it seems likely that one or perhaps two main motifs were dictated by the man, while the rest was left up to the woman. The rhythms of the way the motifs are used are reminiscent of music. The layout used for the patterning is traditional and well defined. A theme is stated in the bottom border or at centre back, variations are played on that theme, a secondary theme may be introduced on the collar or to the sides, and then these main themes are decorated with lesser motifs, imaginatively varied and repeated to enrich the whole.

When the painted coats, with their elaborate designs, are considered in the context of the nomadic life of the caribou-hunting people, it seems

Figure 1.   Map of the Quebec-Labrador peninisula.

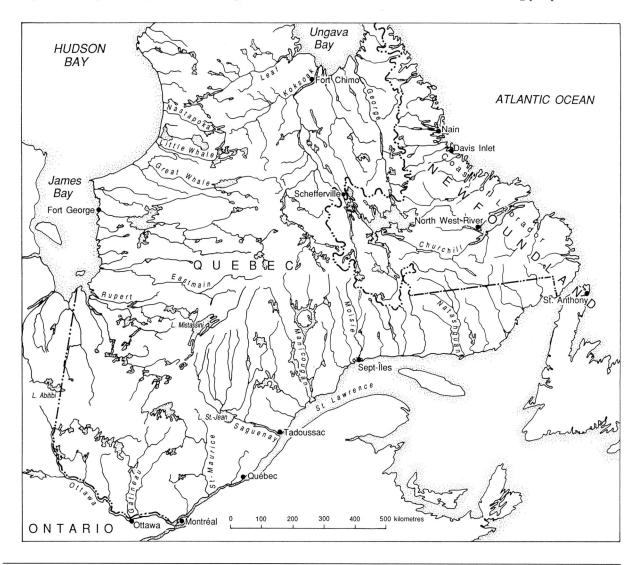

a miracle that, in spite of the well-recognized craft skills of many native women, this painting could be done without even a smooth drawing surface. What did the makers lay the skin on when they drew those firm and fine lines? This is not craft work on a small scale, it is a major art creation. It must not be forgotten that life largely depended on the success of the hunt. Hunting was a "holy" occupation,[8] and these coats could be considered to be holy vestments, one of the ritual elements that would ensure the success of the hunt. The hunters believed that the Lord of the Caribou[9] would send the animals out from the Magical Mountain where they were believed to live, and that the caribou would be pleased to give themselves to the hunters. The hunters would treat the slain caribou in a correct manner, so that their spirits could return to the Magical Mountain and be released again for a future hunt. This extreme simplification of a very complex set of beliefs and observances gives some indication of the reason for expending the time and effort necessary to create one of these special coats.[10]

As is true of so much of the skilled work done by native women in all parts of Canada, the best of it seems to date back to a time when the Christian missionaries had not yet managed to impose the concept of one man-one woman. In earlier days, not only could a good hunter afford to support more than one wife, he needed more than one to do the work of a good hunter's camp.[11] Where there were several wives, one with special skills could be released from cooking, caring for the children, chopping the firewood, and other chores, so that she could withdraw for however long it took to paint the coat that would ensure her husband's success on the next caribou hunt.

The population of the area was never large, so that even if each hunter had two new coats a year, one for the summer hunt and one for the winter hunt, the number of coats made over the years would not have been great, and the chances of destruction in use must always have been close to one hundred per cent. The reason that any of the coats have survived at all is that the magic power was considered to have gone out of them by the end of a year. The coat was then no longer of use to its owner and could be sold or traded to someone else.[12] What better souvenir of a tour of duty or a trip to Canada could there be than one of these magnificent garments.

Probably just as many furred winter coats were made as the light summer ones, but because caribou fur sheds readily, the winter coats were less attractive as souvenirs. No winter coats survive prior to those collected by Lucien Turner in the early 1880s. The coats that found their way to Europe with early travellers were usually placed in private collections and later acquired by various European museums, where they have been safely preserved. We are fortunate that not all of them left Canada and that some of those that were carried away have now been brought home.[13]

The research for this book started with the careful cataloguing of the Royal Ontario Museum's fourteen painted coats. Measured diagrams of the cut of each coat were made, as well as detailed descriptions and photographs. The same recording methods were used to describe coats held by other Canadian museums, and then, as a larger body of evidence became desirable, the effort was extended to museum collections in other countries. For publication purposes information had to be kept to a reasonable size, and with sixty examples it has been possible to present all the coats that appear to be early and all the coats that have histories or possible suggestions of histories in the middle period, plus a number of outstandingly beautiful examples that appear to fit with the datable items, and then to finish with a good series, mostly drawn from Canadian collections, of 20th-century material. The sixty coats presented here represent somewhat less than half of the known surviving examples;[14] most of those omitted are of late date and are similar to ones that are included, and would add little to this catalogue.

All available information that might concern the date of the making of a coat and its area or origin, even if nebulous and on its own unprovable, has been weighed and combined with known provenance in order to work out a logical development and place the sixty coats in sequence.

There are verifiable histories for most of the coats that have a date later than 1880. For earlier periods there are just enough coats with possible, or probable, histories to provide guideposts to which other, less definite information can be attached (Nos. 5, 9–10, 12, 18, 23, 28, 31, 33, 36, 39).

A very evident development in the painting style, concerning both the motifs used and the skill and complexity with which they were delineated, helps greatly in determining date. The fact that two distinct types of motifs were used, one based on a quadrate layout and the other on the double curve (see Design Motifs section), is useful for suggesting area of origin.

The making of measured diagrams, which give the exact shape of each coat, has been of great use in establishing the series. It has shown that there is continuous development in the cut of the coats, which, coupled with the evolution of the painting style, creates a sequence that roughly, but quite obviously, reflects the look or shape of contemporary European fashion.[15]

The first four coats in the series have painting that is probably of very early type. Their cut is comparatively straight, which fits with illustrations of European costume that could have been worn in Canada during the latter part of the 17th century (see Figure 7).[16]

The coats that follow the earliest ones in the series have skirts with a very marked flare, which echoes the shape of European men's coats of the late 17th to early 18th century (see Figures 8, 9). Strong, skilled painting with great variety in the way the double-curve motif is drawn characterizes this group.

As time went on, the cut slimmed down. The shape of coat No. 39, which dates from about 1840, is very like that of a coat on a military man of slightly later date (see Figure 14). Coats of this period are well made and well painted, but by this time the double-curve motif had assumed a standardized form, which was repeated and repeated with little variation.

Continuing further in the development, coats became straighter and shorter, not unlike contemporary *capot* styles (see Figure 15). With the introduction through trade of "laundry blue" in about the middle of the 19th century, the colour scheme changed; the subtle colours of the earlier period gave way to a strong blue used with an equally strong red (see Colours section). Skill in the layout of the design is still evident, but the painting is much coarser than on the earlier coats. Eventually, towards the very end of the period of their making, the coats came close in shape to that of an early 20th-century hunting jacket (see Figure 17).

HISTORY

Once the detailed analyses of the existing coats had been worked out as described in the Introduction, it became apparent that there was a sequence of style that followed the visual appearance of garments worn by Europeans in the areas where the painted caribou-skin coats originated. This helped with the dating of the existing coats, but did not provide a historical context. There is not much evidence concerning what was worn by the native people of the area at the time of contact and shortly afterwards. All that can be done is to present the few facts that are known.

Probably the most basic fact is that, as a rule, considerable common sense is used when a simple body-covering garment is made from a given material. Whether that material is cloth or skin, its size and shape are usually taken into account and used to the best possible advantage.[1] Cutting a coat shape from caribou skin makes no sense at all. Caribou skins are not very large, and to cover the body of a man two skins are required, one for the back and one for the front. It would be much more practical to make a garment that could be pulled over the head, like Athapaskan or Inuit clothing,[2] rather than to cut the front skin in half in order to make an open coat, which then has to be tied closed again. That practical considerations were not foremost strongly suggests that the very special cut of the painted caribou-skin coats is not indigenous to its most recent northern area of use. This does not necessarily mean that the use of the coat shape is based solely on the influence of European garments—there are other possibilities. During the period when the first coats in our series were made, the range of the caribou stretched well down to the St. Lawrence area, but moose were common there too. A coat shape is quite logical when cut from the skin of a moose, for a single skin is large enough to wrap around a man's body, starting and finishing with an opening at centre front. Comparatively early painted moose-skin coats of this type are well known, and this basic cut was also used farther west with buffalo skins. Figure 2 shows a moose-skin coat of about 1780 and the way it is cut.[3] All the maker had to do to shape the skin into a coat was to square off the irregular outlines and put two vertical slits in the upper edge to accommodate the insertion of sleeves. It seems more than possible that the coat shape initially used with caribou skin was borrowed from the area of the moose.

The evidence given by the first few coats in the catalogue series reinforces this possibility. To make coat No. 1, a large skin, in this case the skin of an exceptionally big male caribou, was cut in the same basic way as the moose-skin coat in Figure 2, except that the skirt part was enlarged by the insertion of gussets, a feature discussed later in this section. If the cuts of Nos. 1–2 are compared, the second coat shows the same influence but in a less obvious way. The sleeves are inserted into slashes in the top of the back; this coat was made from a caribou skin of normal size, and so the front sections had to be extended with pieces cut from another skin. The cut of coat No. 3 is the same as that of No. 2.[4] The similarities between the coats that we believe to be the earliest in our series and those made of moose skin reinforces the possibility that the coat idea moved north into caribou country from the more southerly moose country.

The north shore of the St. Lawrence River was an area in which French fashion ideas might be expected to be very strong during the 17th and 18th centuries. Various early French writers give useful information concerning the clothing that they saw on the native people of the area and, incidentally, suggest ways that their own clothing may have been influencing that of the native people.

At the beginning of the 17th century Champlain wrote: "The women make all the clothes, but not neatly enough to prevent one seeing the skin under the armpits; for they have not the skill to make them fit better."[5] Champlain apparently didn't quite understand what he was seeing and dismissed it as careless work, but his comment gives a vivid picture of the wearing of separate sleeves, which was customary with simple native costume in many parts of North America.[6] Later he noted: "Further they have a robe of the same fur, shaped like a cloak, which they wear in the Irish or Egyptian fashion, and sleeves which are tied behind by a cord."[7] Here he noted the use of separate sleeves, but his illustration of this passage, Figure 3, ignores them and shows a

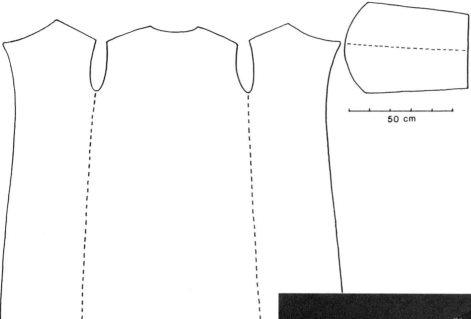

50 cm

Figure 2. Painted moose-skin coat, about 1780, probably from northern Ontario (Canadian Museum of Civilization, Hull-Ottawa, Speyer Collection, IIIx229, neg. 74-120), and diagram showing the cut of the coat.

very European-looking man wearing a knee-length coat with conventional set-in sleeves. Probably the illustrator didn't believe Champlain's words and simply drew his own version of a nice, warm, fur-lined coat. No skin coats contemporary with Champlain survive, but likely they would have been as described rather than as illustrated. A sleeveless moose-skin garment, similar in body cut to the one in Figure 2 but with separate sleeves, would come very close to Champlain's description of the cloak worn in, "Irish or Egyptian fashion," and would be just a little more untidy looking than the illustration.

Champlain also described the painted decoration: "They make bands in many ways, as they fancy, in places putting bands of red or brown paint amidst those of the glue which are always pale, and do not lose their markings however dirty they may get."[8] In the same passage he says that the women "are clad like the men except that they always gird up their robes, which hang down to the knee."

In early Canadian history there were other "fashion commentators." A particularly rich source of information is the *Jesuit Relations*, the fascinating letters that were sent back to France year after year to keep up interest in New France and to keep support coming for the Jesuits' missionary work there. Father Biard in Acadia in 1616 wrote: "They often curry both sides of elk skin, like our buff skin, then variegate it very prettily with paint put on in a lace-like pattern, and make gowns of it."[9] In the same letter he says that the native people wear French *capots*, and in the winter, bed-blankets. Imported goods were already supplanting the native garments.[10]

Biard's mention of the French *capot* is of consid-

Figure 3. Champlain's version of man wearing a native coat. From *Voyages de la Nouvelle France occidentale*, Samuel de Champlain, 1632. (National Archives of Canada, Library, Ottawa, C 103128)

erable interest, for it suggests a type of garment that may well have been an influence on the development of the painted caribou-skin coats. We do not know exactly how a 17th-century *capot* was cut, but it was a simple hooded coat and, as with heavy, warm topcoats from other countries, it was probably of a straight cut, based on the width of the available woven materials.[11] When the material was wide blanket cloth, as it often was, the cut was very close to the typical moose-skin cut. From the time of Biard these hooded woollen coats were basic winter wear in Canada and were used by voyageurs, habitants, the military, Hudson's Bay Company employees, and the native people. In Figure 4 this practical garment is worn by a late 17th-century fisherman in Newfoundland, and in Figure 5 by an early 19th-century man in Quebec.

Figure 4. Detail from an early map showing a fishing station in Newfoundland, with a European fisherman wearing a heavy, hooded coat. From *Amérique septentrionale et méridionale*, N. de Fer, Paris, 1698. (National Archives of Canada, Ottawa, NMC 26825)

Also in the *Jesuit Relations*, Father Paul LeJeune, when writing about the Montagnais with whom he spent the winter of 1634, said: "During the Winter all kinds of garments are appropriate to them, and all are common to both women and men, there being no difference at all in their clothes; anything is good provided it is warm."[12] In the same letter he mentioned separate sleeves and repeated: "Observe that there is no difference between the garments of a man and those of a woman."[13] LeJeune also gave a vivid description of more special costumes worn in Quebec City in 1637–1638:

The day of the glorious Assumption of the Virgin . . . Monsieur our Governor overlooked nothing of all the magnificence that could be displayed, to do honour to this procession. It was a beautiful sight to see a company of Savages marching behind the French, in their painted and figured robes, two by two, and very modestly.[14]

In spite of the "modesty" observed by LeJeune on this occasion the native people were obviously wearing their most magnificent garments in a very European way, formally and to impress the beholder.

These and other passages describe the dress of native people in the St. Lawrence and Acadian areas previous to the time when the earliest of the existing painted Montagnais-Naskapi coats were made. They record that painted skin garments, called robes, were of sufficient quality to be admired by the French. The use of separate sleeves is mentioned, and it is stated repeatedly that men and women dressed more or less alike. But none of this helps us to understand how it is that a strictly male garment, made of caribou skin and in the shape of an open coat, was in existence by about 1700.

Royal gifts suggest a possible origin. In the *Jesuit Relations* for 1639 there is an account of the son of a chief who returned from a visit to France with six magnificent suits, given to him by the king and queen. The recipient of the gift brought them to Quebec City for distribution. "There happened to be present, at the time, Huron, Algonquin and Montagnais savages."[15] Three of the suits remained with the man who had gone to France. The rest were given to other native men, but at the request of those who received them the suits were left in the care of the Jesuits, to be worn only when there was an important procession in honour of the king. These suits would have been very impressive, and the idea that special garments should be created and worn for the purpose of doing honour to someone important like the king . . . or for that matter, the caribou

Figure 5.   A Canadian man wearing a hooded *capot*. Detail from *Sketchbook I of Sempronius Stretton*, Quebec, 1805. (National Archives of Canada, Ottawa, C 14818)

. . . could well have germinated in this way. It is to be noted that it was to men only that the coats were given.

The giving of presentation coats was a custom that was kept up by the French and later by the English right into the 19th century. Wool broadcloth or silk coats, in the high fashion of Europe and often lavishly decorated, were bestowed as very special favours on important native men. A rare illustration, Figure 6, shows an Iroquois wearing a magnificent late 18th-century coat. He is from farther south than the Montagnais-Naskapi, but comparable coats were given in all areas.[16]

There is little to work with other than the factors described above—the basic moose-skin cut, the shape of the *capot*, French fashion, and particularly the possible influence of presentation coats—to

bridge the gap between the descriptions of skin robes worn by men and women alike during the first half of the 17th century and the appearance of the strictly male and very special painted caribou-skin coats by the end of that century. It is possible that there were earlier transition garments that have not survived, but the first coats that we know of, Nos. 1–4, may date from the very beginning of the use of this type of special garment. With the ten to twelve coats that follow next in the series after that first small group, certain aspects of the way the motifs are drawn, particularly the double curves, seem rather tentative compared with the almost routine later production. This suggests that the art form was still in a developmental stage. We assume, but we are not sure, that these early coats were used in the same way as the later examples, which are known

Figure 6. "Grand Chef de Guerriers Iroquois" wearing a presentation coat and medal, a tricorn hat, and a European linen shirt. From *Moeurs, loix et costumes des sauvages de Canada*, M. J. Grasset, Saint Sauveur, late 18th century. (National Archives of Canada, Library, Ottawa, C 106279)

to have been worn to influence the outcome of the caribou hunt.

Our coat series begins after a rather abrupt change in the shape of European men's clothing, which occurred about 1665. Bulky, knee-length trousers and short jackets went out of style and were replaced by slim, slightly fitted coats, long enough to cover narrowly cut knee breeches. This shape of coat, known as a *justaucorps*, was not only fashionable, it was also a practical garment and was in use in Canada during the latter part of the 17th century. There are no pictures to show what the native men looked like when wearing the painted coats of that early period, but Nos. 1–4 must have presented an outline quite close to the shape of the turn-of-the-century *justaucorps* (Figure 7), which has a cut somewhat modified from the earlier versions of the fashion, making the garment looser and more suitable for wear in the wilds of North America. Further development in men's fashions produced a silhouette fitted at the waist and with considerable flare to the skirts of the coat. This shape is seen in an illustration of Frenchmen from 1697 (Figure 8). A slightly later picture shows a Canadian man on snowshoes said to be going to war (Figure 9).[17] His coat also has a fitted waist and a flared skirt; the coats that follow coat No. 4 in the series reflect that shape.

We can make a well-based guess that the shape of the early coats mirrors the slim lines of the *justaucorps,* but when the extreme flare of a coat such as No. 11 is considered, the comparison with European fashion is obvious. It must be emphasized, however, that the influence of European fashion, although strong, was only visual. The shape of Montagnais-Naskapi coats followed the outlines of contemporary European styles, but they were not actually cut and made up in the same way as the European coats. When the cut of an everyday cloth coat of the mid 18th century (Figure 10)[18] is compared with the cuts of contemporary Montagnais-Naskapi coats, it is plain that, although the outline is similar, the parts that make up that outline are different. The European coat has an open vent in the back to make it suitable for wear while riding a horse, not a necessary requirement in the back country of Quebec-Labrador; native coats are always closed at the back. The European coat has three triangular inserts pleated into the side seams to increase its flare; sometimes when skins were too small, a single simple gusset was added at the side seam of the native coats. The neck and sleeves of the European coat are very much shaped; on native coats these parts are almost

Figure 7.   Man wearing a late 17th-century version of the *justaucorps.* Detail from the 1739 re-engraving published by J. F. Bernard of an early map from *Amérique septentrionale et méridionale,* N. de Fer, Paris, 1698. (National Archives of Canada, Ottawa, NMC 23330)

Above: Figure 8.   Frenchmen admiring Niagara Falls.
The triangle at the centre back of the coat is formed
not by an inserted gusset but by pleats on either side of
an open vent. From *Nouvelle découverte d'un très grand
pays situé dans l'Amérique entre Le Nouveau-Mexique et la
mer glaciale,* Louis Hennepin, 1697. (National Archives
of Canada, Library, Ottawa, C 113049)

Right: Figure 9.   A Canadian man going to war. From
Histoire de l'Amérique septentrionale, Bacqueville de la
Potherie, Paris, 1722. (National Archives of Canada,
Library, Ottawa, C 113193)

straight. When they were worn, the European fashion and the native coats would not be unlike in shape, but the influence of the one on the other was superficial only (compare Figures 10 and 21).

Most importantly, there is a hidden but constant feature of the native coats that has nothing whatever to do with European influence. At the centre back of each coat a slim triangle of skin is cut out and another triangle of skin inserted. In the descriptions of the individual coats this piece is called the *back gusset*. The obvious reason for its insertion is to add fullness, so that the wearer could tie the coat firmly around the waist and yet walk comfortably on snowshoes or kneel in a canoe, *but the inserted piece is not always wider than the piece that was cut out* and whether it adds width or even takes away from it, as it does on some of the later coats in the catalogue, this back gusset is put into every painted caribou-skin coat from the entire Quebec-Labrador area from the start of their use to almost the end. There has to be a reason other than the practical one of adding width. It seems likely that this back gusset, which is shaped like a mountain peak, was the symbolic centre of the coat's power and that it represents the Magical Mountain where the Lord of the Caribou lived and from the fastnesses of which the caribou were released to give themselves to the hunter. For further discussion concerning this theory, the reader is referred to the publications of Alika Podolinsky Webber.[19]

With the passing years the painted caribou-skin coats slimmed down, as did the European coats. A well-known late 18th-century illustration, the frontispiece for Captain George Cartwright's *Labrador Journal*, shows Cartwright tending his fox traps. He wears what is obviously one of the painted caribou-skin

Figure 10. Diagram of the cut of a man's cloth coat, 1730–1750. (Gallery of English Costume, Platt Hall, City of Manchester Art Galleries, M/C CAG 1954-1106)

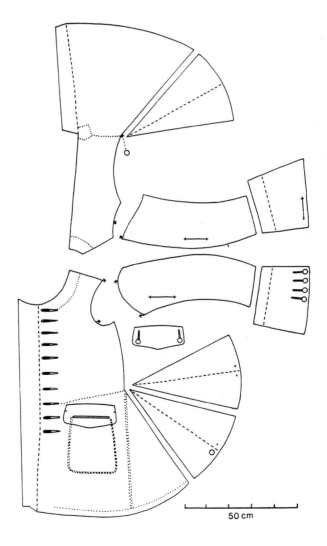

50 cm

coats, with the addition of a warm, European-style tippet and hood (Figure 11). He may well have acquired the coat from one of the "Nescaupick, or Mountaineer Indians" who visited him in October 1778.[20] A vignette on a French map of just about that same time shows three men wearing European coats of similar form (Figure 12).

The outlines changed gradually to a 19th-century shape such as that shown in a watercolour by J. Crawford Young (Figure 13). The painted coat worn by the man in the foreground has apparently been acquired by a non-native owner. Its long, slim shape with stand-up collar is close to coat No. 35 yet similar

Right: Figure 11.   Coat in the same plain style as coat No. 29. Frontispiece from *A Journal of Transactions and Events During a Residence of Nearly Sixteen Years on the Coast of Labrador,* Captain George Cartwright, 1792. (Metropolitan Toronto Public Library, Baldwin Room)

Below: Figure 12.   Detail of a scene depicting the arrival of Jacques Cartier in Canada, an event that occurred more than two hundred years before the execution of this drawing. Note that the men are wearing late 18th-century European clothing. A vignette from the edge of a map, *Carte d'Amérique,* Jean-Baptiste-Louis Clouet de l'Académie Royale de Rouen, 1782. (National Archives of Canada, Ottawa, NMC 11879)

to the Euro-Canadian coats worn by the other men in the picture. At this period it is likely that the coat originated well to the north of the St. Lawrence River. We do not know precisely when but the use of these coats ceased in the south, remaining important only in the northern area, where the large herds of caribou were the mainstay of the Naskapi people until well into the 20th century. Many of the surviving 19th-century coats were collected by men who worked in the northern areas for the Hudson's Bay Company.

In the Catalogue, No. 39 is a coat that can be dated fairly accurately to the 1840s. The cut is typical

Figure 13.   Man (on right) wearing a painted caribou-skin coat. Watercolour by J. Crawford Young, a British army officer, who painted this scene while on duty in Canada between 1825 and 1836. (Courtesy of the McCord Museum of Canadian History, McGill University, Montreal, M21231)

of mid 19th-century coats, and its length and width provide a good parallel with the slim military coat of somewhat later date (Figure 14).

Euro-Canadian coats, which would have been seen by the native people, became shorter, plainer, and more in the utilitarian *capot* style of the 19th century (Figure 15). By the latter part of the century an evolution that had little to do with outside fashion and more to do with the deterioration of the native lifestyle was simplifying both the cut and the decoration of the painted coats. A rare photograph (Figure 16), said to have been taken about 1880 in Labrador, shows a group of native men in their winter coats. Three of the coats are plain and furred on the outside, while two are painted, sewn closed in front, and obviously furred on the inside; the two painted coats

are similar to coat No. 41, which was collected at about the same time. The man on the left has lifted his painted coat to reveal a second coat underneath.

When F. W. Waugh was doing research at Voisey Bay, near Nain, in 1921–1922, he collected two of the furred and painted winter coats (Nos. 54–55), but his photographs indicate that the end of use for that type of coat was near. All his pictures show men wearing short shirts or windbreaker-like garments of either plain skin or white canvas, as in Figure 17. A faint echo of the painted coats is there in a coloured border of lines around the bottom of each coat.

A shirt of similar shape, from about the same time, is shown in Figure 18. It is cut from one large caribou skin and is decorated with painted stars on each shoulder.

Figure 14. Ambrotype of Captain Richard C. Price, 100th Regiment, Quebec, about 1858. (National Archives of Canada, Ottawa, PA 126689)

Right: Figure 15. Man wearing a *capot.* Watercolour by William Smyth Maynard, New Brunswick, 1853–1854. (National Archives of Canada, Ottawa, C 122471)

Below: Figure 16. Photograph of a group of Naskapi men said to have been taken in Labrador about 1880. Canadian Museum of Civilization, Hull-Ottawa, Neg. J. 6542)

Figure 17. Men wearing short shirt- or windbreaker-like garments. Photograph taken by F. W. Waugh near Nain, Labrador, about 1921. Canadian Museum of Civilization, Hull-Ottawa, Neg. 54588)

Figure 18. Diagram of man's caribou-skin shirt, probably about 1920–1930. (Royal Ontario Museum, Toronto, Speck Collection, 958.131.69)

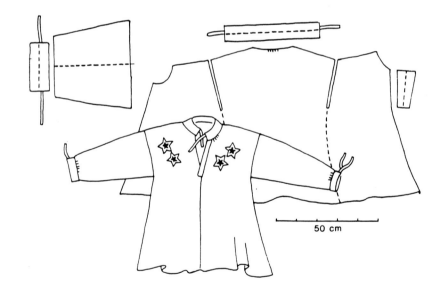

50 cm

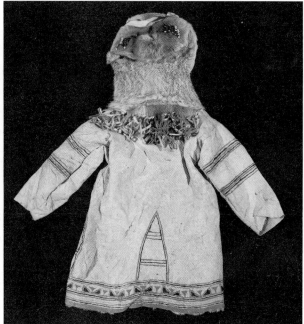

By the early 1930s, with all the changes that were taking place in the lives of the native people of the area, the making of the painted coats came to an end. But there is a quite delightful postscript: the making of small garments for baby boys (Figure 19) continued for a few more years. The fine skin of an unborn caribou was used, and the hood was made from the little caribou's head. There is simple, painted decoration and, although the characteristic back gusset has not been cut out, the shape has been carefully painted on at centre back.

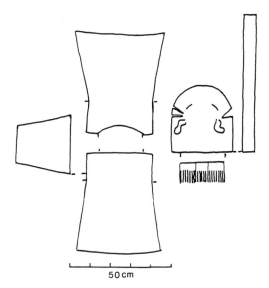

50 cm

Figure 19.   Front and back of a baby boy's painted coat made from the skin of a caribou foetus, probably about 1930 (Royal Ontario Museum, Toronto, Speck Collection, 958.131.641), and diagram showing the cut of the coat.

CARIBOU

The painted coats that we are concerned with in this study owe their existence to the caribou, both for why they were made and for the raw material from which they were made. The caribou is an animal of regal bearing with a head supporting stunningly decorative antlers on female as well as male (Figure 20).[1] Although few people today have had the opportunity to see a live caribou, except in a zoo, Canadians are familiar with them through the excellent portrait head on our twenty-five cent coin.[2]

Caribou are well adapted to their environment. Even in large numbers they can survive in what would appear to be a comparatively barren land. During the warmer months they move constantly, living on lichens growing both on trees and on the ground, mosses, mushrooms, grasses, and low plants such as blueberry, cranberry, Labrador tea, and dwarf willow and birch.

The caribou did not come quite as close to extinction as the better known buffalo; the once vast herds have declined in numbers, and their range has been much reduced, but the herds are still free and on the increase again.

There has been considerable difference of opinion among authorities as to the correct name for the caribou of the Quebec-Labrador peninsula.[3] As this study concerns itself only with a product made from the skin of the animal, the scientific name may seem comparatively unimportant; it is significant to note, however, that the caribou in the north behave quite differently from those in the south. In the tundra area they congregate and migrate in large herds,[4] presenting an opportunity for the native people, acting together, to intercept them and slaughter them easily and in sufficient quantities to ensure food for a whole season.[5] In the more wooded areas of the south, caribou always seem to have been less numerous, occurring only in comparatively small groups. In the winter, in both north and south, caribou scatter, spreading out in their search for food. Their large feet help them to move over the snow and they survive by using their sharp hooves to uncover lichens from under the snow. Caribou fur has remarkably good insulating properties; it provides excellent protection for the living animal and then a warm winter coat for the hunter.

Figure 20. Woodland caribou, *Rangifer tarandus caribou.* From *The Mammals of Eastern Canada,* Randolph L. Peterson, 1966, fig. 183, p. 331, drawing by Paul Geraghty.

It is easy to understand the great veneration of the caribou in the north, where the animal was the mainstay of life and where, if the hunt failed, starvation was all too likely. Because the native people were intensely aware of the importance of the caribou to their survival, they enlisted supernatural aid through various means, including the making and wearing of the special painted coats, to ensure a successful hunt. In the south the use of the painted coats came to an end long ago, so it is impossible to know if they were worn with the same feelings of veneration in that area where the caribou were not as numerous or as vital to subsistence. The decoration and cut of the coats that probably come from the southern "Montagnais" area are of similar type to the more modern "Naskapi" coats of the north. In the north the special coats were worn when the hunt connected with the huge autumn migration was on, but furred coats with similar painting were made to be used when hunting the scattered caribou in the winter. There were no hard lines dividing the north from the south in this area, and possibly it was felt by native people throughout the peninsula that the hunter needed all the help he could get in providing caribou meat for his family, and so called upon the power of the special painted hunting coat in both summer and winter, in the south as well as the north.

The preparation of the skins was mostly done by the women and required skill and much hard work.[6] Repeated dryings, scrapings, wettings, workings, and anointings with by-products of the hunt, such as decomposing caribou brains and liver, were involved. The results were excellent and the fine, soft, dehaired skins became a popular article of trade with the Hudson's Bay Company. Many a fashion-able "Beau Brummell" of the Regency period, who thought his skin-tight white breeches were normal homegrown chamois leather, may well have been clad, in fact, in the more exotic caribou skin.[7]

The skins that were destined to be used for the painted coats were not smoked, but were kept as light in colour as possible. There is some slight evidence of smoking on the inside of later coats, but only one coat in the whole series (No. 23) has been made of fully smoked skin, which gives it a very unusual dark look.

Because many of the best skins were used for trade, most of the coats in the series have skins that are marked with the scars made by warble fly. It is not to be wondered that this pest nearly drives the caribou wild, for it lays its eggs on the fur, and when the larvae hatch they burrow under the skin and make their way to the rump end of the back, where they are warm and comfortable until about May or June. Then, when they are about 125 mm in length, they work their way out through the skin and drop to the ground, leaving holes that take some months to heal and leave nasty scars on the skin.[8]

It wasn't until the autumn that the holes were sufficiently closed for skins to be useful for making garments. Infestations were heavy, with an animal often being the host for more than a hundred of the pests at a time. The worst of the skins were undoubtedly used for things such as tent coverings, but many of the quite special and elegant coats are fairly heavily scarred. Since the scars are concentrated towards the tail, the researcher can tell, even with dehaired skins, that most of the backs of the coats have been cut with the tail end up and most of the fronts with the tail end down.

CUT OF THE COATS

In ethnographic literature the painted caribou-skin coats of the Quebec-Labrador peninsula have frequently been described as being "tailored," which is a misuse of the term. The garments were "shaped" and probably also "fitted" to the measure of the men who were to wear them. The word "tailoring" suggests a much more complex process.[1]

Each coat required a caribou skin for the back, a second skin for the two sides of the front, and a third for sleeves, collar, cuffs, and inserts. Figure 21 gives the basic shape of each part and notes some common variations. The garment parts do not relate in any way to the shape of the animal skin and do not provide a very efficient covering for the body.[2]

The back was cut from the centre of a skin, which usually had its tail end up. Neck opening,

shoulders, and armholes were straight. Some shaping was used on coats of late date, such as No. 60. Straight sides tapered in towards the waist, then flared to the bottom. At centre back a slim triangle was cut out and another triangle of skin, the *back gusset*, was inserted. As has been explained in the History section, it is probable that this insert was the centre of the coat's power and that it represented the Magical Mountain of the Lord of the Caribou.

The fronts were cut from the two sides of a skin that was split down the middle and usually had its tail end to the bottom. The shoulders were straight and slightly sloping. Sometimes the neck opening was rounded. The armholes were straight and the sides flared from waist to bottom. If the skin was not considered to be wide enough, *side gussets* were

Figure 21.   Diagram showing the basic parts used in the making of a painted caribou-skin coat. *A*, Front made from a single piece of skin. *B*, Front with added gusset set into the side seam. *C*, Straight sloping shoulder with no neck shaping. *D*, Straight sloping shoulder with rounded neck. *E*, Cut at centre back for insertion of back gusset; occasionally this is simply a straight slash, but usually it has a width of at least 5 cm. *F*, Triangular back gusset for insertion in centre back; this is usually wider than the piece that was cut out, but sometimes it is just about the same width, and occasionally it is narrower. *G*, The tip of the inserted back gusset is almost always cut off. *H*, The tip fits into a similar square cut in the centre back. *I*, Sleeves are frequently made of a single piece of skin with straight shoulder and sides. *J*, Sleeves may be made of two or more pieces; the shape may be identical to that of the single-piece sleeve, or the sleeve may be slightly more shaped. *K*, Cuffs, when used, may be just a simple turn-back of the sleeves. *L*, Straight bands were often added to the sleeves to provide cuffs. *M*, Many of the coats have falling collars, most of which are attached only across the back of the neck; the collars occur in a variety of shapes, but a pentagonal collar was usual.

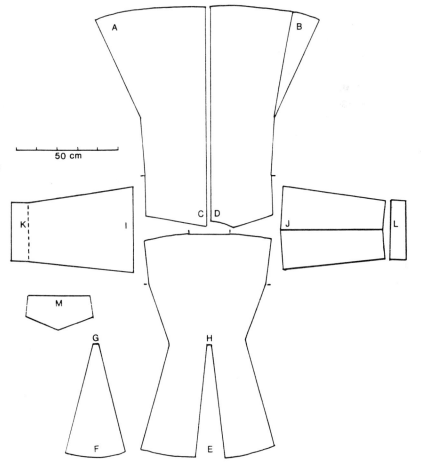

inserted in the seams, but these seem to have had no other significance than to provide fullness.

Winter coats were cut in the same way, but the fronts were sewn together again after painting.

Sleeves, which might be of one, two, or more pieces, were cut straight and tapered towards the wrist. Cuffs, if used, were turned-up bands; sometimes the cuff was an extension of the sleeve but more often it was an addition.

Most of the coats have falling collars, which seems a little strange. Collars were not customary with native garments, yet their use cannot be attributed to the influence of European men's fashion coats of the 17th and 18th centuries because, with the wearing of large wigs, collars were not used. Perhaps the influence came from another European source. The hood of a *capot* was often worn thrown back on the shoulders (Figure 22), providing warmth to the neck, and in this position it looks very like the pentagonally shaped collars used on so many of the painted coats.[3]

A few of the coats have a stand-up band collar (Nos. 34–35), which appears to be a straight copying from contemporary European coats.

Furred winter coats often had a hood made from a caribou head. To shape the skin, small darts were cut at either side and then sewn closed, leaving the small cut triangle of skin dangling by its tip (Nos. 52, 54). The eyeholes were always closed either with sewing or patches, but the earholes were left open.

A few of the coats are very small. It seems most

Figure 22. Man (on right) with the hood of his coat thrown back on his shoulders. The effect is quite similar to that produced by the pentagonal collars often used on the painted coats. From *Travels Through Lower Canada*, John Lambert, 1810. (National Archives of Canada, Ottawa, C 113669)

probable that No. 5 was deliberately made in a child's size to be sent to France as a royal gift. Nos. 9, 19, and 21 may also have been made as gifts for honoured visitors, but they are of a somewhat larger size and could have been for a boy just old enough to be included in the hunting party, or possibly for a very small man.

On coats of late date (Nos. 41–42, 49, 52–53, 55–57), there are small projections at the centre bottom of the fronts. It has been suggested that these small tails may be a feature borrowed from Inuit costume.[4] All examples except No. 56 are on furred coats (Figure 23). The tails do not occur on any earlier coats, but then no furred coats earlier than Nos. 41–42 are known to have survived.

Although the cut of the coats remained fairly constant during the two centuries of their use, there was subtle but continuous development. In order to document this, measurements were taken at the waist and the bottom of each coat, and the proportion of the flare of the skirts, as indicated by the difference in these two measurements, is given with each catalogue entry. At the high end of the scale this ratio is almost 1:3 (Nos. 6, 9, 11); a little later many coats have a ratio of about 1:2 (Nos. 14–38); the proportion is then reduced to about 1:1.6 (Nos. 41–42, 44, 46–47); near the end of the catalogue most coats have hardly any flare (Nos. 48–49, 56, 58–59).

It would be wonderful if we could take this measurement of proportion as a firm guide to dating, but there are many variables, such as area of origin, personal preference, unusual variations in length (e.g., No. 35), or degree of overlap of the coat fronts

Figure 23. Detail showing bottom border and points on coat No. 55. (Canadian Ethnology Service, Canadian Museum of Civilization, Hull-Ottawa, III B 20)

when the coat was worn (e.g., No. 8). As few of the early coats have a reliable history, any help in establishing a sequence of dating is of importance. Combined with the complexity of the painted pattern layout, the skill of the painting, and the choice of motifs, the measure of the flare of a coat does help greatly in determining where that coat fits in date and has contributed very considerably to the formation of the coat sequence in this catalogue.

An incidental benefit of making a detailed record of this range of costumes, which are from an extended period of time but a single area, is that it gives information on the stature of the wearers. Two measurements were taken, the centre back of the neck to the bottom of the coat and the centre back of the neck to the wrist. The former measure does not necessarily indicate the wearer's height because the coat may have been worn above or below the knee, according to personal taste or current fashion. Judging from the neck-to-wrist measurements, it seems that the average man was about 175 cm (5 feet, 9 inches) tall, and a few men were up to 185 cm (6 feet) tall. There seems to have been little change in the average height over the entire period, which is interesting considering the increase in stature of European men between 1700 and 1920–1930.

SEWING

Sinew, according to the *Concise Oxford English Dictionary* (1982), is a "tough fibrous tissue uniting muscle to bone." It is the sinew that lies along the backbone of the caribou that provided the strong thread used for almost all the sewing done on these coats. Lucien Turner who was at Fort Chimo between 1882 and 1884, gives a good description of the first step in the process:

The sinew, which lies along the lumbar region just below the superficial muscles, is exposed by a cut, and with the point of a knife or tip of the finger loosened from its adherent flesh. One end, usually the forward end, is detached and a stout thong tied to it, and it is jerked from its attachment by a vigorous pull. It requires a strong person to remove this tendon from the body of a lean animal. A stroke of the knife frees the wide layer of sinew from blood and particles of flesh. This is . . . laid aside for awhile, then washed to free it from the blood, which would stain it dark in color and also tend to diminish the strength of the fibres by rotting them. It is now spread out and allowed to dry.[1]

At this point the sinew is a flat, fairly wide ribbon consisting of many fibres that lie more or less parallel but look very dry and not too hopeful.

Daniel Williams Harmon, writing early in the 19th century, describes the next stage:

In sewing leather, instead of thread, they make use of the sinews of animals. When this substance is some moistened, they separate a fibre, and by running their finger along between it and the main sinew, they part it to a sufficient length. The sinews of the caribou may be made as fine and even, as fine thread. These fibres, when thus separated, they twist at one end between their fingers, which gives them a sharp stiff point, when they are dry. They use awls, which they obtain from us, or an instrument of bone which they construct themselves, in sewing.[2]

The first director of the Royal Ontario Museum, Dr. C. T. Currelly, while training to be a Methodist minister worked as a missionary in Manitoba in 1898–1899; in his autobiography one of his stories of that period concerns the use of sinew.[3]

The sewing was all done with sinews. The big sinew was taken out from each side of the back of the deer and dried,

then small pieces were pulled off in lengths easy for sewing. They were moistened by running them through the mouth and rolling them on the knee. This made a sewing thread that was very strong, although of course it would not stand boiling. All of this was "women's work," and I caused great laughter by sitting with the women and patiently learning to roll a sinew. Not all the women knew how.

Currelly goes on to say that on his circuit, in getting his horse across a swollen river in very cold weather, the fronts of his heavy woollen mitts were almost torn off. He went to the nearest house hoping to get a leather patch put over them:

A fine grown-up girl came to the door, I held up my hands, and she bemoaned the fact that although there was a whole moose hide in the house she did not know how to roll a sinew and her mother was away. She was certainly surprised when I told her I could roll a sinew . . . and I soon had a thoroughly good pair of mitts.

With basic sinew sewing, an awl was used to punch a hole in the leather; the stiffened sinew could then be pushed through the hole to make a stitch. The process sounds slow and laborious, but with practice and skill many a fine seam was sewn by this means. The last surviving Beothuk native of Newfoundland, a woman named Shananditti, spent some time in St. John's before she died of tuberculosis in 1829. A friend described Shananditti's method of sewing:

I never saw her with a needle, but I often saw her stitch by passing the thread through a hole made with a sharp point or awl.[4]

Awls appear on many lists of early European trade items but needles are also mentioned. From the evidence of finished coats it is difficult to be sure how the sinew was carried through the skin. Three of the early coats, Nos. 1–2 and 5, all of which are very finely sewn, have "needle" holes, which appear to be tiny slashes, either straight or slightly rounded, and which may have been made by a locally produced bone awl. Almost all of the other coats have triangularly cut holes, most likely made by an imported glover's needle. Although many native people like Shananditti sewed using only sinew and awl, eyed needles of bone or copper that date to pre-contact times are known. Some of these were likely quite delicate and may have been used for the sewing only, while a stronger awl would have been used to make the hole in the leather.[5]

To make the seams on the coats the two right sides were placed together and joined by overcast stitching, with all the sewing on the inside of the coat. The neatness and quality of the stitching is generally excellent. All the stitch counts in the catalogue descriptions are based on a 5-cm length of seam and range from a low of about fifteen to a high of thirty-five. Seven stitches to the centimetre is incredibly fine sinew sewing and occurs on what are probably the two earliest coats (Nos. 1–2), but many of the coats have four to five stitches per centimetre. The coarser sewing is found on late coats and, understandably, on those that are furred.

There seems to be a standard order for making up the coats. *Before painting*, the back gusset was inserted; if there were gussets to put in at the sides, they were attached and the side seams sewn up. If the sleeves had two pieces, one seam, usually the top one, was sewn *before painting*. This gave fairly large sections that could be spread out flat for the painting, although one cannot help wondering where the women found sufficient firm, flat space for a suitable "drawing board." *After painting*, the sewing of the coat was completed: the front and back were sewn together at the shoulders, the second sleeve seam was sewn, and the sleeves, cuffs, and collar were attached.

As the coats were examined, detailed notes were made, and a strange departure from the usual order of making up was noted. On some coats the side seams were sewn *after* the painting was done. Those with this feature seem to be from approximately the middle period in date (Nos. 19–23, 28, 31–39). It must have been very difficult to draw the lines and motifs of the separate sections of a border design with the accuracy necessary to make them come together neatly when the side seams were sewn, but on many of these coats the joining is so good that it can be detected only by careful examination. The question is why, when the usual practice was to join before painting, should the painter be subjected to all this seemingly unnecessary strain? It has been suggested that lack of space in the living area is probably the answer.[6]

A subtlety of sinew sewing can occasionally be seen at the bottom of a finished seam. Coats were

Below: Figure 24.   Detail showing tags of sinew at the bottom of the seams on the outside of the back gusset on coat No. 7. (Canadian Ethnology Service, Canadian Museum of Civilization, Hull-Ottawa, III B 590)

Bottom: Figure 25.   Detail showing tags of sinew at the bottom of the seams on the inside of the back gusset on coat No. 7. (Canadian Ethnology Service, Canadian Museum of Civilization, Hull-Ottawa, III B 590)

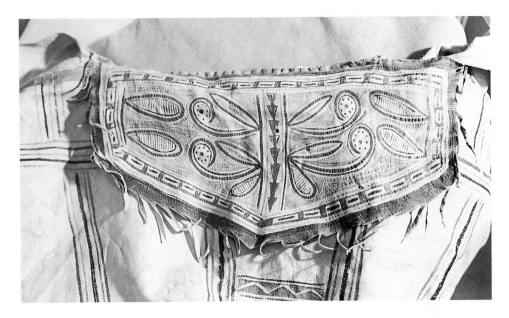

Figure 26. Detail showing the coarse running stitches used to attach the collar on coat No. 16. (Canadian Ethnology Service, Canadian Museum of Civilization, Hull-Ottawa, III B 642)

made to the measurements of the intended wearer. If the length cut was not quite right it could be changed when the lower line of decoration was laid out, but by that time the main coat seams were already sewn and neatly finished. A sinew seam was ended off by working the sinew back under the last five or six stitches—probably a fussy operation. When trimming the length of the skin to fit the painted pattern, the worker spared herself the trouble of redoing the seam end by cutting neatly around it instead of through it; this left an unobtrusive little tag of sinew sewing to hang below the bottom of the coat (Figures 24–25).

Most collars, and the cuffs as well, were joined to the coat by overcast stitching with the inner side of the coat placed against the right side of the collar, so that the sewing is hidden under the collar when it is turned back. On Nos. 1–3, and on several somewhat later coats (Nos. 13–17), the collar has been attached in a much more primitive way. The wrong side of the collar was simply placed against the right side of the back of the neck and these two edges were joined by a running stitch, with all the sewing showing on the outside of the coat (Figure 26). This does not match at all with the careful sewing of the rest of the garment. It is almost as though the makers of these early coats had seen collars, or as we suspect, the hood of a *capot*, and wanted to add one to the caribou coat but didn't quite know how to do it. Also, the presence of this primitive collar attachment on some of the earlier coats but not on later ones suggests that the method of making up the coats went through a period of development before it became standardized.

QUILL WRAPPING AND BEADING

Most of the painted caribou-skin coats have no decoration other than painting; a few, however, are decorated with beads or porcupine quills, and sometimes with both.

The cuffs on Nos. 1–3 are edged at the wrist with a line of beads attached as shown in Figure 27.

Figure 27. Diagram showing the way beads were attached to the cuffs on coats Nos. 1–3.

Sinew is sewn through the caribou skin at the edge of the turn-back of the cuff, a bead is threaded on to the sinew, another stitch is taken through the skin, another bead is added, and so on around the cuff.

Quill-wrapped and beaded fringes have been set into the shoulder and sleeve seams of coat No. 28. The epaulettes consist of long fringes, which serve as warps for ten rows of bead weaving in blue and white (Figure 28).[1] Below the woven band of beads the loose fringes are wrapped with white quill and threaded with blue, white, and brown beads.

Figure 28. Detail of bead-woven band and quill-wrapped fringes forming epaulette on coat No. 28. (Canadian Ethnology Service, Canadian Museum of Civilization, Hull· Ottawa, III B 633)

31

Figure 29. Detail of very handsome quill-wrapped fringes forming epaulette on coat No. 29. (British Museum, London, 2613)

Figure 30. Diagram showing attachment of beads to fringes on coat No. 29.

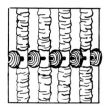

Very handsome quill-wrapped fringes have been inserted into the shoulder and sleeve seams of coat No. 29, and epaulettes (Figure 29) combine yellow and white bands of quill wrapping with two rows of beads attached in an unusual way: sinew is passed right through a fringe, then threaded with a bead passed through the next fringe, threaded with another bead, and so on across the width of the epaulette (Figure 30).

On coat No. 58 a sparse line of beaded strings has been sewn in across the back of the shoulders.

LAYOUT OF THE DESIGN

The areas on the coat that were to be filled with painted designs were first laid out using the yellow fish roe medium. On most of the coats this was done with a painting tool with more than one prong, usually one that made a triple line (see Tools section). The idea that the pattern areas should be enclosed by more than one line seems to have been so basic that when a multiple tool was not used the multiple line was faked by a careful repetition of single lines on both early and later coats (Nos. 1–2, 43, 50).

The first coats in the catalogue use a pattern layout that was already established. Tradition was very strong, and the patterned areas and the ways of filling them are surprisingly constant. Figure 31 shows the standard pattern areas as used on an early 19th-century coat (No. 31). There is considerable

simplification in the patterning layout towards the end of the use of the coats.

A wide border that follows the curved line of the bottom carries one of the main design themes.

At centre back there is a triangular pattern area, the *central gore form*. On most coats the outline of this area covers and hides rather than coinciding with the line of the inserted *back gusset*. (*Note:* It is essential in considering these coats to differentiate clearly between the piece that is inserted into the centre back of the coat, the *back gusset,* from the design area that covers it, the *central gore form.* The terminology used throughout this study is *gusset* if it is cut and inserted, *gore form* if it is painted on.) The design in this central gore form is usually of equal importance to that of the bottom border, sometimes

Figure 31. Diagram showing the pattern areas on coat No. 31. The coat is early 19th century, but the layout is typical of coats dating from the mid 18th to the mid 19th century. In later coats the layout though similar was simpler.

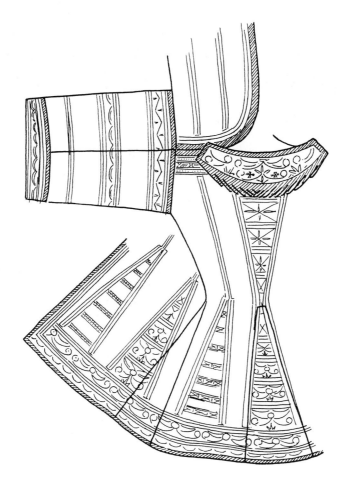

carrying the same motif, sometimes bringing in a second theme.

On coats that date from before the middle of the 19th century, with only one exception (No. 20), the central gore form narrows to the waist and then spreads out up the shoulders in a V-shape, which usually joins a band that crosses the back of the shoulders.[1] Painting may be quite minimal in this enclosed triangle, and even when complex it is often left unfinished under the collar.

On later coats the central gore form often coincides accurately with the inserted back gusset; the decoration is minimal and, with only a few exceptions (Nos. 47–48, 51, 56, 60), the form does not extend upwards towards the neck but terminates in a blunt point at the waist.

There is always at least one additional painted gore form to either side of the coat. These triangles of pattern do not relate in any way to gussets that may be inserted in the side seams. On most coats from before the middle of the 19th century, there are two or three gore forms to either side of the central one, making five or seven surrounding the coat. Two coats, Nos. 5 and 12, are the only ones known with nine. The two sides of the coat are symmetrical, with more elaborate patterning in the central gore form than in the pairs of gore forms to either side, although one of the side pairs often uses a simpler version of the design in the centre.

The side gore forms often have an extension, usually quite a simple band, running up to the shoulder. A point worth noting is the finish, or lack of it, at the waist. On Nos. 1–4 the tops of the side gore forms are carefully rounded, suggesting that they were meant to be seen and that those coats were worn open, with no belt. On most of the coats, however, the finish at the waist is not very tidy. The layout of the design is usually done with a 3-prong tool; with the gore forms, two triple lines converge at the waist and stop there quite abruptly. The continuation to the shoulder may grow out of one of the pairs of lines in the gore form, but more often it is simply centred over them, and sometimes is completely separated from them (No. 16). This rather clumsy transition confirms the thought that most of the coats were worn with a sash covering this part of the design.

Collars are usually an important design area, very often filled with double-curve variations and sometimes having small, significant motifs such as crosses and circles fitted into the corners. Surprisingly, several fairly elaborate coats have simple collars painted in a less expert way than the rest of the coat (Nos. 13, 17, 30).

Front borders are usually narrow and simple but may have unusual motifs, such as the triangles on coat No. 7. Sometimes the front borders depart from the usual complete symmetry of the coats in that the motifs differ slightly between the two sides (Nos. 9–11). Very often the front border turns just below the neck and extends horizontally towards the armhole; the patterning on that extension may be the same as or different from that on the front border.

Occasionally, sleeves are covered with painted decoration (Nos. 2–3, 8, 29), but more often they have a band of decoration at the top, another at the elbow, and, if there is no cuff, a third at the wrist. As the patterning becomes simplified on the latest coats, the sleeve bands are reduced to a token decoration of simple lines across the front face of the sleeve only (Nos. 52–53, 55, 58).

Many coats have patterned cuffs. When the double curve is a main design motif, it may be inverted on the cuffs, so that the wearer sees it the right way up, probably following the widespread tradition of orienting the pattern on moccasin vamps towards the wearer rather than the viewer (Nos. 12–13).

The outer borders are neat bands, usually about 2 cm wide, painted around parts of the outside edges of all except two of the coats. Of these two, No. 27 has fur bandings that are apparently original, and there is no paint under them; No. 59 has only minimal painting. Red is by far the most common colour for the outer border, but occasionally brown is used, and on one coat (No. 58) the border is dark blue.

Markings in the form of lines, usually narrower than the borders and roughly painted in red, occasionally in brown, were applied to various parts of the coats where they join together – at the shoulder seams, the armhole seams, the side seams, and sometimes the upper sleeve seams. One unusual occurrence of this type of marking crosses the seam at the blunt top of the inserted back gusset on coat No. 36. Usually the paint was applied over a seam after it was sewn, but there are exceptions where the paint was applied before sewing. These markings appear on all the coats in the last third of the catalogue except No. 59. That they have significance is proved from examination of No. 54, which is furred on the outside, has a simple border design painted around the inside of the bottom of the coat, and has rough red markings on the shoulder seams far up inside the coat where they are completely hidden. Is it

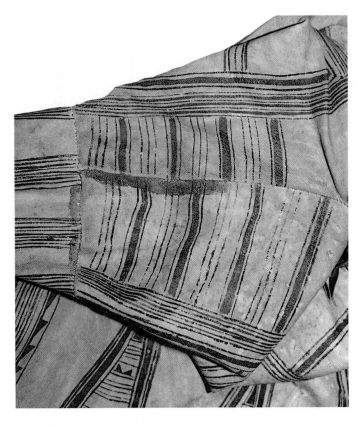

Figure 32. Detail of groups of vertical lines used on both front and back of shoulders and tops of sleeves on a coat No. 15. (National Museums of Scotland, Edinburgh, L.402)

possible that these markings were used to make a symbolic joining of the parts of the coat suggesting that, ideally, the garment should be of a single skin?

On an earlier group of coats (Nos. 12–21) the rough markings have been used on the shoulder seams in conjunction with groups of vertical parallel lines that fill the space between the shoulder bands and the shoulder seams. Similar vertical parallel lines may be used at the top of the sleeves (Figure 32). Although these vertical lines are carefully painted, there was no attempt to make those on the front continuous with those on the back where they meet at the shoulder seam. No clue to their significance has yet been found.

COLOURS

The colours used for painting the caribou-skin coats are yellow, red, browns of various earth colours, some black, blue (which is particularly strong on the later coats), and very little green.

Lucien Turner recorded the painting methods used during his stay at Fort Chimo between 1882 and 1884:

A favorite vehicle for the paint is the prepared roe of a sucker (*Catastomus*) abounding in the waters of the district. The female fish are stripped of the mass of ova which is broken up in a vessel and the liquid strained through a coarse cloth. The color is a faint yellow which becomes deeper with age. The fluid is allowed to dry and when required for use is dissolved in water. It has then a semiviscid consistence and in this condition is mixed with the various pigments. When a yellowish color is desired the fish-egg preparation is applied alone.[1]

The Department of Ethnology of the Royal Ontario Museum was able to acquire frozen fish roe of the right type from Labrador.[2] When thawed, mashed, and strained, it produced a truly excellent painting medium. Some of the medium was placed on the palm of the hand, and a 3-prong painting tool of antler from the museum's collection was drawn through it. With the medium that adhered to the tool it was possible to draw a triple line fully 20 cm long on a fine piece of chamois leather. Lines on the coats had been studied and even with magnification it had not been possible to detect when the tool had been lifted to pick up more medium to extend the line. Our experiment answered this question. The medium remained quite juicy at the end of the line, giving sufficient time for the tool to be remoistened and laid down again before the first application dried. The join was thus undetectable. Nothing fancy was tried. The experiment included drawing straight lines, both multiple and single, and a few curved single lines around a template. We now know that the fish roe medium works, makes a permanent bond with the animal skin, and can be used with the known tools to paint the multiple lines that are characteristic of the painted caribou-skin coats. Although the experiment provided answers to some of the technical questions, it did nothing to reduce the awe with which the painted designs are viewed.

As Lucien Turner said, when yellow was the required colour the medium was used alone. This made it the simplest colour to produce and as such it is logical that yellow should be the most-used colour. As a general rule, at all periods the pattern areas were laid out with yellow, very often with a 3-prong tool; yellow was also used for most of the fine crosshatching that fills in much of the background.

Lucien Turner's statement that the yellow colour darkens with age has been quoted over and over again in the literature, but our experiment showed that when the fish roe was thawed and ready for use, it was about the colour that is found on most of the coats. Possibly the freezing had already darkened it.

There are a few coats painted with a much lighter-coloured medium, which is probably not from fish eggs but from birds' eggs. The Canadian Conservation Institute in Ottawa (CCI) has tested the pigments used on many articles of native manufacture including painted garments from the Quebec-Labrador peninsula.[3] All the CCI tests can tell us about the yellow is that it is protein with no pigment in it. They cannot differentiate between fish eggs and birds' eggs.

Red, bright and clear in colour, is achieved with vermilion, obvious to the eye, but also borne out by the CCI reports. Vermilion could be obtained by trade from the earliest times of contact. Red is almost always the colour used with a single-prong tool to outline the pattern motifs.

On some of the later coats, such as those collected by Frank G. Speck in this century, there is a strong red, definitely not local, that tends more to the blue side of the spectrum than vermilion. On a test of one of Royal Ontario Museum's coats (No. 56), the CCI's preliminary report lists this colour simply as red lead.

Brownish reds and browns were made with local pigments obtained from the earth. Low, in a report for the Geological Survey of Canada in 1896, mentions that near Lake Chibougamau there was a place called "Paint Mountain, from the rusty colour of the rocks, due to the decomposition of iron-pyrites in them," and that on the Koksoak River there was "a large exposure of bedded iron ore (a mixture of magnetite and haematite) about twenty-five feet thick."[4] Similar local deposits of soft rock and red earth were scattered through the peninsula. Ground down to fine powder and mixed with the fish roe, they made excellent colours, although the reds were brownish rather than bright like vermilion. The CCI reports verify that the reddish browns and browns on a number of the coats in the series are haematite held in protein.

Black is used sparingly for small details and occasionally for the outlines of motifs. Nothing has been found in the literature to suggest an origin for the black pigment, but a present-day artist has suggested that burnt bones might be a source. As bones were often traditionally disposed of by fire, this could well be an answer.

Blue is another pigment that was supplied by trade and used to some extent at quite an early date. Some early blues have been tested by the CCI and have been shown to be Prussian blue, although the pale blue on No. 8 is listed as silica.

About the middle of the 19th century there was a distinct change in the colour of blue used on the coats. The change originated with the introduction of "laundry blue," which came as a compact powder in neat little cakes. Its original purpose was to make a blue-tinted rinse for use when laundering white linens. The rinse counteracted the tendency of linen to go yellow with age and assured the careful house-wife of sparkling white tablecloths. Laundry blue was a popular trade item for native use in many parts of the world. An excerpt from a letter from Reckitt & Colman (Canada) Limited gives an interesting comment on the trade.

Our Company history would indicate that the most probable point in time during which production and distribution of Blue would have reached sufficient volume to have come to the attention of the Hudson's Bay Company for its trade with the Indians would be between 1852 and 1863. These dates are most probable since in January 1852 some ultra-marine was bought by the then Reckitt's Company and the first sales of Laundry Blue manufactured from it were made in February of that year. The Company history also relates that it was not until 1863 that the sale of Blue had reached almost equal proportions to that of starch which in those days was the Company's mainstay in the commercial field.[5]

This strong laundry blue was obviously in use by the time that Lucien Turner was collecting coats in the area of Fort Chimo, and it dominates the decoration of most of the coats made after that period.

There is a limited use of green. On two of the early coats in the National Museum of Civilization in Hull-Ottawa, Nos. 7 and 10, a most unusual strong green is used. The colours on No. 10 were not analysed, but the CCI lists the pigment of the green on No. 7 as copper salt and states that the later greens are simply Prussian blue pigment held in the yellow fish roe.

PAINTING TOOLS

The native people of Quebec-Labrador did not use soft brushes when doing their painting but stiff, hard tools made of antler or bone. The coats were worn to honour the animal on which life largely depended – the caribou. The skin that was used to make the coats was caribou, and it was seemly that the tools used in the painting should also come from the caribou.

Painting tools exist in a number of museum collections, the curved ones made of antler, the small straight ones usually of bone.[1] Only those made very recently are of wood. The examples illustrated were collected by Frank G. Speck. Figure 33 shows single-prong tools that terminate in a small, curved, blade-like edge capable of producing either a fine, straight line or a tight curve. In Figure 34 there are two 2-

Figure 33. Bone painting tools for making single lines, probably about 1930. Lengths approximately 10 cm. (Royal Ontario Museum, Toronto, Speck Collection. *Top to bottom:* 949.186.6c, 958.131.98)

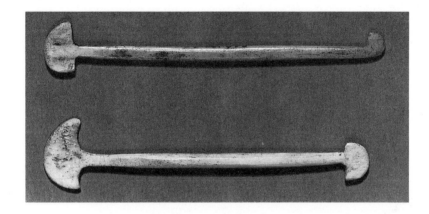

Figure 34. Painting tools of caribou antler for making double or triple lines, probably about 1930. Lengths approximately 7 to 13 cm. (Royal Ontario Museum, Toronto, Speck Collection. *Top to bottom:* 958.131.69, 958.131.65, 958.131.66, 949.186.6a)

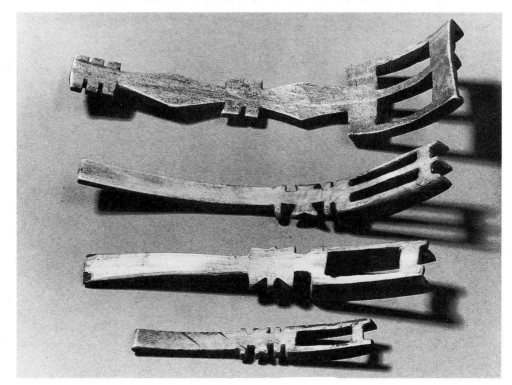

prong and two 3-prong tools of the type used to make the multiple lines that delineate the pattern areas on most of the coats. They are of caribou antler. The natural curve of the antler has been utilized to produce a tool that is beautifully shaped for its purpose. When a curved tool moistened with the painting medium is placed on the skin, the movement of the curve as the tool is drawn across the skin lengthens the line that it is possible to draw with one sweep.

Figure 35 shows small paint cups that were never used and were probably made especially for Speck, but they are similar to those illustrated by Lucien Turner[2] and would have been used for mixing the pigments and the fish roe medium preparatory to painting.

Each woman probably owned a number of painting tools, and because they were important possessions they would have been buried with her.[3] In 1968 Alika Podolinsky Webber wrote a very interesting article based on information from Walter Kenyon, a Royal Ontario Museum archaeologist.[4] The article described various tools found at grave sites that had been thought to be pottery markers, but which Kenyon and Podolinsky Webber considered to be painting tools. All had been casual finds and had entered the Royal Ontario Museum collections at very early dates. Each tool had a record of approximately where it was found—the locations were in Brant, Wentworth, Simcoe, and Hastings counties of Ontario—but none had any more specific information, so that, although they were dug up from the

Figure 35. Wooden paint cups, probably about 1930. Diameter of cup on right approximately 5 cm. (Royal Ontario Museum, Toronto, Speck Collection. *Left to right:* 958.131.115, 958.131.414)

Figure 36. Painting tools of uncertain date dug from the ground in Ontario. Lengths approximately 13 to 27 cm. (Royal Ontario Museum, Toronto. *Top and centre:* From Baptiste Lake, Hastings County, David Boyle Collection, donated in 1891, 10505, 10506. *Bottom:* From Simcoe County, gift of the Reverend J. W. Annis, 11674)

ground, there is no certainty of their ages. This material has been examined again,[5] and three of the pieces are illustrated in Figure 36. The tools from Brant and Wentworth counties are not included; it was decided that they have too short a working face for painting and are, as originally thought, for marking pottery. The others are undoubtedly for painting, either people or animal skins. The face of each of these tools is grooved, not to provide multiple separate lines, but to hold a supply of paint. The top one, from Baptiste Lake, Hastings County, has two separate prongs which would produce parallel lines, one wider than the other. The middle one is from the same area, and the bottom one is from Simcoe County.

A much more precise archaeological find was made during excavation of the Amerindian cemetery beside the chapel on the site of the 17th-century Jesuit mission at Sillery, Quebec. The circumstances of the find and tool itself are well described in an article by Gérard Gagné,[6] who gives a native name for this tool, *pechahigan*. The tool is very like the modern tools and, like them, is curved by the natural shape of the antler. It has four prongs, two wide (4 mm and 5 mm) and two narrow (2 mm) and the working sides of all the prongs are grooved like the Ontario examples. None of the recent tools that have been examined have grooves, but lines painted on many of the early coats show definite striations in the paint. The striations are particularly noticeable with wider lines, such as those on Nos. 6–7, and are undoubtedly the result of using a grooved tool like the one found at Sillery.

Top left: No. 1. Hunterian Museum, The University, Glasgow (E.128). Detail of bottom border. *Top right:* Detail of shoulder band. (See pp. 104–107)

Above: No. 2. Pitt Rivers Museum, Oxford (1952.5.01). Collar.
Left: Medallion. (See pp. 108–111)

43

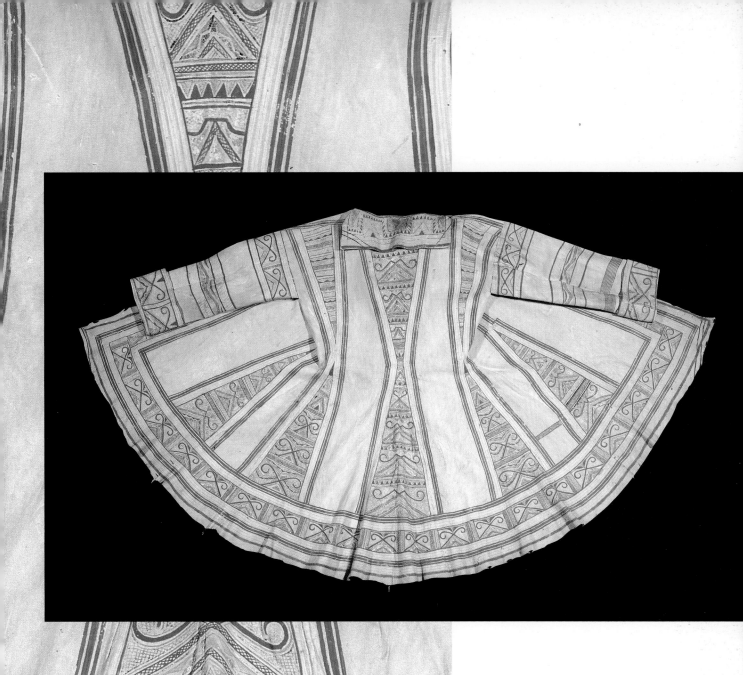

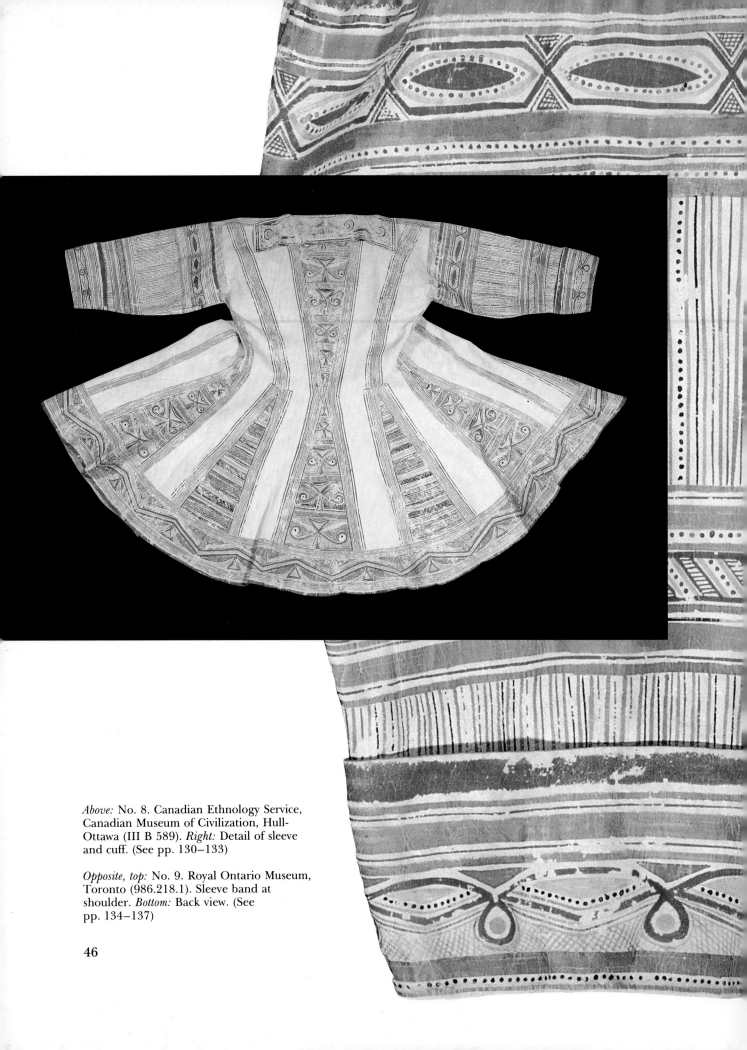

Above: No. 8. Canadian Ethnology Service, Canadian Museum of Civilization, Hull-Ottawa (III B 589). *Right:* Detail of sleeve and cuff. (See pp. 130–133)

Opposite, top: No. 9. Royal Ontario Museum, Toronto (986.218.1). Sleeve band at shoulder. *Bottom:* Back view. (See pp. 134–137)

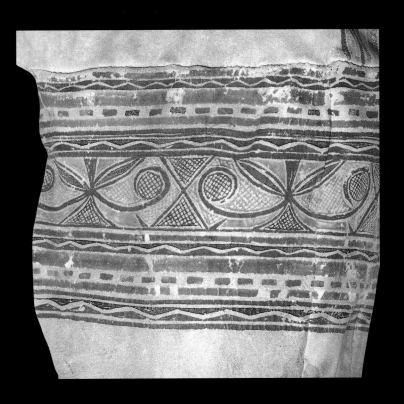

Above and right: No. 10. Canadian
Ethnology Service, Canadian Museum of
Civilization, Hull-Ottawa (III B 632). Back
and front views. (See pp. 138–141)

Opposite, top: No. 14. Royal Artillery Institution, Woolwich, London (UN 828).
Shoulder. (See pp. 153–157)

Opposite, bottom: No. 15. National Museums
of Scotland, Edinburgh (L.402). View of
lower back. (See pp. 158–161)

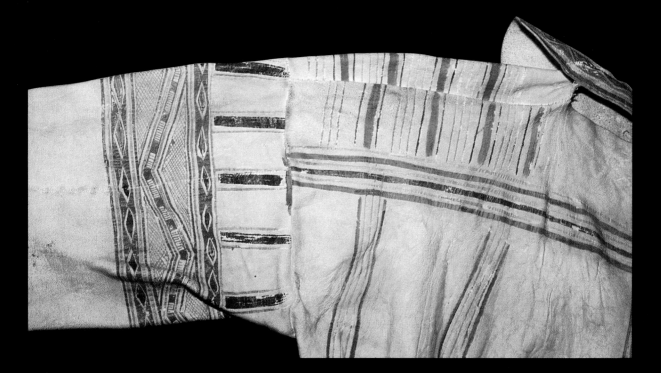

49

Above: No. 16. Canadian Ethnology
Service, Canadian Museum of Civilization,
Hull- Ottawa (III B 642). *Right:* Detail of
lower back. (See pp. 162–164)

50

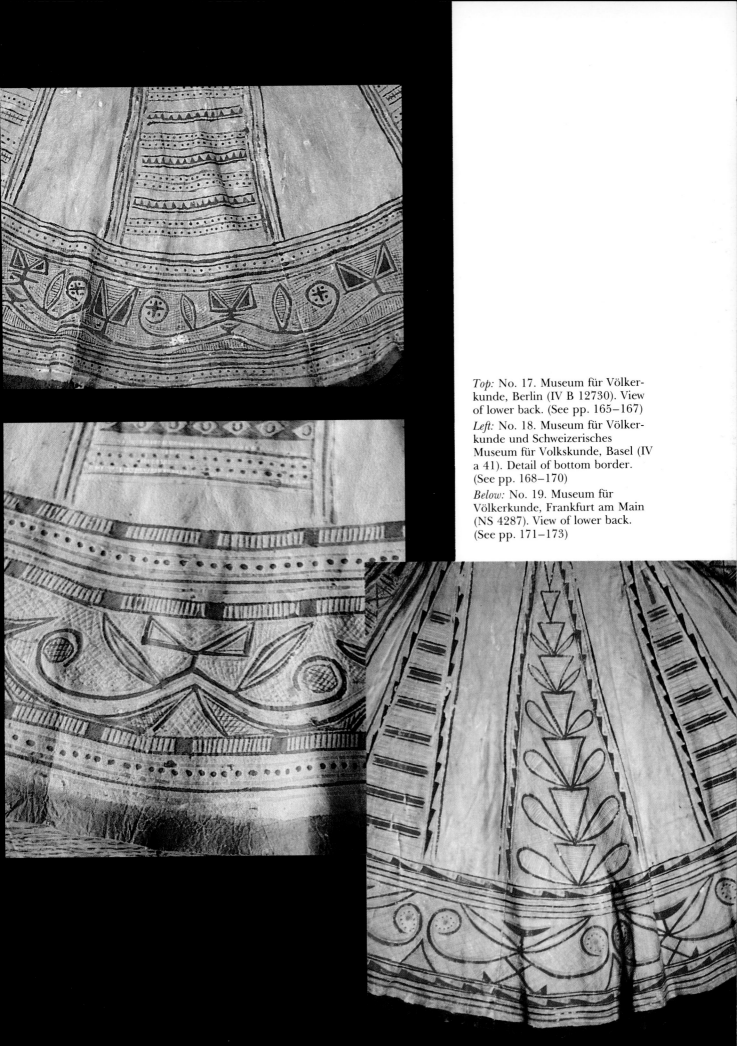

Top: No. 17. Museum für Völkerkunde, Berlin (IV B 12730). View of lower back. (See pp. 165–167)

Left: No. 18. Museum für Völkerkunde und Schweizerisches Museum für Volkskunde, Basel (IV a 41). Detail of bottom border. (See pp. 168–170)

Below: No. 19. Museum für Völkerkunde, Frankfurt am Main (NS 4287). View of lower back. (See pp. 171–173)

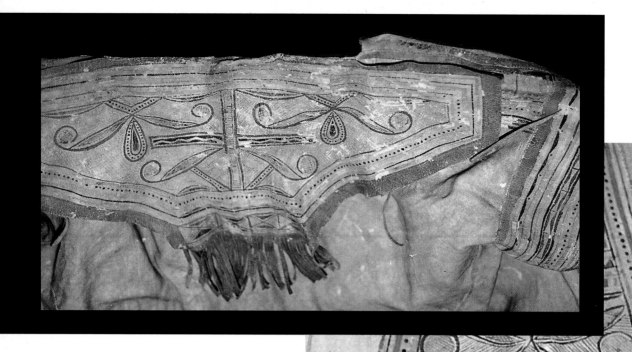

Above: No. 20. British Museum, London (1954 w Am 5 964). Collar. (See pp. 174–176)

Right: No. 22. Pitt Rivers Museum, Oxford (1906). Detail of centre back. (See pp. 180–183)

Opposite, top: No. 25. Musée de la civilisation, Québec (68.2875). Detail of borders at front. (See pp. 190–193)

Opposite, bottom: No. 26. Deutsches Ledermuseum/Schuhmuseum, Offenbach am Main (11569). View of upper back. (See pp. 194–196)

52

54

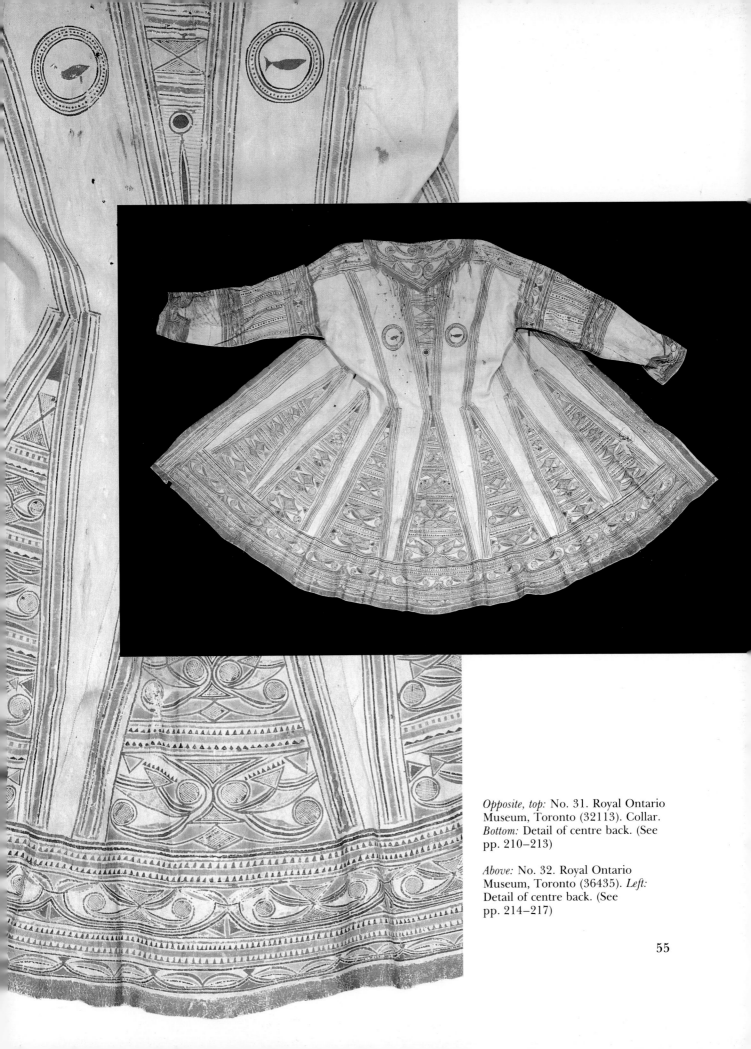

Opposite, top: No. 31. Royal Ontario
Museum, Toronto (32113). Collar.
Bottom: Detail of centre back. (See
pp. 210–213)

Above: No. 32. Royal Ontario
Museum, Toronto (36435). *Left:*
Detail of centre back. (See
pp. 214–217)

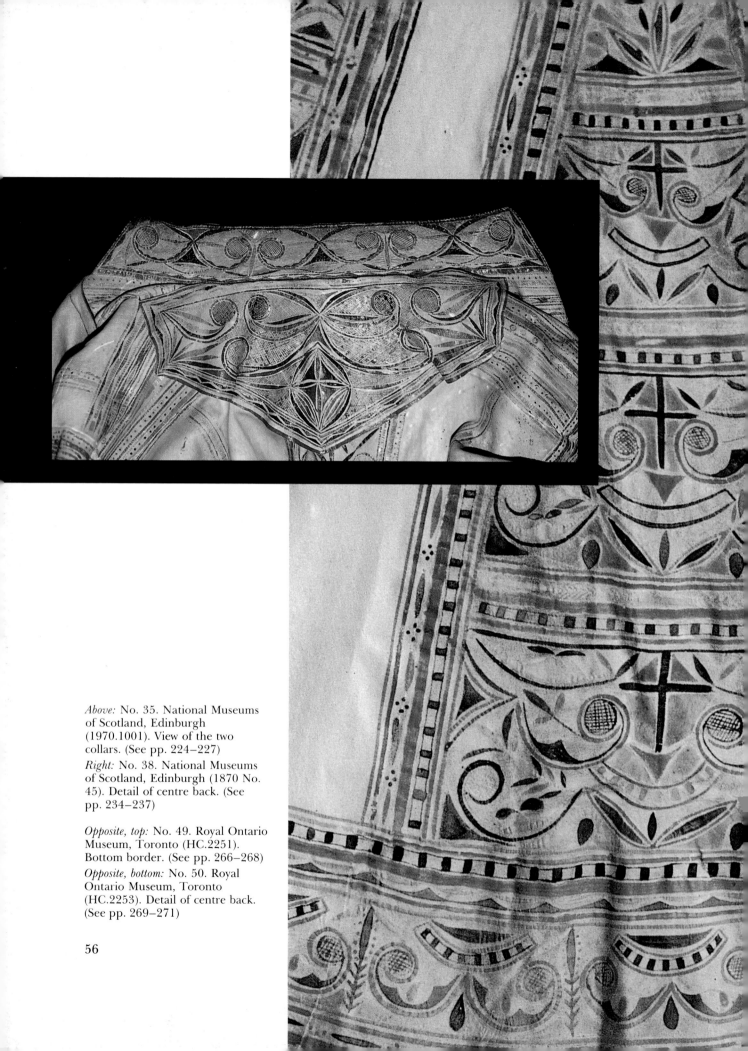

Above: No. 35. National Museums of Scotland, Edinburgh (1970.1001). View of the two collars. (See pp. 224–227)

Right: No. 38. National Museums of Scotland, Edinburgh (1870 No. 45). Detail of centre back. (See pp. 234–237)

Opposite, top: No. 49. Royal Ontario Museum, Toronto (HC.2251). Bottom border. (See pp. 266–268)

Opposite, bottom: No. 50. Royal Ontario Museum, Toronto (HC.2253). Detail of centre back. (See pp. 269–271)

56

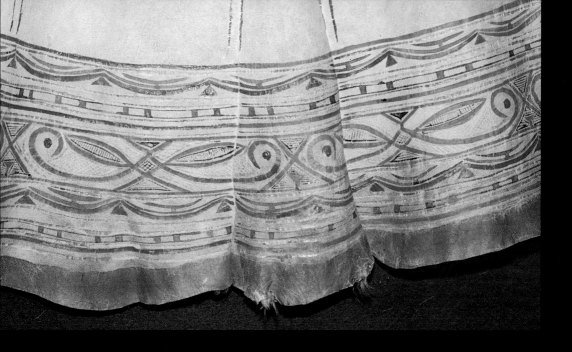

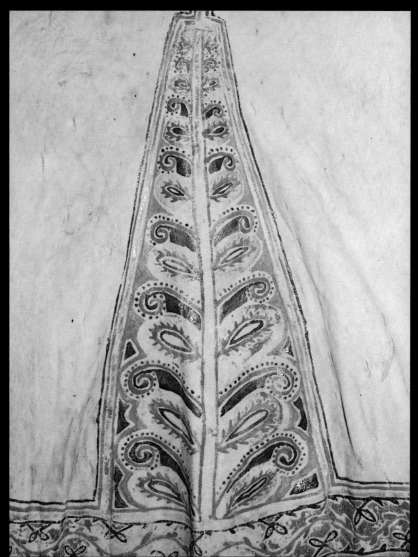

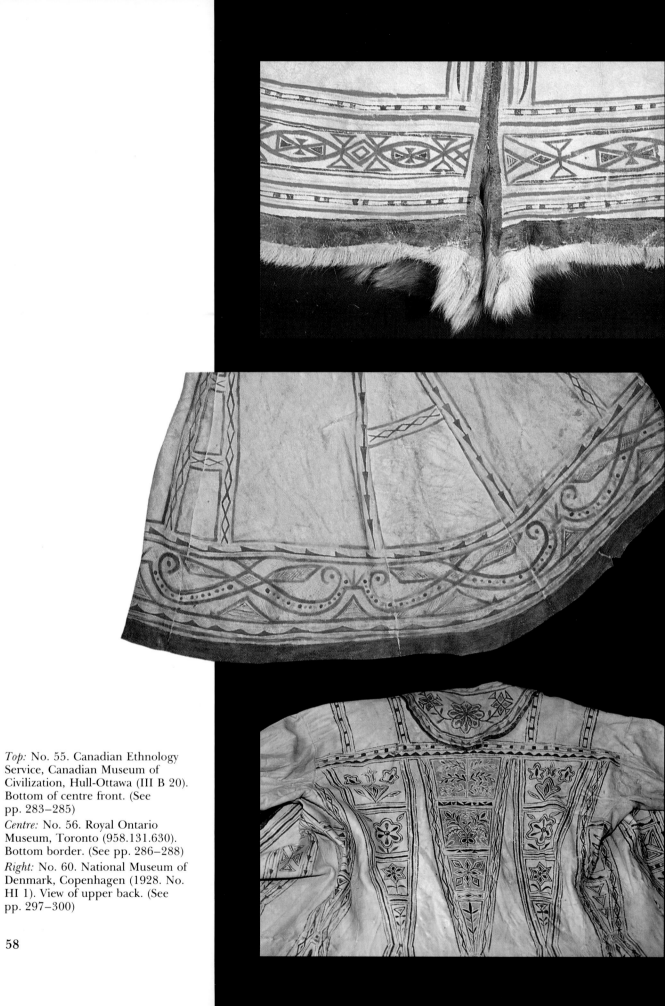

Top: No. 55. Canadian Ethnology
Service, Canadian Museum of
Civilization, Hull-Ottawa (III B 20).
Bottom of centre front. (See
pp. 283–285)
Centre: No. 56. Royal Ontario
Museum, Toronto (958.131.630).
Bottom border. (See pp. 286–288)
Right: No. 60. National Museum of
Denmark, Copenhagen (1928. No.
HI 1). View of upper back. (See
pp. 297–300)

DESIGN MOTIFS

Two types of design dominate the painted decoration of the coats: those based on a quadrate layout and those based on double curves. The two traditions may have developed separately but on these coats they are often intermingled.

Supporting and enriching these two basic themes there appears to be great complexity of patterning, but only nineteen other motifs have been isolated: chevrons, circles, crosses, crosshatching, diagonal crosses, dots, growth patterning, hearts, leaves, lozenges, ovals, parallel lines, realism, rectangles, scallops, stars, tracks, triangles, and zigzags. Some of these motifs are used on many coats, some only rarely. They are described in alphabetical sequence after the two main design traditions.

Although separation has been attempted, it has not been possible to pigeon-hole the motifs neatly, for there is considerable overlapping. Zigzags, for example, may be seen as just a line of chevrons joined together, or a row of lozenges as two interlocking lines of zigzags. While some motifs are definitely leaflike and others are simply ovals, there are those that lie in between and are difficult to classify as either. Growth patterning, while not a motif in the strictest sense, pervades so many design areas that it seems wise to have a separate entry for the kinds of patterning that suggest a feeling of growth.

Frank G. Speck tells us that the motifs that would give a hunter power when painted on his coat appeared to him in a dream. The hunter passed the dream instructions on to his wife and she, probably with little understanding of their symbolism, was left to translate them into reality.[1] From examining many of the coats it seems likely that the man's instructions were quite simple: he probably requested one or possibly two themes, while the woman filled out and enriched those themes with lesser motifs, the success of the coat depending on her skill and artistry.

The first question people always ask about these designs is What do they mean? The motifs undoubtedly had specific meaning for the man who dreamed them, but that significance was not always recognized and agreed upon by others. For example, a motif might be interpreted as a flower by one person, a celestial body by another, and a "soul" or "heart" by a third.[2] It is quite obvious, from the location of the motifs and their frequency of use on a coat, that some motifs are more important than others, but it is quite impossible to know or even to suggest what meaning the original owner of the coat attributed to the motifs or what power they might have given him.

Certain of the ethnologists who have done extensive fieldwork concerning the native life and the religion in the Quebec-Labrador peninsula have published information given to them relating to the meaning of some of the motifs. When possible this information has been added as notes to the descriptions of the individual motifs.

Note: In the following descriptions of the individual motifs, the coats in this series are referred to by their catalogue entry number. If the number is in bold type, the reader will find an illustration adjacent to the text, and if the number is in normal roman type, the reader should refer to the catalogue entry for that coat for illustration.

QUADRATES

Motifs based on a quadrate layout provide one of the two basic design types used by the native people of the Quebec-Labrador peninsula to decorate their caribou-skin coats. It seems most probable that this quadrate type of patterning is based on the widespread and ancient art of biting a design into a thin piece of folded birch-bark. Some examples of motifs produced in this way are shown in the accompanying photographs.[3]

Birch-bark biting is a woman's art and one that is done for fun, often as part of a social gathering, sitting in a group around a fire. It was practised wherever birch-bark was available, from Newfoundland to the Plains, and it is still done in some areas. It has been said that the elderly women who had few teeth left were the ones who excelled. A small piece of bark is peeled down to a thin fine layer, which is folded in half, folded at a right angle in half again, and then folded diagonally from the centre to make eight thicknesses. The woman takes this small folded triangle of bark and moves it around while she bites it. She does not bite through to make a real hole but just squeezes the layers tightly together. When the piece of bark is unfolded, there, like magic, is a pattern of considerable complexity. Some women were, of course, far better at it than others; some were more ambitious and with additional folds could produce fairly realistic floral motifs with stems and leaves, butterflies, bugs, or even animals.[4] Most examples have rosette designs based on the three basic folds, and it is this type of motif that seems to be the inspiration for many of the quadrate patterns used in decorating the caribou-skin hunting coats.

There is no suggestion that birch-bark bites were copied exactly when painting a coat, but the symmetry and the size of the individual motifs on the coats certainly suggest a close connection of thought with the birch-bark bites. Frank G. Speck put it well when he said: "While the connection is vague, it would be no more so than that between sketch book and the finished picture . . . of the modern artist."[5]

Birch-bark bites by Angélique Merasty. *Left, top to bottom:* Royal Ontario Museum 957.49.20, 957.49.24, 957.49.46, 957.49.18, 957.49.25.

The most elaborate use of quadrate patterning is found on the first four coats in the series (Nos. 1–4), all of which were probably made by Montagnais in the southwestern part of the Quebec-Labrador peninsula. Coat No. **1** has two different quadrate motifs in the bottom border, the simpler one of which has a layout like a "Union Jack."[6] There are also complex quadrate motifs in the central gore form and its extension.

1

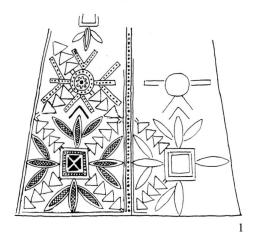

1

Small motifs used on the shoulders and sleeve bands of coat No. **2** provide obvious comparisons to birch-bark-bite designs; less obvious, but still surely connected, are the lozenge motifs and the scrolls that surround them in the gore forms. The layout for the medallions on the back could also owe something to the inspiration of a birch-bark bite. Interestingly, many areas of the patterning on this coat are outlined with tiny dots that seem to suggest a series of bite marks.

Coat No. **3** also has motifs with a quadrate feeling in the bottom border, too complex to be a direct copy of a birch-bark bite, but with the symmetry and the size of that type of motif. The quadrate feeling pervades many of the other patterned areas on that coat as well, particularly two of the side gore forms.

2

2

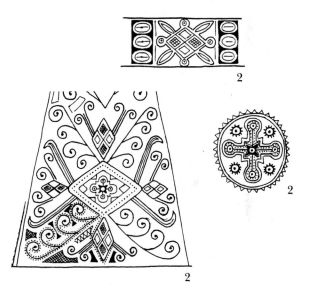

2

3

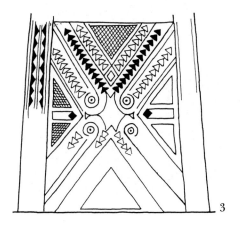

3

4

The collar on coat No. **4** has five motifs across its width, and although they incorporate rather primitive forms of the double-curve motif, they have a quadrate layout. The pattern of the medallions on the back of the coat divides neatly into eight, like motifs made when using the three basic folds of a piece of birch-bark.

4

Considerably further along in the sequence of development, coat No. **24** has quite unusual patterning. The bottom border with its lozenges could be taken to have a quadrate connection. A four-petalled motif is used repeatedly in the gore forms, while the collar decoration, although topped by a great sweeping double curve, has a definitely quadrate combination of leaves and ovals in the centre. This coat, which does not fit in well with any other of its period, may also come, like Nos. 1–4, from the western part of the peninsula.

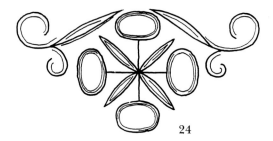

24

Quadrate patterning shows up again on coats collected later by Lucien Turner and Robert Flaherty. Both men apparently gathered material in the Fort Chimo area, where native people came together from both east and west. Among the coats they collected are ones with the double-curve designs of the Naskapi and others with a completely different style of design—many of the motifs, although very clumsily drawn, are recognizably quadrate in form. The quadrate tradition, now seemingly forgotten in that area, probably moved up the western side of the peninsula, surviving long enough to inspire the painted patterns on these coats of the late 19th and early 20th centuries.

On Nos. **43–44** the bottom border designs are quadrate-based with four-petalled motifs enclosed in squares. Dividing a gore form into two halves, with similar, fairly small quadrate motifs on either side of a vertical line, was a layout used on No. 1 and is repeated at this late date on three of the Lucien Turner coats, Nos. **43–45.**

43

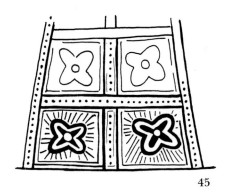

44

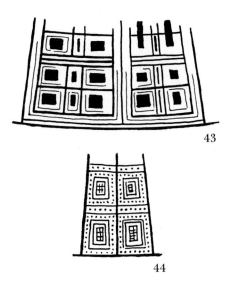

43

44

The connection with quadrate patterning is not quite as obvious with the two Flaherty coats, Nos. 50–51. They are quite different in style from the usual Naskapi double-curve type, and the colour and many details of the patterning—for instance, the quadrate leaf motif in the side gore forms on No. **50**—seem to tie them in with the more western coats.

50

DOUBLE CURVES

Spirals and curves, used singly, doubled, or in groups, occur in many parts of the world. A particular form of double curve is of immense importance in the Quebec-Labrador peninsula; it is one of the two main types of patterning used in the area and undoubtedly the most significant of the motifs painted on the coats.

In the basic form (left), two matching arms curve out and up in opposite directions from a central point, to terminate in tight curves. A template, probably just a firm piece of birch-bark, was used to draw double curves. The artist could lay the template down and draw one curve; then she could flip it over to produce the reverse curve. It is possible when examining a coat to isolate the curve of the basic template or templates. The repetition is obvious, but the artist also had freedom to use the template as she wished. Sometimes only part of the length of the line might be used, or possibly another template with a slightly different curve was substituted, but the two arms of a double curve always match in reverse. The terminals of the arms often vary slightly and were probably drawn freehand.

There are three groups of coats that make use of this motif in three different ways.

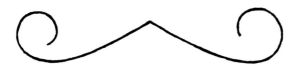

On Nos. 1–4, coats with designs based on birch-bark bites, and on Nos. 43–46 and 50–51, the much later coats that show a survival of that type of patterning, double curves are not important. The collar on No. 1 has a double curve but it is so leaflike that it is not readily recognizable. On No. **2** slender curves grow out from the central lozenge motifs and from the fantastic blossoming stem, while in gore forms 1 and 5 paired curves grown down between the leaves. Curves are fitted in around the motifs on No. **3** but more remarkable is the small double curve of basic form at the centre back. On No. **4** single curves surround the central gore form and a double curve is

2

2

3

4

used on the collar, although it is almost hidden in the foliage. Of the later coats, No. **45** has a strange double-curve variation and on No. **51** there is a decadent survival of the motif.

45

51

The coats in the second group, Nos. 5–11, are early in date. Double curves are a main motif of each of these coats but they are used with a wealth of variation. It almost seems that the usual motif, repeated and repeated in later years, had not as yet been set and that the artists were still free to use this powerful motif in inventive and personal ways. There are many double curves on coat No. **5**, but those in the bottom border are upside down while those in the gore forms are fragmented. On No. **6** the curves are used singly, attached to the chevron motifs, and on the collar there is a double curve with extra curves hanging from it. On No. **7** double curves are either inverted or have an additional angle in the centre. No. 8 is the exception in this group for its double curves are of standard form. On No. **9** the curves are either doubled or reversed in the gore forms but are standard double curves on the collar. No. **10** has an unusual and very strongly drawn version, with the curves swelling into leaves, a form that is repeated on No. 11.

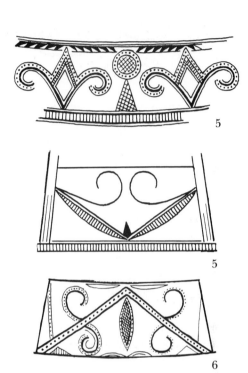

5

5

6

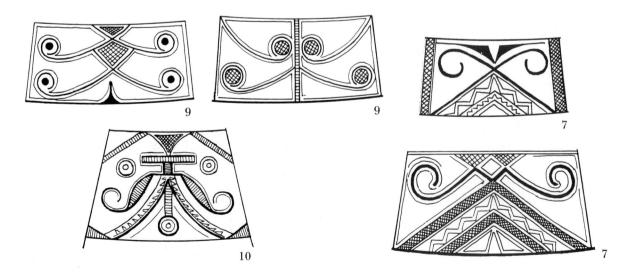

9

9

7

10

7

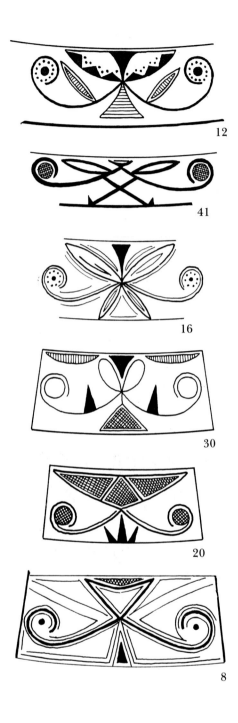

The third group is composed of thirty-five of the forty-eight coats that follow No. 11 in the series and range in date from the late 18th century to about 1930, when the making of the coats ended. All have basic double curves, some rounded, some long and slim, some large, and some small. The proportions may vary but the motif is still the simple standard double curve. Variations on the theme may be added, but the basic double curve is also there.

During this long period the double-curve motif remained fairly constant, but the subsidiary motifs varied considerably, although the choice of what to use and where to place it does not seem to relate to any sequence of dating. To give a few examples, at all periods paired leaves may be poised on the arms of the curve as on No. **12** and the much later No. **41**. Leaves may also grow from the tip or central point where the curves meet as on Nos. **16** and **30**. The double curve is usually supported in some way, possibly by a triple leaf (No. **20**), a triangle used either point up (No. **8**) or point down (No. **22**), or a diagonal cross (No. **40**). Sometimes the diagonal cross extends to make a secondary double curve as on No. **15** and, at the other end of the period, on No. **56**.

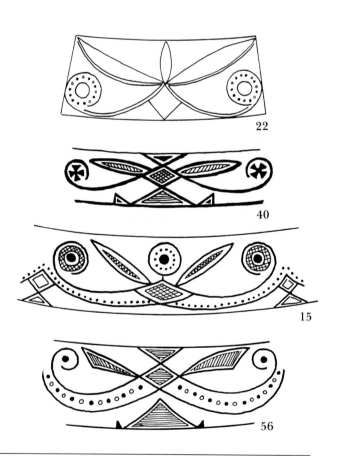

The terminals of the arms of the double curves are not left empty; at any period they may be filled by a crosshatched circle, a single dot, or a dot surrounded by smaller dots. On two coats, Nos. **17** and **40**, a small cross is used in this position.

The arms of the double curve may end where they meet or cross and continue up in a V-shape to the top of the pattern area as with No. **15**. If they terminate where they meet that point usually supports a subsidiary motif such as the circle on No. **39**, the ovoid on No. **20**, or the triangle on No. **34**.

The collars of the coats often have the most carefully drawn of the double-curve designs and quite frequently have additional single curves moving either in or out at the sides. The collars of Nos. 12–16, 18, 34, **36**, and 40 all use the same pattern layout in which curves grow out to either side of a central line.

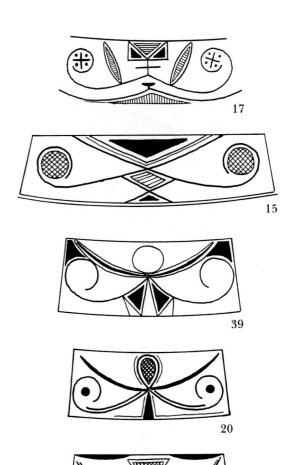

17

15

39

20

34

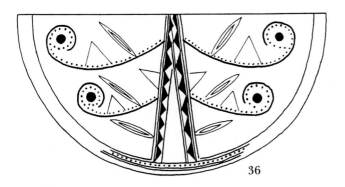

36

The way double curves are used seems to split the Quebec-Labrador peninsula in two. It may be reading too much into the very scanty evidence, but the designs based on birch-bark bites are probably Montagnais rather than Naskapi and probably come from the southwestern part of the area. Also to the west, but much farther north, there is a survival of that type of decoration on coats collected by Lucien Turner and Robert Flaherty. On all these probably western coats double curves are used only in minor variations, while to the east, on coats that can be considered to be Naskapi, double curves of basic form provide the most important motif and survive right to the end of the period.[7]

CHEVRONS

Chevrons are rare, occurring only on five of the coats in this series. They are used in two different ways: as a single bent line combined with other motifs, or continuously one above the other to fill a whole area.

On coat No. **6** chevrons are the most noticeable feature of the design, used singly in five of the seven gore forms to support double-curve variations. A similar though not as obvious use occurs on No. **10**, where the chevrons are slightly curved.

Chevrons are used continuously as the central line of the front borders on coat No. **2** and are repeated on a larger scale right up the centre back of No. **27.**

The latest use is on coat No. **46.** The painting of this coat is fairly minimal and clumsy, with chevrons filling the two side gore forms.

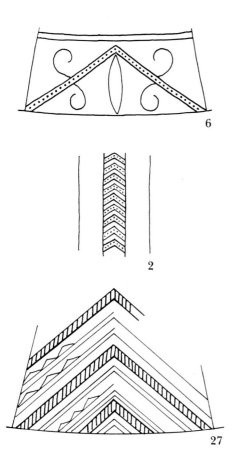

6

2

27

46

CIRCLES

Circles are not a common motif but are of early date and when used seem to be of importance. There are two types: those with simple outlines, and those surrounded by short radiating lines, which strongly suggest that the artist intended to indicate the sun.

On coat No. **5** a plain circle is balanced on a sharp point as one of the main motifs of the bottom border.

Freely floating circles are used to the side of the main motifs on coat No. 10, and to either side of the collars on Nos. 12, **22,** 25, and 27.

Infrequently circles hang from the centre of a double curve, as on Nos. 10, **11,** and 25, but in its most usual position the circle is supported by or floats just above the centre of a double-curve motif, as on Nos. 15, 22–23, 28, **31,** 37, and 39. The filling of the circle usually matches that of the terminals of the supporting double curve.

On the back shoulders of coat No. 32, circles surround the only realistic motifs that have so far been recorded on painted caribou-skin coats. The fish and the bird that the circles enclose are undoubtedly the significant part of the motif and the fact that they are enclosed in circles is purely incidental.

It should be noted that all the coats mentioned above date from no later than the mid 19th century.

Rayed circles, or "suns," are even rarer and earlier than the plain circles, occurring on all four of the earliest coats (Nos. 1–4) and only once at a later date (No. 51).

One of the motifs of the bottom border of coat No. **1** looks rather like a "Union Jack" (see Quadrates), but there is a circle in the centre, and the surrounding crosses are probably rays. One of the two motifs in the central gore form also has a circular centre, but with V-shaped rays.

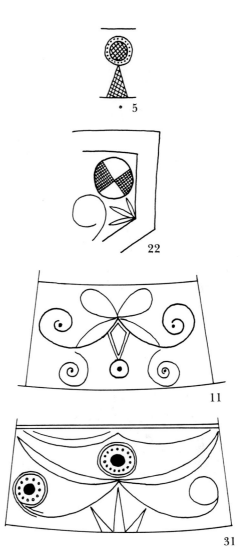

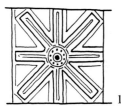

1

1

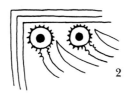

2

2

On coat No. **2** the medallions on the back shoulders have rays of small zigzags around them and enclose four small rayed circles. In the corners of the collar there are pairs of rayed circles. Similar motifs occur at the top of gore forms 2 and 4, while each of the lozenges in the vertical bands on the sleeves contains a small rayed circle.

On coat No. **3** rayed circles are used on the shoulders and the front borders. There are daisylike motifs, which are probably also "suns," on the centre-back extension, the sleeve bands, and the cuffs.

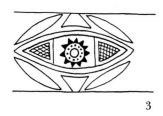

3

3

3

4

A most important use of rayed circles is for the beautifully designed medallions on the back of coat No. **4.** The design theme is repeated in the bottom border and on the shoulder band.

4

There seems to be only one use of the rayed circle or "sun" motif at a later date. It occurs on a small scale but with importance in the centre-back gore form of coat No. **51,** where rayed and plain circles are combined with double curves in a very confused and coarsely drawn design. The coat dates from about 1910 and probably comes from northwestern Quebec, where there seems to have been a survival of the earlier types of patterning.

51

CROSSES

Crosses are used on fifteen of the coats described in the catalogue. Most are on coats of early date and are small in size but placed in important positions. All except those on coat No. 38 are of native type.

Crosses with arms of equal length and with a short crossbar at the end of each arm are used on coat No. **1.** They are very small in size and are grouped at the centre bottom of the collar; the delicate little motifs made of lozenges and placed beside them probably have the significance of a cross also. The theme is repeated at the centre top of the collar, where five tiny circles are arranged in cross form. A similar motif, with small circles in the middle and at the ends of the arms, occurs again in simple form on the shoulder band of the same coat. A slightly more elaborate form is used as the centre of the medallions and many of the motifs on No. **2** and again above the bottom border of No. **4.** A unique use of this type of cross is the large central motif on the collar of No. **24.**[8]

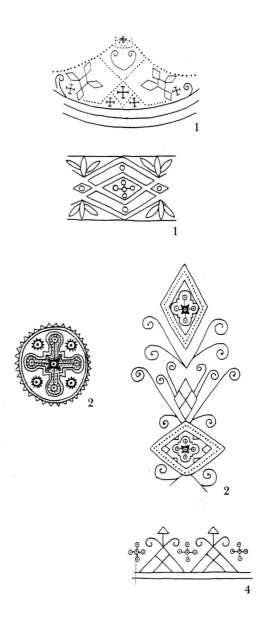

1

1

2

2

4

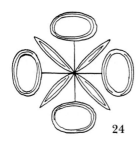

24

Plain crosses with arms of equal length are used on the sleeve bands of Nos. 1 and **3.** Cross forms are used in the terminals of the double curve on No. **17** and at the centre of the collar on No. **35.**

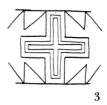

3

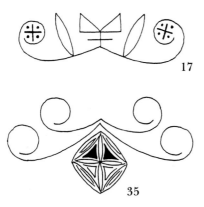

17

35

27

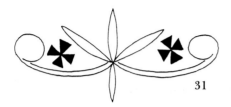

31

On the collars of three coats (Nos. 22, 25, **27**) there are pairs of circles; all the circles are divided into four parts by straight cross lines, but since all the lines run on the diagonal, perhaps these should not be considered to be cross motifs.

Four small triangles radiating from a central point make a cross motif. These are used with double curves on the collar of coat No. **31** and in the bottom borders of Nos. **40** and **45.**

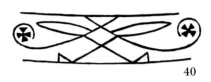

40

45

The only use of crosses that are most probably of Christian type is on coat No. **38.** Those in the central gore form are obvious, while those in side gore forms 2 and 6 are less well defined. On the same coat, tiny examples of the native type of cross made up of four triangles are used in gore forms 1 and 7.

38

38

CROSSHATCHING AND HATCHING

Crosshatching is used in two ways. The more common one is with fine yellow lines providing colour in the background of many patterned areas. This probably has no other purpose than to enrich the overall effect. On some coats background crosshatching is combined with solid filling, also done in yellow.

Crosshatching is also used to fill motifs, particularly the circles that are in the terminals of so many double curves, as on the collar of coat No. **31.** Black or some other strong noticeable colour may be selected for this purpose. The same kind of treatment may emphasize other essential parts of a design. Crosshatching used in this way may have significance.[9]

How much or how little crosshatching was done on a coat would have depended on the amount of time the painter was able to spend, and that was probably quite limited on the later coats. The maker of coat No. **22** did not stint with her time. Crosshatching and hatching completely fill three of the gore forms, the bottom border, and the large collar on that coat. The painter's effort cannot be ignored, for as well as the usual pale yellow much of the fine work has been done with quite strong blue and red.

Crosshatching was also used to make decorative bands, such as those used for the front borders and the sleeve bands on No. **7,** and in the side gore forms of Nos. 8–9 and **10,** all early in date, and of No. 33, at a somewhat later date.

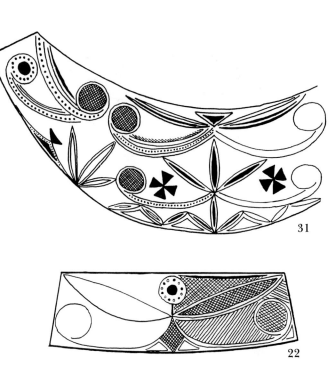

31

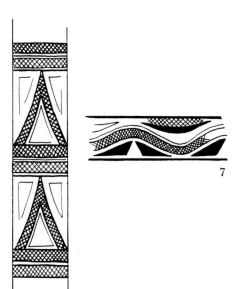

22

7

7

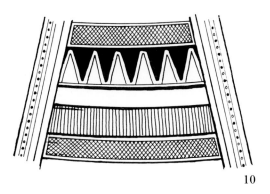

10

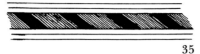

35

Hatching is far less common than crosshatching. When used in background areas it may just be that the cross lines were never completed or do not show up. On coat No. **35** a band with careful, close-set diagonal hatching alternating with heavy lines, rather like a barber pole, is used in the bottom border and repeated in some of the gore forms and on the very careful inside painting on the stand-up collar. The "barber-pole" theme also appears in wider form on No. 8, where it has been used with hatching on the sleeves and without hatching on the front borders.

DIAGONAL CROSSES

The crossing of two diagonal lines to form an hour-glass shape is a decorative motif of very widespread global use. It is used in the painted decoration of many of these coats, not as a main motif but in an important supporting role and probably with considerable significance.[10]

On the early coats in this series (Nos. **1–2,** 3–4) diagonal crosses occur in a fairly elaborate way but only as part of the quadrate layout of the motifs.

From the second half of the 18th century on, whenever the main motif is a double curve, the diagonal cross motif may be used in three different ways.

Frequently it provides the foundation on which the double curve sits (Nos. 15, **19,** 21, 28, **36,** 41, **49,** 54).

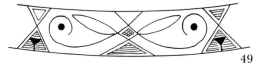

Less often the diagonal cross is used as a divider between the motifs in border designs, as on the sleeves of coat No. **9** and in the bottom borders of Nos. 30, 40, and 49.

The third method of use strongly indicates that the diagonal cross is a condensed form of the double curve. In the gore forms the compartments of design narrow as they approach the waist. When there is no longer sufficient width for a double curve, the smaller compartments are commonly filled with diagonal crosses. This can be seen on Nos. 5, 8–9, 15, 18, 20–23, 25, 28, 30–34, 36–37, 39, and 50. On Nos. 31–34 and 37 diagonal crosses continue up the centre-back extension. The diagram taken from the centre back of coat No. **31** shows the transition of the double curve into a simple diagonal cross at the waist and out again into a more decorative form of the motif as the space widens towards the shoulders.

1   2

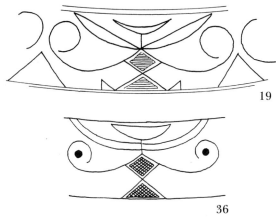

19

36

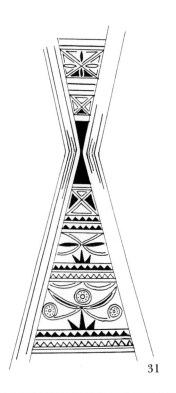

31

49

9

9

15

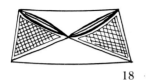

18

Variations on the theme of the diagonal cross are used in the side gore forms of Nos. **15, 18,** 19, and 21, and in smaller form in a band across the side gore forms of No. 31, on the cuffs of No. **18,** and on the collars of Nos. 20, **32,** and 33.

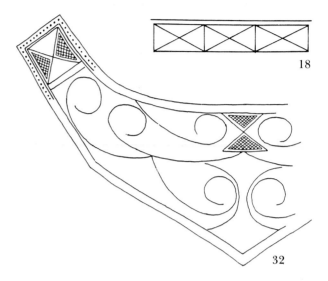

18

32

Probably all of these versions of the diagonal cross motif are used to reiterate and reinforce the power of the more recognizable double curve.

DOTS

Dots are a simple and frequently used design element. Singly they make a centre point for a motif or fill the terminal space of a double curve. When used for that purpose they are often surrounded by a ring of smaller dots, a feature of double-curve designs dating particularly from the latter part of the 18th to the first half of the 19th century and occurring on Nos. 12–14, 19, 21–22, **31,** and 36, as well as at a later date on No. 48.

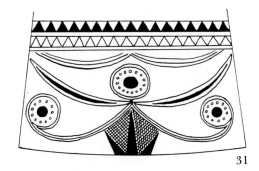

31

Dots arranged in a row are one of the most common of the various line decorations that were used to edge and enrich the pattern areas of the coats.[11] The bottom border of coat No. **31** is typical of the way in which rows of dots are used on a good two-thirds of the coats in this series. Whether or not these lines of dots have any great significance, they add greatly to the overall richness of the decoration, often carefully alternating between red and some other colour. As might be expected, use is particularly lavish on coats dating from before the middle of the 19th century.

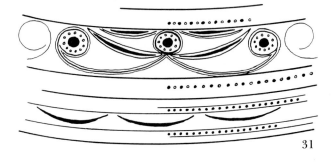

31

A special form of line-and-dot decoration occurs only in the bottom border and on the top sleeve bands of coat No. 22, and more noticeably on No. **38,** where it is used in the surrounds of many of the gore forms. It has a narrow leaflike line alternating with a group of four small dots. It must have been quite fussy to paint, so perhaps it is not surprising that it is so rarely found.

38

One other rather unusual type of dot is surrounded by a small circle. It is used in great profusion on coat No. **13** and more sparingly on No. 16. Dots were probably made by using a small round stick as a painting tool. A stamp for the circles could easily have been made from a slightly larger bit of pithy wood with the pith pushed out, or possibly something like a goose quill could have been used. Small circles without dots are used to centre the lozenges that cross the side gore forms of No. 18.

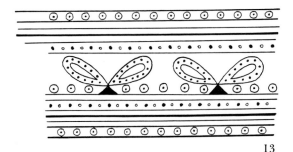

13

GROWTH PATTERNING

Although growth patterning is not perhaps in the strictest sense a motif, because it is a dominant element in the painting of caribou-skin coats, it seems to belong here in the Design Motifs section. Those who have lived through a winter in the interior of the Quebec-Labrador peninsula tell us that when the first signs of new leaves appear in the spring, the reaction to the renewal of life and growth is quite overwhelming, and it is natural for that joy to be reflected in the designs painted on that most important garment, the coat that was worn for the caribou hunt.[12]

Growth patterning is an integral part of the early quadrate designs, escaping as small leaves and tendrils from the centre of many of the motifs, as on coat No. **2**, unfolding in great fernlike sweeps, as on the collar of No. **1**, and zigzagging or curving upwards to breathe life into the surrounds of the gore forms, as on Nos. **2** and **4**. Similar growth motifs are repeated many, many years later on coats that were collected by Lucien Turner (Nos. **45, 46**) and by Robert Flaherty (Nos. **50–51**).

2

1

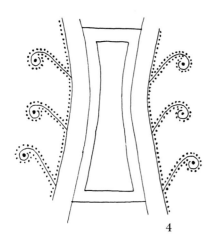

4

45

50

50

51

With the quadrate-based designs, growth takes the form of leaves, sprouts, and tendrils — all vegetal, but there is growth also with animals. The double curve in itself has a very obvious feeling of growth. The thought behind the double curve may be animal, and is considered by many to be caribou, but many versions support pairs of leaves, as on Nos. **22** and **49,** and occasionally the arms of the double curves swell out into leaf forms, as on No. **11.** In the most popular type of collar design, leaves and double curves grow out from a central line; an excellent example is No. **16.** This same coat provides a good illustration for another type of growth pattern in which pairs of leaves reach up and out to fill the central gore form.

A feeling of growth, to a greater or lesser extent, is a part of the decoration of every coat in this series, except those that have only simple line decoration.

6

HEARTS

Hearts, or more correctly motifs that look like hearts, are used occasionally. Rather than hearts as they are known in European design, these motifs are probably another shortened form of the double curve. In the centre of the collar of coat No. **6** there is a large double-curve variation, and to either side of it small heartlike motifs are drawn in the same way. They are undoubtedly small variations of a double curve, even though the terminals curve up and in, to create a motif that appears at first glance to be a heart. No other double-curve motif simulates a heart shape quite as closely as this, but any of the double curves, if their arms are pushed up from the centre point, will eventually make a heart shape.

Small "hearts" are also fitted into the zigzag pattern of the bottom border of this same coat, No. **6**, and are used in a similar way on No. **9,** which has a wealth of double-curve variations in all parts of the coat except the bottom border. These "hearts" probably reiterate the strong double-curve theme of both coats.

Another heartlike motif consists of paired, fat leaves and is used in the bottom borders of Nos. **10** and 13, on the sleeves of No. 13, and at the centre of the double-curve motifs on Nos. **11** and 30. Pairs of fat leaves also fill the central gore forms of Nos. 16 and 19. Are these possibly double curves in disguise? They are, after all, in an area usually reserved for double curves.

6

9

10

11

A further use of heart-shaped motifs can be seen in the bottom border of coat No. **43.** The way they are drawn makes them very similar to the paired leaves in the side gore forms of the same coat — more double curves?[13]

43

43

Very, very few of the design motifs on these coats show European influence, and so, with the evidence of the not-quite-closed heart form on No. 6, which seems undoubtedly to be a double curve, it seems most likely that the other heart-shaped motifs are also of native origin; some may well carry the significance of a double curve.

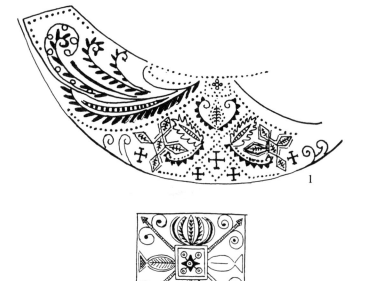

1

LEAVES

Leaves are fitted in around other motifs on most of the coats in this series. Many are completely stylized, but a few are drawn with more freedom and detail and possibly represent the leaf of an actual tree or shrub.[14]

Leaf forms are richest and most detailed on the first few coats in the series. On the collar of coat No. **1** there is a foliated double curve and a pair of tiny leaves with serrated edges; there are also other small precise leaves in the bottom border. Similar leaves form the lattice on the collar of No. **3.** On No. **2** there are three types of leaves in the bottom border, while in the gore forms leaves grow out and down from a central stem. The theme of a branching stem is repeated at a late date on Nos. **43, 45–46,** and **50.** These coats probably all originated in the northwestern part of Quebec, where there seems to have been a survival of early designs. The leaves on No. 50 are startlingly similar to the small leaves with serrated edges on the collar of No. 1.

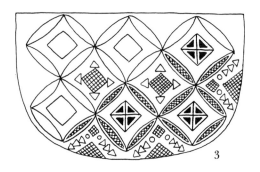

1

2

2

3

43

50

Many of the coats from the late 18th century on use pairs of leaves above the double-curve motif. These may be fairly large as on coat No. **22** or slimmer and curved as on No. **31.** On No. **18,** in addition to the usual pair of leaves, there are wedge-shaped triangles which probably also represent leaves.

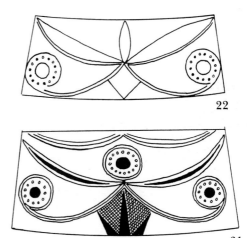

22

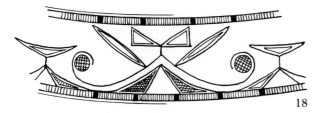

18

31

The collar design on coat No. **16** has lanceolate leaves as well as broader rounded ones at the side of a type also used on Nos. 13, 19, 23–24, and 30.

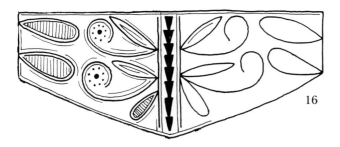

16

On coat No. **11** the arms of the double-curve motif swell into leaf forms, and where they meet they support a pair of broad leaves that forms sort of a heart motif. As has been mentioned in Hearts, this motif may be a condensed form of double curve.

The collar of coat No. **28** has unique leaf sprays, perhaps native in origin, but possibly influenced by the weeping willows that were fashionable in European design at the beginning of the 19th century when this coat was made.

The sleeve band on coat No. **35** has clumps of small lanceolate leaves, a theme that is repeated on the collar and in the side gore forms of the same coat.

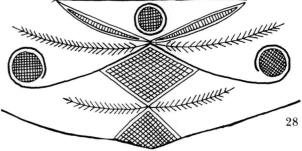

11

28

35

30

Most unusual small leaf sprays punctuate the zigzags on the shoulder band of coat No. **30** and are used lavishly on the collar and in all the gore forms of No. **38.**

38

50

The undulating vine with small sprouts on coat No. **50** is perhaps more of a growth motif than a leaf. On the same coat, similar sprouts extend to either side of a line up the centre of the back and are also used around the side gore forms on No. 51.

No. **48,** an early 20th-century coat, has complex designs that incorporate many traditional leaf motifs. The diagram shows the collar with its double-curve variation mounted on a sort of tree with blossoms and paired leaves. No. **60,** which dates from 1926, has similar, fairly traditional designs in the bottom border, but much of the patterning used in its gore forms shows the influence of contemporary Canadian design.

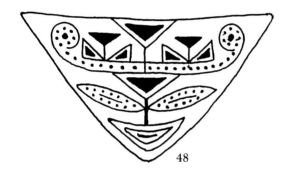

48

60

60

LOZENGES

Lozenges (diamonds, rhombs) are motifs that were used extensively and at all periods.

Single lozenges are rare. They are used as the centre of motifs that were probably inspired by birch-bark bites, as on Nos. 1–2 and **3.** At a later date there are single lozenges in all the side gore forms of coat No. **32** and above the double curves in the bottom border of No. 35. Otherwise, when a single lozenge occurs, it is either as the result of a space created by more important motifs, as on the collars of Nos. **27,** 28, and 38, or clumsily drawn between diagonal crosses, as on No. **44.**

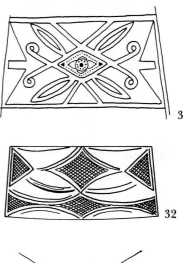

3

32

44

27

While the use of single lozenges is rare, lozenges arranged in rows occur on almost half of the coats, early and late, in this series. On Nos. 23, **24,** 46, and **53,** they are the main motif of the bottom border, but on most coats the lozenge rows are fairly narrow and are used most effectively to surround and enrich the patterning of the borders, the gore forms, the shoulders, the collars, and the sleeves.

24

53

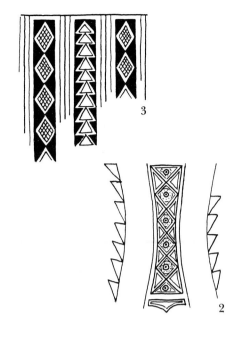

3

On the early coats the most noticeable use of lozenges is on the sleeves of Nos. 2 and **3** and at the centre back of Nos. 1, **2,** and 3. At a somewhat later date a row of lozenges is used for the central vertical band on a number of collars (Nos. 12–13, **15**, 19, 34).

2

15

Lozenge rows may be used as the main decorative motif when side gore forms are filled with horizontal bands (Nos. **13,** 15–16, 18). The motif had a long life as it is to be found in one form or another on many of the late 19th- and early 20th-century coats.

13

44

Lozenges occur drawn in simple lines as on the collars of Nos. 13 and 19, but more frequently they are reserved against a dark ground as on No. **44.** If fairly small, they are usually left plain but sometimes they enclose a dot or a ringed dot (No. **16**); if slightly larger, as on the collar of No. 15, they may be crosshatched.

16

There are rare variations where the diamond form is elongated and made into something very special, as on the sleeves of No. **8,** in the bottom border of No. 22, and across the shoulders of No. **31.**

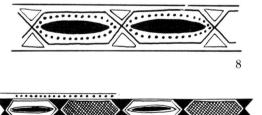

8

31

OVALS, OVOIDS, AND POINTED OVALS

Motifs in this section are called ovals when both ends are rounded, ovoids when one end is rounded and the other is more pointed, and pointed ovals when both ends are somewhat pointed, often giving a very leaflike appearance. None of the forms is numerous.

In this series coat No. **24** has the only example of ovals. They are used at the ends of the arms of the cross on the collar, in just the same way that circles are used on many smaller crosses.

An ovoid motif is also used in a way that is interchangeable with a circle, balanced above a double curve, on Nos. **20**, 21, and **33**. On coat No. **20** an ovoid sits up like a blossom between leaves in the bottom border and another hangs down like a drop on either side of the centre of the collar. The drop form is also important as one of the motifs fitted in with the zigzags on the bottom border of No. **9**.

9

While ovals and ovoids may be interchangeable with circles, pointed ovals are often hard to distinguish from leaves. On Nos. 1 and **3** pointed ovals form a central vertical line in the side gore forms and are combined with paired leaves. On Nos. **12** and 13 the use is similar but the shapes are drawn with more definition and they support a series of double curves.

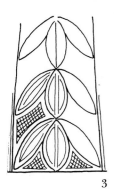

3

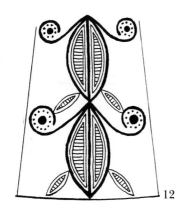

12

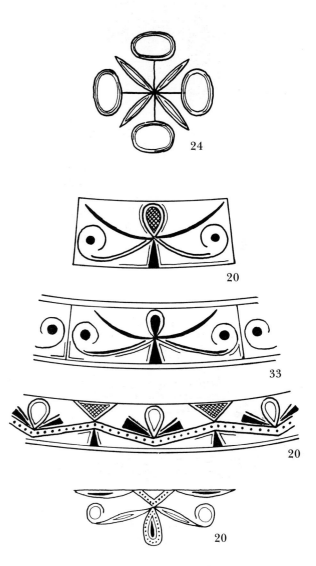

24

20

33

20

20

3

Pointed ovals, rather hidden in the complex patterning, are used as links in the shoulder band and the bottom border of coat No. **3.** On No. **6** much more definite and strongly drawn pointed ovals make a centre for all the compartments in three of the gore forms and on the collar. These are obviously an important element in the coat's overall design, and the way the motif is placed, standing on end, suggests that it is not a leaf but has some other significance.

6

On coat No. **30** similar motifs, quite unlike leaves, are used lying down on their sides to make bands that alternate with parallel lines in all the side gore forms.[15]

30

PARALLEL LINES

Parallel lines are the natural result of the use of painting tools that have more than one prong. Such tools that pre-date any of the surviving coats have been found (see Tools section). It seems that by the time the earliest coats in this series were being made, the tradition that the layout of the pattern areas should be in parallel lines was so strong that on a few coats where only single prongs were used, individual lines were carefully laid down side by side to make it look as though the work was done with a tool with more than one prong (see Nos. 1–2 and at a much later date Nos. 43, 46, 50–51, 59).

The layout of the patterned areas of most of the coats is done in yellow with a 2-prong or more frequently a 3-prong tool. Very often lines in a contrasting colour, made with either a single or a 2-prong tool, are fitted in between the original lines as in the diagram at right.

Parallel lines are not used only to delineate the design areas; sometimes they are the sole decorative element. Coat No. 47 is patterned with triple lines only, some of which were made with a 3-prong tool and some with a single prong used three times over. On No. 42 the line decoration is more elaborate, the result of using both 2- and 3-prong tools; this coat has the minor addition of a single track in the front borders. The entire decoration of No. 29 consists of plain parallel lines combined in the different weights and spacings of 3-, 5-, and 7-prong tools. It is a beautiful coat and has the rare addition of quilled fringes, the wrapping of which is done in bands of colour that reinforce the impact of the line decoration.

On most of the coats between Nos. 9 and 39, parallel lines are used across the side gore forms, sometimes alone but often alternating with one of the small line decorations — dots, crosshatched lines, or rows of small lozenges. Whether this use of parallel lines has some meaning or is just a decorative space filler, probably no one can now say.[16]

The centre-back extensions of many of the coats between Nos. 12 and 29 are similarly filled with horizontal parallel lines, as are the unique extensions of the side gore forms on No. 25.

On later coats, from No. 34 on, the customary bands of decoration on the front borders and the sleeves are often reduced to simple parallel lines, probably a quick and easy way of filling traditional areas of patterning. On two coats that are comparatively early in date and quite elaborately painted (Nos. 17, 30), however, the collars, so often a very important design area, have no ornamentation other than parallel lines.

Parallel lines are also used in groups placed vertically on the shoulders of all the coats between Nos. 12 and 21 (for illustration, see Layout of the Design section and photographs of individual coats). Such groups of lines usually combine the heavy and light lines of two different tools and may occur on the fronts, on the back, and on the tops of the sleeves, or on just one or two of these areas. From a horizontal band below the shoulders they run up and into the shoulder seams. They are not spaced to meet the lines coming into the seam from the other side of the coat, so whatever their function, it is probably not to unify the parts of the coat.

REALISM

Realism occurs in a definite way on only one coat, No. **32.** On either side of the centre-back extension there are medallions, one of which encloses a fish and the other a bird. Although on the bird medallion the paint is quite worn, it is possible to see that the bird is standing on legs of medium length and looks very much like a goose. The designs on all these coats were painted to honour the caribou as the mainstay of life, but fish and birds were also very important as food sources, and this hunter's coat is a rare acknowledgement of that fact.

Much less definite realism occurs with some of the leaf forms that are worked into the designs of the coats. When the painting was being done the artist may well have been thinking of a specific plant, but with most examples, a type — long and slim, short and fat, or even triangular — is as close as they come to realism (see Leaves for illustrations and commentary). One arrangement used on some coats of fairly late date (Nos. 48, **52,** 58, 60) combines two wedge-shaped triangles with a stemmed triangle growing up between them. It is not very realistic, but must surely be intended as a flower between leaves.

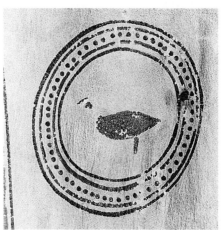

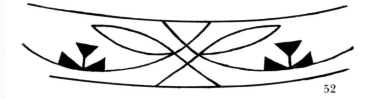

52

RECTANGLES AND SQUARES

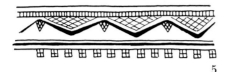

5

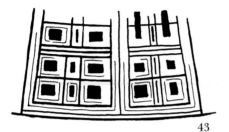

43

The basic rectangle form seems to have little importance in the context of the patterning of Montagnais-Naskapi coats. As a recognizable motif it occurs on only four of the coats in this series. On coat No. **5** the sleeve bands near the shoulder have a most unusual row of very small squares hanging down from them. On Nos. **43** and 44 a more obvious use is the clumsily drawn simple squares or rectangles in the gore forms and borders. These two coats, collected by Lucien Turner, are probably from northwestern Quebec, and their designs may be decadent survivals of the quadrate patterning used on the early coats, Nos. 1–4.

Many of the quadrate patterns on Nos. 1–4 fit into squares or rectangles, but these seem to be divisions for layout purposes rather than motifs. An exception is the square lattice on the collar of coat No. **3,** which is filled with small square motifs.

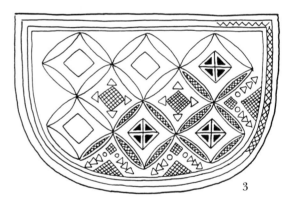

3

The bottom borders on Nos. 7, 11, 25–26, and 33 are divided into rectangular sections, each of which contains a motif of some kind. These divisions are part of the pattern layout and probably have no significance as a motif.

SCALLOPS

Like double curves, scallops are usually made with a template so that the line of the curve can be repeated comparatively accurately. Sometimes the same template may have been used for both motifs when scallops occur under a double curve, giving it support, as on Nos. **13,** 15, 17–18, 28, 30, and 56. In this position scallops seem not to be a motif in themselves but simply incidental to the double curve.

13

A few coats have scallops as an important design motif, evident in the bottom borders of Nos. **37** and 52. Two lines of scallops, one curving up and the other down, make a single row of pointed ovals alternating with lozenges in the border of No. 55, and on No. **57** the same decoration occurs on a smaller scale with simple scallops above and below it.

37

57

Much more remarkable are the few instances of single scallops as a noticeably important part of a design. On coat No. **12** a motif that could be considered to be either a segment of a circle or a scallop is outlined by zigzags and used above the double curves in the bottom border and in four of the side gore forms. A strong single scallop is balanced above the double curves in two of the side gore forms on No. **33,** and a similar single ornate scallop is used in the bottom border and in the central and two of the side gore forms of No. 38.

12

33

Possibly there is also significance in single scallops used as cuplike finials above double curves and other motifs on Nos. 13, **18,** 19, and 36.

18

32

21

A fairly frequent, but subsidiary, use of scallops is on a small scale as line decorations. This use is quite important as the secondary bottom border on Nos. 31 and **32,** and is repeated twice in the bottom border of No. **21,** but more often it is not very notice-able and occurs in design areas such as the sleeve bands of Nos. **15,** 21, 28, 31–32, and 36.

15

49

On the later, more simply painted coats, lines of scallops, which were probably fairly quick and easy to produce, occur drawn in line, or filled in solidly, or sometimes in reserve. On Nos. 41 and **49,** a small triangle is placed between the scallops, and on Nos. 48 and 53 a small triangle sits in each scallop. Scallops were also used cut in half and arranged in a line on Nos. 52 and **56.** On No. 60, a coat with very lavish decoration, half-scallops provide a border for the collar. None of these uses seems likely to have much design meaning, but all add significantly to the decorative effect of the coats.

56

STARS

Star motifs seem to occur late in Naskapi design. There is only one illustration in this book of a garment decorated with stars. It is a shirt and is not included with the series of coats, but is illustrated in the History section (Figure 18). It was collected by Frank G. Speck, probably between 1920 and 1930, and has as its only decoration two five-pointed stars painted on the front of each shoulder.[17]

Stars are of late occurrence, but that does not mean that in their period they were unimportant in the Naskapi context, for with either four or five points, they are used as a main motif on the special ceremonial robes, many of which were collected by Speck and are now distributed in various museums. Robes of this type are not made-up garments but are decorated caribou skins that were used by shamans. Similar but smaller skins, also decorated with stars and made for boys, were collected by Alika Podolinsky Webber in 1962 at North West River.[18]

Star motifs on man's painted caribou-skin shirt, Royal Ontario Museum, Speck Collection, 958.131.69 (see Figure 18).

TRACKS

In its simplest form, the track motif looks rather like a railway track: two parallel lines are joined by crossbars or blocks of colour. Tracks are a very common form of line decoration, occurring on over half the coats in this series. They are fairly evenly distributed through the whole period from the earliest to the latest. Never a major motif, tracks are used to enrich a border, to provide the divides or the surrounds of a gore form, or to edge a collar. They are usually combined with other line decorations, rows of dots, lozenges, zigzags, or parallel lines.[19]

In the following catalogue, if the tracks are plain and have evenly spaced divisions, as on coat No. **3** and many, many of the other coats, they are described as a single track; if the divisions are arranged in pairs, a late feature occurring only on Nos. **49**, 52–53, **55**, and **57**, they are described as a double track. There is one coat, No. **34**, with a track in the bottom border that has the cross lines grouped in threes, a rare triple track.

There are quite a few variations of the design: the divisions may each contain a dot as on coat No. **2** or a dash as on the collar of No. **8** or the bottom border of No. **16**. On the sleeves of No. **9** alternating blocks of colour provide the cross divisions. A single but very wide track with closely set cross lines is used across the side gore forms on No. **10**. A more common variation has blocks of colour alternating with groups of fine cross lines on Nos. **12**, 18–21, and **37**, while No. **28** has a very handsome and unusually wide version of this type of track in the bottom border, and No. **17**, a rather strangely patterned coat, has a track variation that is simply a single line with short evenly spaced crossbars.

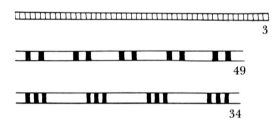

3

49

34

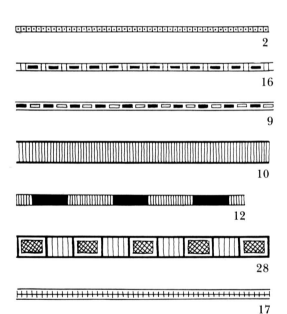

2

16

9

10

12

28

17

TRIANGLES

Triangles are a very common motif, occurring in one form or another on almost every coat in this catalogue.

Triangles are usually subsidiary to a main motif, providing support for double curves (No. **30**), occurring between double curves (No. **19**), or separating scallops, as an accent (No. **41**).

Small triangles abound at all periods. At an early date they are arranged in rows and used to fill in the spaces around the quadrate motifs on coat No. **1**; on the collar, in the bottom border, and on the side gore forms on No. **3**; and surrounding the medallions on No. **4.**

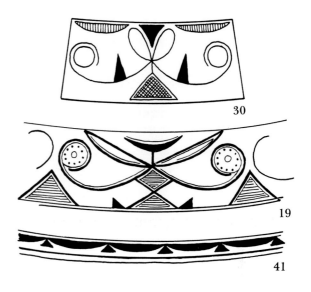

30

19

41

3

4

The sleeve bands on coat No. **31** show how small triangles are sometimes used to emphasize the turning points of a zigzag. The same use is seen on a larger scale in the bottom border of No. **8,** which also illustrates a stemmed triangle. This is an unusual motif at this date, but on later coats it is

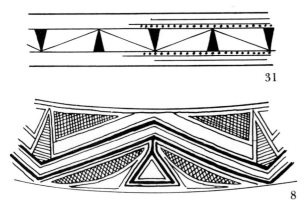

31

8

55

48

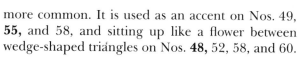

more common. It is used as an accent on Nos. 49, **55,** and 58, and sitting up like a flower between wedge-shaped triangles on Nos. **48,** 52, 58, and 60.

The diagram for coat No. 48 also shows three other uses of triangle motifs: a stemmed triangle between the arms of the double curve, small triangles sitting in the border scallops, and little wedge shapes to either side of the central diagonal cross. Wedges are used in a similar manner on Nos. **13,** 19, 40–41, and 56.

13

When the arms of a double curve extend beyond the central point where they meet, a triangle is automatically formed between them and the edge of the enclosure. Triangles made in this way occur frequently from coat No. 7 on. Sometimes the arms continue in a straight line as on No. **15,** but quite often they bend back in towards the centre and the enclosed triangle appears to be a more separate motif, as on No. **8.**

Triangles are sometimes used in a rather vague way, filling in spaces around the edge of an area or perhaps sitting on the arms of a double curve as on the collar of coat No. **36.**

15

8

A rare version of wedge-shaped triangles occurs on Nos. 15 and **34** where the triangles are doubled and arranged in a line.

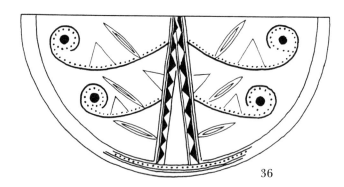

36

34

Despite these many and varied uses, triangles seem to be a motif of individual importance on only a very few coats. On coat No. **4** they are not large but they form a unique secondary border above the main border. On No. **5** they seem almost as important as the circles they support. The front borders on No. **7** consist of a strange vertical line of sharply pointed triangles. Another vertical line of triangles, in this case balanced on their points, is used as the centre of the back gore form on No. **19.** On the collar of No. **33** three individual and very strongly drawn triangles are very noticeable flanking and supporting the central double curve. And on No. **32** small separate triangles are used in an important and possibly meaningful way with double curves and lozenges in all the gore forms.

4

5

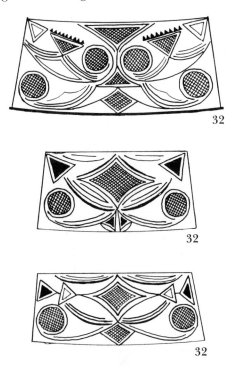

32

32

32

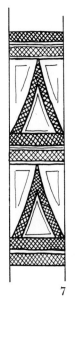

7

19

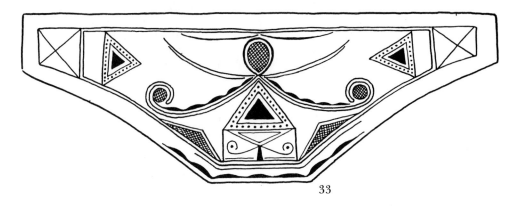

33

ZIGZAGS

Rows of chevrons or V-shapes joined together in zigzag lines are seldom given major status, but they often occur in different sizes and ways, surrounding or separating various areas of patterning.[20] They are fairly common, but examination of the coats in this series shows that their use largely ends by the middle of the 19th century. This should not be surprising: as their function is to enrich rather than to carry the main message of the coat, they have little place on the later plainer coats.[21]

Zigzags are used as the main line of patterning in the bottom borders of Nos. 6, **8–9,** 20, **27,** and, at a much later date, **51.** It is hard to tell whether, when they are used on this comparatively large scale, the zigzags have significance in themselves, as seems probable with the strength of the version on No. 8, or just give support for other motifs, as on Nos. 9 and 20. On Nos. **6** and **27** the extensive use of zigzags in many areas of the patterning certainly reinforces the chevron themes of those coats. One later coat, No. 51, has strong, plain zigzags as the main motif in the border, and the zigzag theme is repeated in a very broken-up way in the side gore forms.

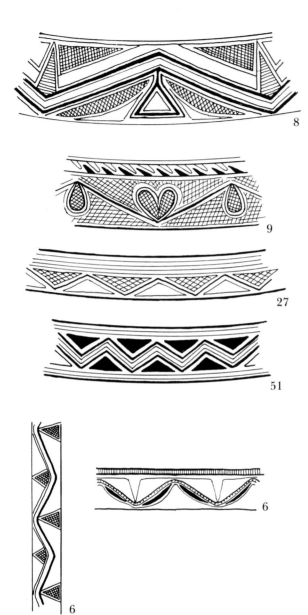

Zigzags in a small but fairly important form are used in various ways, for example, the bands at the elbows on coat No. **1,** above and below the main border pattern on No. 3, and in a leaflike variant on the sleeves of No. **16.**

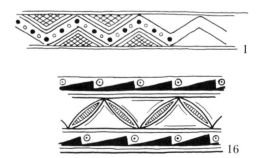

In the side gore forms of Nos. 10 and **11** zigzags are painted with two colours of interlocking triangles; smaller versions of the design, which must have taxed the skill and patience of the worker, are used in the surrounds as well. This subtle interlocking pattern although not very common also occurs on Nos. 7, 10, 20, 30, and 37.

11

All the zigzags mentioned so far have been made of isosceles or equilateral triangles, but there is another form of the motif in which the triangles formed by the zigzag are wedge shapes. The most noticeable example is seen surrounding the central gore form on coat No. **2.** On No. **10,** a coat that uses zigzags in many ways, the front border design is based on a fairly large line of wedge-shaped zigzags. Much more commonly, wedge-shaped zigzags occur on a small scale as surrounds or as interior details of patterning, as on Nos. 3, 5, 7, **8,** 9–10, **12,** 13–16, 19, and 37. It will be noted that all these coats are probably no later than the end of the 18th century.

2

10

8

12

CATALOGUE OF THE COATS

Twenty-seven of the coats described in this catalogue are in the collections of Canadian museums and provided the foundation for this study. To augment the study, thirty-three coats have been added from the collections of seventeen other museums in nine other countries (see Museums in Index of the Coats).

A Note on the Illustrations

Overall photographs of the coats acquired from the various owning institutions are useful to give a general impression of the coats. Back views are provided, and occasionally front views are included as well. But because of the small scale of the motifs used in the painted decoration, the overall photographs give little help towards making an analysis of the development of the painted motifs. Photographs of details were made, whenever possible, when each coat was examined. But photographic conditions were not always ideal, and the results, although of use to the researcher, were not always of publishable quality. By combining these working photographs with magnifications of the overall pictures and with sketches made on the spot, it was possible to produce the line drawings that accompany the catalogue descriptions. Because the drawings were based on photographs, it was not possible to make accurate measurements of the various motifs, but great care has been taken to keep them in balanced proportion. The drawings have made it possible to trace the subtle changes in the decorative motifs during the more than two hundred years when the coats were made and worn.

The cuts of the coats were measured and then drawn to one-tenth scale. For the book they have all been further reduced an equal amount.

The diagrams showing the widths and combinations of lines produced by painting tools used on the various coats were all drawn actual size and are published at that scale.

1. Hunterian Museum, The University, Glasgow (E.128)

Man's painted caribou-skin coat
Probably Montagnais, from southwestern Quebec, probably about 1700

See colour plates page 43

Although this coat is not listed in a catalogue that was made of the holdings of the Hunterian Museum by Laskey in 1813, the museum considers that it most probably was in the original collection of Dr. William Hunter (1718–1783). Hunter, who studied at the University of Glasgow, became one of the leading medical practitioners of his day. He had a thriving practice in London with an aristocratic clientele. Success in commercial speculations made him a wealthy man, and as such he was able to collect much varied, rare, and interesting material. He left his private collection, with funds for housing it, to the University of Glasgow, providing the foundation of the present Hunterian Museum.

If the coat is from Hunter's own collection, it must date from prior to his death in 1783, and from the cut and decoration it probably dates from considerably earlier than that.

This magnificent coat has a wealth of detailed patterning, much of it based on the quadrate layout that results from the influence of birch-bark bites. There is a beautiful double curve on the collar. The coat relates in style of cut and decoration to Nos. 2–4, which probably are equally early and also from southwestern Quebec. The style is repeated in a very degenerate form in much later coats collected by Lucien Turner between 1882 and 1884 (Nos. 43–46) and even later ones collected by Robert Flaherty in the early part of this century (Nos. 50–51).

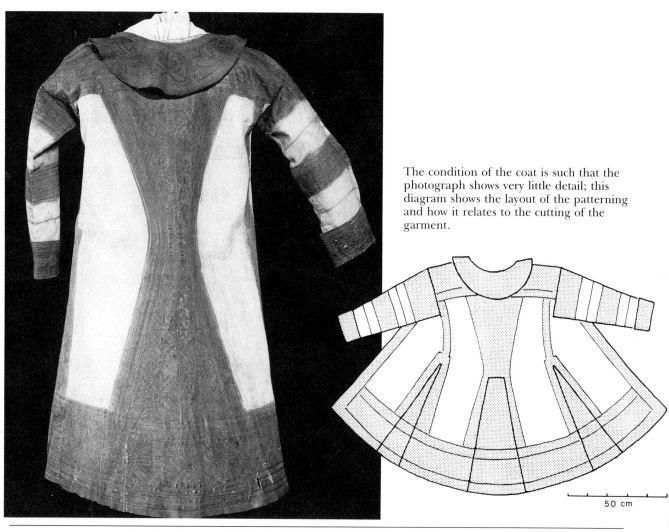

The condition of the coat is such that the photograph shows very little detail; this diagram shows the layout of the patterning and how it relates to the cutting of the garment.

50 cm

Quality: Superb. Medium-weight skin; complex and precise painting.

Condition: Sound but soiled. The condition of the coat made it very difficult to produce a clear photograph, so a diagram has been added to show the pattern layout. At some time white paint was applied to much of the unpatterned areas of the skin. Possibly this was an attempt to make the piece more attractive for display in a "cabinet of curiosities," especially since a part of the coat that would have been hidden if the coat were spread out for display was not painted white.

Cutting: The body of the coat is cut from a single, exceptionally large caribou skin, slashed at the top for the insertion of the sleeves. This is a basic skin-garment type, but few caribou are large enough to be treated in this way, and among Montagnais-Naskapi men's coats this cut is unique. Unlike coats made from the larger skins of moose and buffalo, this one has three slashes up from the bottom, into which three gussets are set to widen the skirt, like caribou coats of more usual cut. From waist to bottom there is a flare of 1:1.8.

Although the cut of the coat is based on an ancient form of skin cut, it shows European influence in the addition of small triangular gussets inserted on either side of the neck opening. This feature, commonly used to strengthen the neck edge of cloth shirts of the type obtained by the native people in trade, certainly indicates that the maker had knowledge of European clothing.[1]

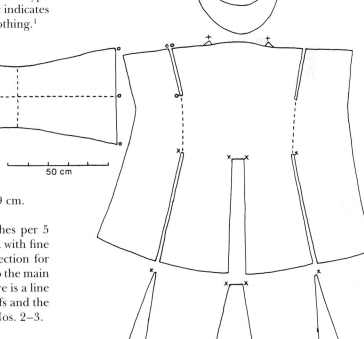

Cut

Size: Length, 112 cm. Back of neck to wrist, 79 cm.

Sewing: Entirely with sinew, very fine, 35 stitches per 5 cm. The collar is joined to the back of the neck with fine running stitches on the outside (see Sewing section for comment); the cuffs are turned up and sewn into the main sleeve seams, and along the turn of the cuff there is a line of small beads. The sewing of the collar and cuffs and the beading of the cuffs are identical to those on Nos. 2–3.

Beading on cuffs

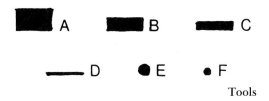

Tools

Bottom border

Colours: The overall effect of the painting is almost entirely the red-brown of the background, but the layout is dull orange-yellow and the motifs are drawn in black or red.

Tools: Probably all single prongs, *A* used double or triple for layout with yellow, *B* also with yellow, *C* with red, *D* with black. Two stamps used for dots, *E* with red and black, *F* with red.

Bottom border: Two alternating quadrate motifs, one with a double-curve variation occurring unobtrusively in the corners; small lines of zigzags above and below.

Central gore form: Filled with two alternating complex quadrate motifs arranged in two rows, one on either side of centre. The surrounds have three rows of small lozenges between parallel lines.

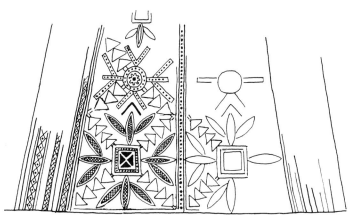

Central gore form

Waist: A double row of small lozenges terminates at top and bottom with double-curve variations. Comparable lozenge designs are used in the same position on Nos. 2–3.

Centre-back extension: Similar to central gore form.

Shoulders: A wide band of lozenges, each centred by a cross composed of five small circles, at both back and front.

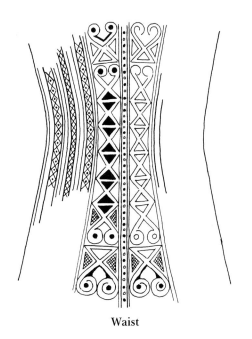

Waist

Shoulders

Collar: Beautifully drawn design with very unusual foliated double curve above various small motifs, which include a group of crosses.

Gore forms 1 and 3: A line of ovals with paired leaves, similar to design in same position on No. 3 and probably relating to bold designs of ovals and double curves on Nos. 12–14. The surrounds, heavy parallel lines that include a row of dots and a row of small zigzags, turn across the top of the gore form without a break and, from that turn, extend as a triple line with two rows of dots to the shoulder. This type of neat finish at the waist, occurring also on Nos. 2–4, suggests that all four coats were designed to be worn open without a sash, which would obscure the decoration at the waistline.

Front borders: Simple parallel lines.

Sleeves: At shoulder, a band of alternating straight and diagonal crosses; at elbow, a band with a double zigzag line filled with dots. Both bands are edged with lines and rows of small dots.

Cuffs: Similar to upper sleeve band. The edges are beaded.

Outer borders: Brown around coat and collar.

Collar

Gore forms 1 and 3

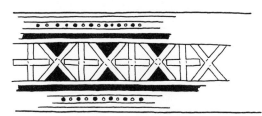

Sleeve band at shoulder

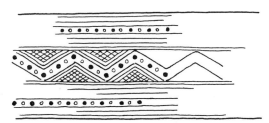

Sleeve band at elbow

2. Pitt Rivers Museum, Oxford (1952.5.01)

Man's painted caribou-skin coat
Probably Montagnais, from southwestern Quebec, probably about 1700

See colour plates page 43

This coat came to the Pitt Rivers Museum from Colonel Shirley, Ettington Park, Warwickshire. The tradition is that it was worn to the coronation of George III in 1761, but no proof of this has been found and the coat is most likely of an earlier date. It is very close in style of cut and decoration to Nos. 1 and 3–4.

This elegant coat has patterning so complex it is almost bewildering, but in spite of the wealth of detail the effect of the whole is very strong. The motifs have a definite quadrate basis that is coupled with spreading curves, not like the usual formal double curves, but with a strong vegetal growing feeling. A native form of cross, with circles at the centre and the ends of the arms, is used in a fairly unobtrusive way, but occurs in many parts of the design: on the collar, the shoulder bands, and the cuffs; in three of the centre-back lozenges; and most importantly as the main motif of the medallions.

Quality: Superb. Beautiful skins; very fine detailed painting.

Condition: Good. Some loss of paint on sleeves.

Cutting: As with No. 1, there are vertical slashes down from the top for the insertion of sleeves, but because this skin was not large enough to encircle the body, additional material had to be seamed on to make the fronts wide enough. It is as though the maker were accustomed to cutting a coat from a large skin, such as moose, and for this coat had to adapt to the smaller size of a caribou. The coat, from waist to bottom, has a flare of 1:1.75.

Size: Length, 122 cm. Back of neck to wrist, 94.5 cm.

Sewing: Entirely with sinew, very fine, 35 stitches per 5 cm. The details agree exactly with Nos. 1 and 3; the collar is attached with running stitches on the outside (see Sewing section for comment); the cuffs are sewn back up into the sleeve seam and the turn of the cuff is finished with a line of beads attached as in the diagram with No. 1.

Colours: The dominant colour is a very bright red, probably vermilion, and it is used for the background of most of the patterned areas. The layout is in a strong yellow and a brownish red. Other colours are blue, black, and olive green.

Tools: All appear to have been single prongs, used to make triple, double, and single lines. No specific notes were made of the weights of these lines but some are very, very fine. There were also stamps used for small dots.

Bottom border: Two alternating motifs; although it is not as obvious as with No. 1, the inspiration is probably birch-bark bites, since one of the motifs is quadrate and the other "folds" along a central line.

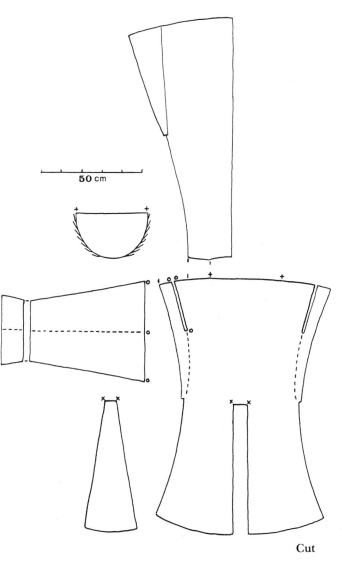

50 cm

Cut

Bottom border

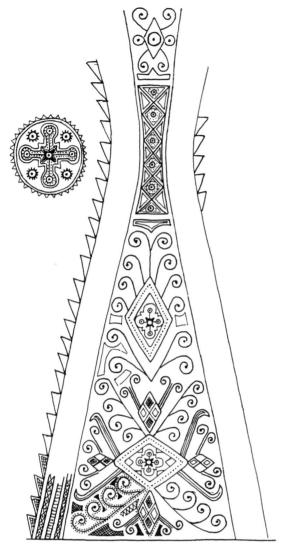

Central gore form: Two very detailed and elaborate motifs centred by diamonds from which curves and double-curve variations grow out in all directions. Many of the curves are outlined with double rows of dots. The motifs have a quadrate base and are strongly suggestive of growth. The surrounds, with strong wedge-shaped zigzags running up the sides, add to the feeling of upward growth. Similar zigzags are used around the central gore forms of Nos. 12–14.

Waist: A line of lozenges similar to those used on the waists of Nos. 1 and 3. On either side is a rayed circular medallion containing a large cross, the arms of which terminate in circles and have small rayed circles between them.

Centre-back extension: Quadrate motifs with double-curve variations growing out from them.

Shoulders: Both back and front are crossed by a wide band with quadrate motifs.

Shoulders

Collar: A stunning design centred on a diamond out of which grow long curved leaves and sprays of double-curve variations. The drawing is strong and fairly free but has been very finely executed. A detail of the section just to the left of the central diamond is illustrated here to show how all the curves are outlined by double rows of dots and how, wherever there is sufficient opening in the background, tiny zigzags or other motifs are fitted in to fill the spaces.

Central gore form, waist, and medallion

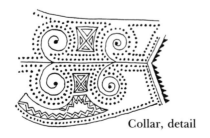

Collar, detail

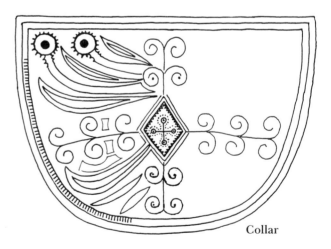

Collar

Gore forms 1 and 5: Paired leaves and double curves grow down from a central line. Although different, this pattern may be related to the vertical lines of ovals and leaves used in the same position on Nos. 1 and 3. As with No. 1, the surrounds of all the side gore forms turn neatly at the waist without a break; from there a single band of lines and tiny lozenges extends to the shoulder.

Gore forms 2 and 4: A quadrate motif at the bottom, similar to those in central gore form, and, growing up from it, a stem of strange diamonds and double curves. At the top are two rayed circles similar to those in the upper corners of the collar.

Front borders: A chevron band.

Sleeves: At the top, a wide band with a cross motif alternating with a diamond. Below the band the sleeves are entirely covered by two types of lozenges arranged in alternating vertical rows. No. 3 has similar sleeve patterning.

Sleeve band at shoulder

Sleeves

Cuffs: Design similar to sleeve bands.

Outer borders: Bright red around coat, collar, and cuffs. Shoulder and armhole seams have wide red bands painted on after the coat was sewn up. They vary in width and sometimes infringe on the previously painted designs.

PUBLICATIONS: Phillips 1987a, fig. 64, p. 75; 1987b, cat. fig. W5, p. 38.[2]

Gore forms 1 and 5

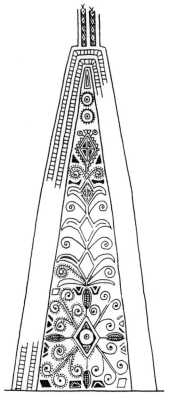
Gore forms 2 and 4

Front borders

3. Indianer-Museum der Stadt Zürich (494)

Man's painted caribou-skin coat
Probably Montagnais, from southwestern Quebec,
probably about 1700

See colour plate page 44

This coat came to the museum with the Hotz Collection with no further information. It is another magnificent example, close in style to Nos. 1–2, and it also probably originated in the vicinity of Quebec City at an early date. As with those coats, the motifs are based on a quadrate form, showing the influence of birch-bark bites. Added to this obvious theme there are other minor themes that repeat throughout the patterning: double-curve variations, rayed circles, a dot within a ring of smaller dots, and, in the bottom border, on the collar, in gore forms 2 and 4, and on the sleeves, repeated lines of small triangles.

Quality: Superb. Excellent skins and painting.

Condition: Good, but skins stiff and soiled.

Cutting: Unfortunately, since it was not possible to handle this coat, a diagram could not be made of the cut, but it appears to be similar to No. 2, with seams well to the front of the armholes rather than at the sides.[3]

Size: Length, 130 cm. Back of neck to wrist, estimated 80 cm.

Sewing: Although the coat could not be closely examined, the sewing is probably standard and done with sinew. It was possible to see that the collar was sewn on with running stitches on the outside and that the cuffs were turned up and sewn right into the sleeve seam with a line of small beads at the turn of the cuff, just as with Nos. 1–2.

Colours: Yellow for layout; a bright red, probably vermilion, for drawing motifs and filling much of background; light blue, dark blue, and brown for details.

Tools: It was not possible to check the tools accurately but there are various single lines, some heavy and some very fine. There is also a fairly heavy triple line which may have been made with a 3-prong tool or, as seems to have been the case with Nos. 1–2, a heavy single-prong tool used three times.

Bottom border: Complex quadrate motifs, very finely drawn, with curves used in an important but rather unobtrusive way, as on Nos. 1–2.

Central gore form: Graduated compartments with quadrate motifs centred on lozenges, all of which enclose a dot surrounded by a ring of smaller dots.

Waist: A line of small lozenges similar to those used in the same position on Nos. 1–2. There is a plain, small, inverted double curve above the lozenges.

Bottom border

Central gore form

Waist

Centre-back extension

Centre-back extension: Compartments with designs based on diagonal crosses. The central motifs in the upper compartment are most probably rayed circles or suns even though they look like daisies.

Shoulders: A band of pointed ovals enclosing a rayed circle centred by a dot surrounded by a ring of smaller dots.

Shoulders

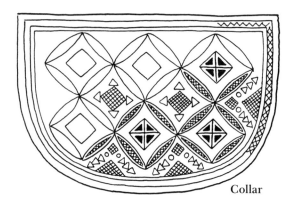

Collar

Collar: An overall lattice design created from rows of interlocking circles, probably resulting from the use of a circular template for laying out the pattern. It is a most unusual design but a similar one is illustrated from a much later date on a Têtes de Boule birch-bark container.[4]

Gore forms 1 and 5: A vertical line of triple leaves, same motif in same position on No. 1 but drawn more clearly here. Both probably relate to the line of ovals used on Nos. 12–14.

Gore forms 2 and 6: The diagram shows the bottom compartment with a diagonal cross formed by a triple line of tiny triangles, which almost hides the curves that come into the centre from the four corners. Above this, three smaller compartments enclose simplified versions of the lower half of the design.

Front borders: Compartments enclose a motif that combines a rayed circle containing a rayed dot within a circle of smaller dots.

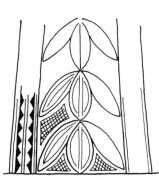

Gore forms 1 and 5

Gore forms 2 and 6

Front borders

Sleeves: At shoulder, a band with a straight, even-armed cross similar to the one in the same position on No. 1. Here it is combined with a motif that looks like a daisy, probably a rayed circle or sun. Below this the sleeve is entirely covered with alternating vertical bands of lozenges and lines of small triangles. The design is similar to that on No. 2, but the execution is considerably coarser and less detailed.

Cuffs: Similar to sleeve band at shoulder.

Outer borders: Red around coat, collar, and bottom of cuffs, and on shoulder seams.

PUBLICATION: Läng, p. 68, pl. IV.

Sleeve band at shoulder

Sleeves

4. Pitt Rivers Museum, Oxford (1921 VII 2)

Back and collar of man's painted caribou-skin coat
Probably Montagnais, southwestern Quebec,
probably early 18th century

See colour plate page 44

There is no history for this coat other than that it was given to the museum by L. C. G. Clarke, a former director of the Fitzwilliam Museum, Cambridge.

The general shape of the back, with its inserts, and the quadrate basis of many of the motifs tie this piece in firmly with the previous three coats (Nos. 1–3), all of which probably came from the southwestern part of Quebec. Remnants of sewing and needle holes give evidence that the coat to which this back belonged was made of two skins with the side seams placed in a normal position under the armhole. This may indicate that its date is slightly later than Nos. 1–3; the bolder painting probably bears this out. The piece may not be as incredibly finely painted as Nos. 1–3 but it is quite stunning and probably predates all the following coats.

The four pairs of beautifully designed medallions on the back are unique and very powerful. The only known parallels are the single pairs used in the same way on Nos. 2 and 32.

Quality: Good. Medium-weight skins, considerably fly-marked; painting well designed and drawn.

Condition: Good, but soiled. Some loss of paint. The piece consists of only the back with back gusset, one side gusset, and two collars.

Cutting: On the left side, just above the side gusset, a short section of seam remains, and there are holes made by sewing on both sides of the back, indicating that there were seams at the sides. The square shape of the back and the wide cut made for insertion of the back gusset are, however, similar on Nos. 1–3. There is a second, stand-up band collar.

Size: Length, 120 cm. Width of shoulders, 70 cm.

Sewing: Sinew, 30 stitches per 5 cm. The collars, although attached with sinew, may have been altered at some point; the band collar is now roughly sewn down with linen thread.

Colours: Yellow for layout; red, probably vermilion, for drawing motifs and also for filling much of background, both solidly and with crosshatching; black and dark green for details.

Tools: The layout seems to have been made with a wide 2-prong, *A*, used double, with the space filled in, giving the effect of a 3-prong tool with a very wide central line. Two single prongs, *B* and *C*, used with red. Other single prongs and stamps for dots, the weights of which were not noted.

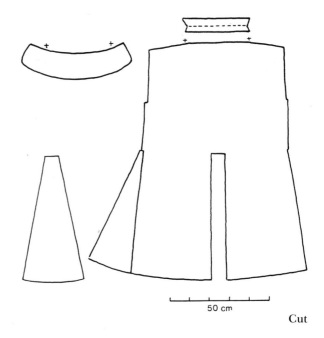

Cut

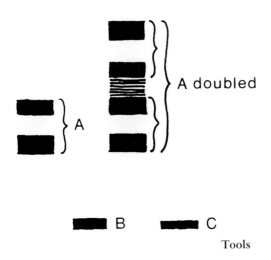

A doubled

Tools

Central gore form

Shoulders

Bottom border: Above main border of circles with radiating leaves, an unusual additional border of triangles surmounted by double curves and small crosses.

Bottom border

Central gore form: Graduated compartments in which various quadrate motifs form complex lattices. From the surrounds of parallel lines, curves jut out and up, giving a strong feeling of growth.

Centre-back extension: Two compartments with motifs similar to those used in gore forms 1 and 3.

Additional: Four pairs of beautifully drawn medallions are carefully spaced on either side of central gore form and its extension. Each medallion is centred by a rayed circle and surrounded by rays which are alternately triangular and leaf shaped.

Medallion

Shoulders: A lattice of dotted lines on which are superimposed two alternating motifs, one with circles on a diagonal cross, the other with lozenges.

Collar: Five compartments contain motifs that combine a quadrate form with double-curve variations. The second collar is a plain narrow band, folded double.

Collar

Gore forms 1 and 3: Graduated compartments. The bottom one has a diagonal cross made with rows of small lozenges and hidden curves very similar in arrangement to those on gore forms 2 and 4 on No. 3. The other compartments are filled with complex arrangements of ovals and lozenges. The surrounds are simple parallel lines that turn in a neat and unbroken way across the top of the gore form. Bold, wedge-shaped zigzags, similar to those used around the central gore form on No. 2, jut from the surrounds and also edge the extension line that runs up to the shoulder.

Outer borders: Red on shoulders, around bottom and collar, and entirely covering second collar.

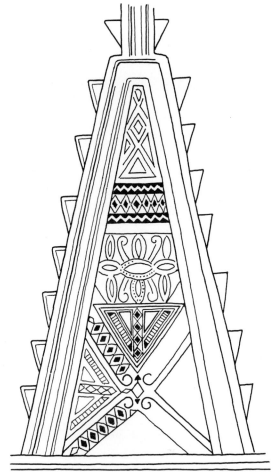

Gore forms 1 and 3

5.   Musée de l'Homme, Paris (34.33.10)

Small boy's painted caribou-skin coat
Probably Montagnais, southern Quebec, probably
early 18th century

Traditionally this coat is thought to have been sent
to France for the education of the royal children.
The very small size of the coat bears this out. A
passage in the *Jesuit Relations* of 1638 states that the
king of France (Louis XIII) sent suits of clothes in
the French fashion as gifts for the native people, who
responded by giving the Jesuits a *petite robe* for the
king's son, who might take pleasure in seeing how
the native children dressed. The account goes on to
say that, as smallpox had broken out, it might be
unwise to present the gift, which might carry infec-
tion.[5] It is not known if the gift was given or not, but
in any case the date of the above account is really
too early for this coat.

There was a later royal child who might well
have had a similar gift bestowed upon him. Louis
XV was born in 1710 and became king at the age of
five. The cut of this coat suggests a date in the early
years of the 18th century, and the size is suitable for
Louis XV either just before or just after he became
king. It is an intriguing possibility but as the records
seem to be gone it will probably never be proved.

Whether or not this was a royal gift, it is a charm-
ing and most unusual piece, with nine gore forms,
more than any other coat that has so far been
recorded, except No. 12.

Quality: Good. Unblemished skins; excellent, strong, but
fairly simple painting.

Condition: Good. Some loss of paint; a few small holes.

Cutting: Flare of 1:2.5. The back gusset is unusual in that
it is pointed and set into a straight slit. The neck edge has
a slight extension, which is turned under and held in place
with running stitches, and there is a narrow skin facing on
the edge of the wrists — two details of construction that
suggest European influence.

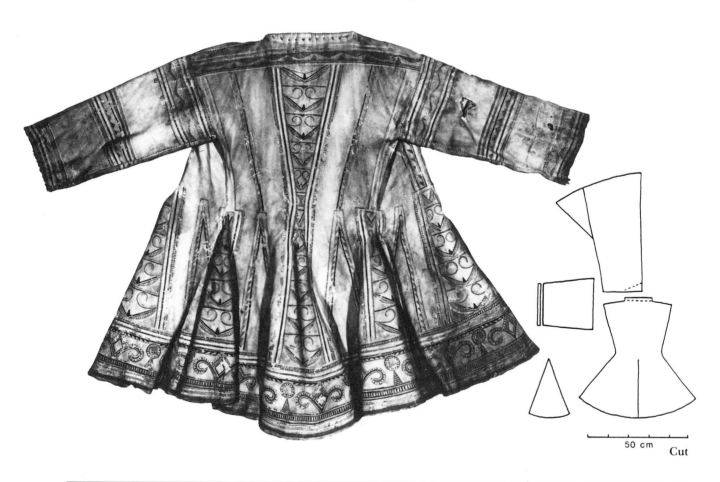

50 cm

Cut

Size: Length, 56 cm. Back of neck to wrist, 42 cm.

Sewing: Sinew, 28 stitches per 5 cm. Also some linen thread, Z,2S, handspun, used to turn down top corners of fronts and to hem wrist facings.

Colours: Very pale yellow for layout; red, probably vermilion, for drawing pattern; faded black.

Tools: A 2-prong, *A*, for layout. Several single prongs, the weights of which were not noted.

Tool

Bottom border: Strong double curves in an unusual inverted variant centred by a lozenge. The motifs are separated by a circle balanced on a triangle. There are wedge-shaped zigzags and a single track above the band of motifs, and a wider single track below.

Bottom border

Central gore form: Graduated compartments each with a strong, simple double-curve variation, with curves facing in, above paired leaves. The surrounds are narrow parallel lines and a single track.

Centre-back extension: Repeats patterning of central gore form.

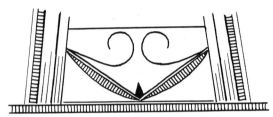

Central gore form

Shoulders: Crossed by a band of zigzags.

Shoulders

Gore forms 1, 3, 7, and 9: Double-curve variations, identical to those in central gore form; surrounds of parallel lines and a single track come together at waist in a blunt point, from the centre of which an extension runs up to shoulder. The extensions of gore forms 1 and 9 are wide bands of wedge-shaped zigzags, while those of gore forms 3 and 5 are simple parallel lines.

Surround of gore forms 4 and 6

Gore forms 2, 4, 6, and 8: There is no decoration inside the gore forms, but they have a strong surround of wedge-shaped zigzags. All gore forms terminate in a blunt point at the waist, 2 and 8 without extension, 4 and 6 with a band of wedge-shaped zigzags to the shoulder.

Sleeve band at shoulder

Front borders: A zigzag band.

Sleeves: At shoulder, zigzags with an unusual row of small protruding rectangles; at elbow, a simple zigzag band; zigzags repeated at wrist; no cuffs.

Outer borders: Red around coat and wrists.

Sleeve band at elbow

PUBLICATION: Phillips 1987b, cat. fig. W4, p. 37.

6. British Museum, London
(1963 Am 5)

Man's painted caribou-skin coat
Montagnais-Naskapi, Quebec, probably early
18th century

See colour plate page 44

This coat was purchased from Miss M. Niven; there is no further information concerning its history.

A number of things about this piece suggest that it should be placed early in the sequence of development. The extreme flare of the skirts fits with European fashion of the beginning of the 18th century, and, even allowing for a considerable time lag for the fashion to reach Canada and have any effect on native work, an early date is still indicated.

The second factor confirming this dating is that the double-curve motif has not as yet developed into the rather rigid form that dominates later design — it is still almost experimental. Tools with wide lines, striated to hold the painting medium, are also an early feature, while the strength of the drawing and the skill and care lavished on the work certainly suggest a culture that was still comfortably in balance.

The design themes of the coat are interesting. Double-curve variations are used in five of the seven gore forms but are almost overwhelmed by the chevrons and V-shapes used to support them. The angular feeling is reinforced by a lavish use of large and small zigzags. A less obvious motif, but one that is placed in a prominent position, is the single vertical pointed oval or leaf form, which centres all the double-curve variations. It is a magnificent coat!

Quality: Excellent. Good skins; careful, precise painting.

Condition: Excellent. Some slight soiling.

Cutting: An extreme flare of 1:2.95.

Size: Length, 100 cm. Back of neck to wrist, 80 cm.

Sewing: Entirely with sinew, 23 stitches per 5 cm.

Colours: Whitish yellow used for layout; darker yellow for crosshatching, which fills background of most of patterned areas; red, probably vermilion, for drawing motifs; black; olive green.

Tools: A 3-prong, *A*, with a very wide striated central line, with yellow for layout. A 2-prong, *B*, with yellow and red. A 7-prong, *C*, with yellow across gore forms 2 and 6. Several single prongs, the weights of which were not noted, with red, yellow, and black. Small stamps for red and black dots.

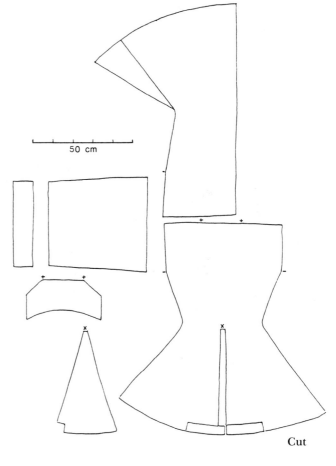

50 cm

Cut

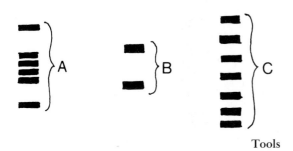

Tools

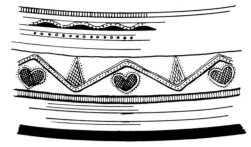

Bottom border

Central gore form

Bottom border: Large zigzags enclosing a "heart" motif; single track and rows of dots and small zigzags above, and single track below. The zigzag and "heart" relate fairly closely to the border design of No. 9. If these "hearts" are compared with the half-closed double-curve motif on either side of the collar, the relationship of a heart-shaped motif to a double-curve motif becomes evident (see Hearts in Design Motifs section for comment).

Central gore form: Graduated compartments each with a large chevron supporting a double-curve variation. The surrounds are parallel lines and a row of dots.

Centre-back extension: Repeats motif of central gore form but reversed, with V-shape pointing down rather than up.

Shoulders: Simple horizontal parallel lines.

Collar: A strongly drawn double-curve variation; on either side a small double-curve motif bent in until it almost resembles a heart.

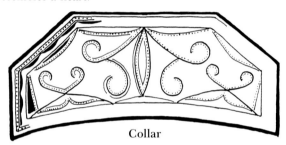

Collar

Gore forms 1, 3, 5, and 7: Similar to central gore form. The surrounds of all side gore forms are parallel lines, which come together at the waist in a blunt point, from the centre of which a single band of lines extends to the shoulder.

Gore forms 2 and 6: Horizontal 7-fold parallel lines alternate with lines of single track.

Front borders: A zigzag pattern with triangles.

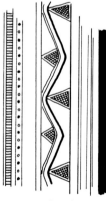

Front borders

Sleeves: Bands at shoulder and elbow both repeat the zigzag theme and are enclosed between parallel lines and an assortment of single tracks, small zigzags, and rows of dots.

Cuffs: A simple double curve between parallel lines and rows of small dots.

Outer borders: Red around coat and collar.

———————————

PUBLICATION: Coe, no. 91 (picture with caption).

Sleeve band at shoulder

Sleeve band at elbow

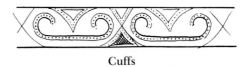

Cuffs

7. Canadian Ethnology Service, Canadian Museum of Civilization, Hull-Ottawa (III B 590)

Man's painted caribou-skin coat
Montagnais-Naskapi, Quebec, probably early
18th century

See colour plates page 45

This coat was purchased from the Speyer Collection. The story connected with it is that Herr Speyer, Sr., collected it from a German museum, where it was about to be discarded. There is no record identifying the museum.

The strongly designed and skilfully drawn pattern is dominated by the double-curve motif but in a version that is quite unlike the later use of the motif. As with No. 6, angled lines are very strongly evident.

The design is so beautifully laid out that it is remarkable to find two details that depart from the usual perfect balance: above the cuff the right sleeve is encircled by a line made with a 9-prong tool, *C*, which is used nowhere else on the coat, and on the right side a narrow crosshatched band joins the two side gore forms. Both features appear to be part of the original painting.

Quality: Excellent. Heavy soft skins; beautifully designed and executed painting.

Condition: Very good. Only slight loss of paint.

Cutting: Flare of 1:2.1. The back gusset is pieced with a seam down the centre.

Size: Length, 105 cm. Back of neck to wrist, 82 cm.

Sewing: Entirely with sinew, 22 stitches per 5 cm. At the bottom of several seams there are tags of sinew sewing (see Sewing section for comment).

Colours: Pale yellow for layout and for background cross-hatching; strong red for drawing motifs; a most unusual strong green, also used on No. 10.

Tools: A 3-prong, *A,* with wide striated central line, with yellow for layout, and with red, repeating layout lines. A 7-prong, *B,* with yellow. A 9-prong, *C,* with red. Two single prongs, *D* and *E,* with red. Another very fine single prong, *F,* with red, green, and yellow for details and cross-hatching.

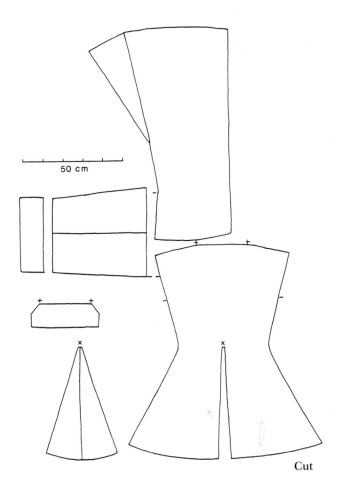

Cut

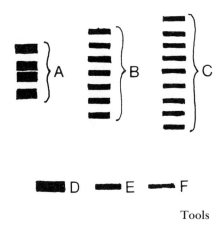

Tools

Bottom border: Compartments each contain an inverted double curve with the stems of the curves extending to form a triangular base, which encloses two lines of zigzags. Above and below there are parallel lines in yellow and red.

Bottom border

Central gore form

Collar

Front borders

Central gore form: Graduated compartments each carry a double-curve variation balanced on a triangular base. At the waist the double curve reduces to an open "heart" motif (see Hearts in Design Motifs section for comment). The surrounds are triple parallel lines, first in yellow and then in red.

Centre-back extension: Repeats the design of central gore form.

Shoulders: Horizontal parallel lines.

Collar: An unusual pattern with an angled line of small zigzags enclosing fairly large triangles.

Gore forms 1 and 5: Similar to central gore form with yellow and red triple-line surrounds that meet at the waist in a blunt point. From the centre of the point a band with a single yellow triple line between the red lines extends to the shoulder.

Gore forms 2 and 4: Graduated compartments each with an inverted double curve similar to those in bottom border but with rounded lines of zigzags in background. The surrounds of yellow and red parallel lines meet at the waist and then diverge into a full, wide extension filled with horizontal crosshatched bands alternating with lines of small zigzags.

Gore forms 2 and 4

Front borders: Repeated steep triangular motifs.

Sleeves: At shoulder, a wide band with same inverted double-curve motif as bottom border; at elbow, a band of rounded zigzags.

Sleeve band at elbow

Cuffs: Double-curve motifs similar to those of bottom border. The cuffs have been sewn on so that the curve on the left cuff is inverted while the one on the right is not.

Outer borders: A heavy red line within skin edge around coat and across top and bottom of collar.

Additional: On collar and bottom of fronts there are some dark brown lines that cut across the design for no apparent reason. Possibly the skin was marked for cutting and then plans were changed.

Inside on right front there is a faint line drawing in red of a sword of 18th-century style, 14 cm long, and near the bottom of the coat a floral motif with a heart and curling leaves, 9 cm long. These drawings appear to be of European rather than native workmanship.

PUBLICATIONS: Brasser, cat. no. 143; Benndorf and Speyer, cat. no. 40.

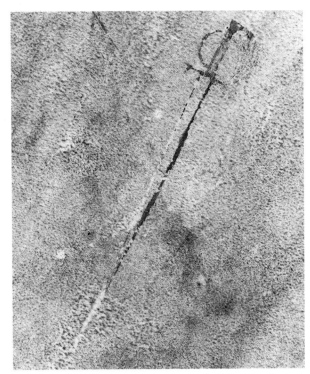

Drawing of 18th-century-style sword, inside right front of coat.

Drawing of floral motif, inside right front of coat.

8. Canadian Ethnology Service, Canadian Museum of Civilization, Hull-Ottawa (III B 589)

Man's painted caribou-skin coat
Montagnais-Naskapi, Quebec, probably early
18th century

See colour plates page 46

This coat was purchased from the Speyer Collection. Before it was acquired by the Speyers it is said to have been in the collection of the Grand Duke of Baden.

Quite standard double curves are used in three of the gore forms and on the collar, but visually the strong zigzags of the bottom border dominate, while the richness and variety of the minor motifs give the coat its stunning impact.

Quality: Good. Beautiful, medium-weight white skins; elaborate, bold design.

Condition: Excellent. Only slightly soiled; some loss of paint, particularly on collar.

Cutting: The fronts are unusually wide, providing for considerable overlap. The measuring to establish the proportion of flare to the skirts of the coat is thrown off by this overlap, and the expansion from waist to bottom is probably greater than the 1:2 that it actually measures. A greater flare fits in with a date in the early part of the 18th century.

An unusual feature is the back gusset, which is cut to a sharp point and inserted into a straight slash, as is the case with another early coat, No. 5.

Size: Length, 103 cm. Back of neck to wrist, 79 cm.

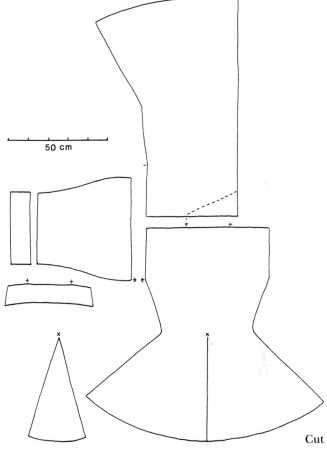

50 cm

Cut

Sewing: Entirely with sinew, 23 stitches per 5 cm. The coat fronts have been turned back and sewn down with coarse running stitches to make lapels. A thong is carried across the back of the neck and through the lapels to make front ties.

Colours: A very strong yellow, which appears to have been quite sloppy when applied; red for drawing motifs and for details; two shades of blue that both tend towards a slate colour, one very pale, the other quite strong.

Tools: A 3-prong, *A*, with all three lines striated, with yellow for layout. Fine single prongs, *B, E,* and *F,* with red; *C* with yellow; *D* with dark blue for crosshatching. A small stamp, *G,* with blue for dots.

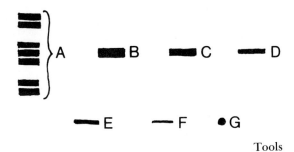

Tools

Bottom border

Bottom border: Bold zigzags with a stemmed triangle hanging from upper bend; simple parallel lines above and below.

Central gore form: Graduated compartments each with a double-curve motif supporting a triangle. The horizontal divides are crosshatched bands; the surrounds are simple parallel lines.

Centre-back extension: Repeats design of central gore form.

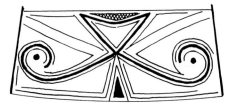
Central gore form

Shoulders: Crossed by horizontal lines.

Collar: A double curve growing out from a central line with another curve on each side.

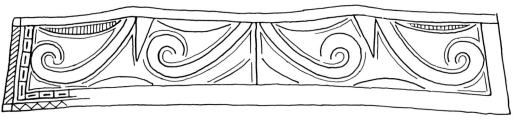
Collar

Gore forms 1 and 7: Horizontal crosshatched bands alternating with groups of parallel lines. The surrounds are simple parallel lines that meet at the waist in a blunt point, from the centre of which an unusually wide band of lines enclosing a single track extends to the shoulder.

Gore forms 2 and 6: Similar to central gore form. The surrounds of parallel lines meet at the waist and continue without a break to the shoulder, one to the front of the armhole, the other to the back.

Gore forms 3 and 5: Similar to gore forms 1 and 7 but only simple parallel lines extend to shoulder.

Additional: Four vertical bands of parallel lines extend from bottom border to shoulder between front borders and gore forms 1 and 7, and between gore forms 1 and 7 and gore forms 2 and 6.

Front borders: Parallel lines on either side of a "barber pole" with wedge-shaped zigzags.

Front borders

Sleeves: Entirely covered with patterning. At shoulder, a band of lozenge variation, and, just above cuff, a band with dots and parallel lines centred by a "barber-pole" band of dots and shaded lines. Between the bands are vertical parallel lines and rows of dots. The use of vertical lines to cover the sleeves is similar to the sleeve treatment on two earlier coats, Nos. 2–3, and on one later one, No. 32.

Cuffs: A scallop variation.

Outer borders: Red, narrow, around bottom, top of sleeves, and cuffs.

PUBLICATIONS: Brasser, cat. no. 92; Benndorf and Speyer, cat. no. 39.

Sleeve band at shoulder

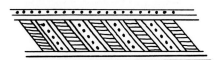

Sleeve band at elbow

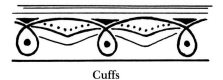

Cuffs

9. Royal Ontario Museum, Toronto (986.218.1)

Boy's, or very small man's, painted caribou-skin coat
Montagnais-Naskapi, Quebec, most likely
1765–1775

See colour plates page 47

This coat was purchased from Lord Strange with the assistance of the Government of Canada, under the Cultural Property Export and Import Act, Department of Communications. It was collected by one of Lord Strange's ancestors, either Colin Drummond, who served at Quebec City as paymaster-general of the forces in Lower Canada from 1765 until his death in 1776, or by his son, Sir Gordon Drummond, who had a distinguished military career, two stretches of which were in Canada, 1808–1811 and 1815–1816.

Both Colin and Gordon Drummond collected aboriginal artifacts while in Canada, but this coat, with its extreme cut, which fits with a date in the 18th rather than the early 19th century, is undoubtedly from the father's time.

An intriguing letter from Adam Drummond, another of Colin's sons, written from school in England to his mother in Quebec in 1778, says, "I have received the Guinea and Mackasons [sic] which I return you many thanks for but I want a pair of leggins [sic] and the rest of the savage dress." This letter was written after Colin Drummond had died and before the family returned to England in 1780, and it rather suggests that the boy knew that leggings and "the savage dress" were in his mother's possession. The fact that the coat is a boy's size tempts one to conclude that this is the "savage dress" that Adam Drummond asked his mother to send. The coat remained in the possession of descendants of the Drummonds until purchased by the Royal Ontario Museum in 1986. A copy of Adam Drummond's letter was sent to the museum with the coat.

With the extreme flare of the skirts it would seem logical to date this coat quite early in the 18th century, when European men's coats had a similar shape, but the rather firm history, which places it between 1765 and 1775, cannot be ignored. The size of flare of all the coats described has been worked out and recorded and it has proved to be a useful tool in the developing of a dating sequence. But flare

is only one factor among several that indicate date and as the personal tastes of maker and wearer must have had considerable effect on the finished garment, we can use width of flare, with some reservations, only as a guide to age.

This little coat presents other problems. It would probably fit someone only about 150 cm (5 feet) tall but is traditional in every way; it is elaborate in both cut and decoration and has a lavish use of the double-curve motif. It is possible that it was made specially for a non-native wearer, as with No. 5, but it does seem unlikely that a hunting coat as perfect as this would have been made deliberately for sale. Was it made for an unusually small man or is it possible that a promising boy may have worn it when first included in a caribou-hunting party? Whatever the answer, it is a superb example of the elaborate painting that the Montagnais-Naskapi were using on their hunting coats during the 18th century.

Quality: Excellent. Good lightweight skins; complex painting.

Condition: Not very good. Skins stiff; considerable loss of paint.

Cutting: An extreme flare of 1:2.97, greater than any other coat examined.

Size: Length, 86 cm. Back of neck to wrist, 75 cm.

Sewing: Entirely with sinew, very fine, 32 stitches per 5 cm. Tags of sinew sewing at bottom of several seams (see Sewing section for comment).

Colours: Yellow for layout and for extensive background crosshatching; red, probably vermilion, for drawing motifs; brown; black.

Tools: Two 3-prongs with yellow for layout, *A* for gore forms and *B* for borders and sleeves. A 2-prong, *C*, with red and brown. Four single prongs, *D* and *E* with red, *F* and *G* with yellow.

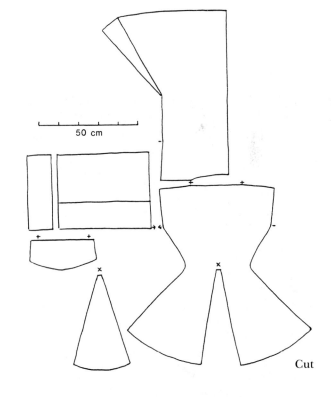

50 cm

Cut

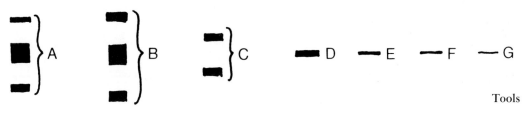

Tools

Bottom border

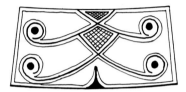

Central gore form

Bottom border: Repeated zigzags and a "heart" motif, probably a shortened form of double curve (see Hearts in Design Motifs section for comment); fairly similar to bottom border of No. 6.

On this coat the crosshatching used to fill many background areas is unusually strong and noticeable. It has therefore been included in this diagram, but not in the others, because it would confuse the delineation of the motifs.

Central gore form: Graduated compartments each contain a doubled double curve. The surrounds and horizontal divides are simple parallel lines.

Centre-back extension: Repeats motif of central gore form.

Shoulders: A crosshatched band.

Collar: Double curves growing out from a central line. This arrangement of motifs is repeated in many variations on the collars of later coats.

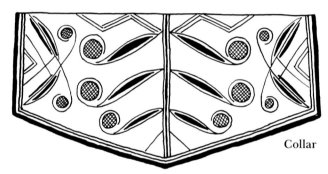

Collar

Gore forms 1 and 7: Similar to central gore form. The simple surrounds of all the side gore forms are parallel lines that terminate at the waist in a blunt point, from the centre of which a narrow band extends to the shoulder.

Gore forms 2 and 6: Repeated crosshatched bands.

Gore forms 3 and 5: Graduated compartments each contain a double-curve variation with curves going both into and out from a central line.

Gore forms 3 and 5

Front borders: A zigzag design on left side of coat and a row of lozenges on right.

Sleeves: At shoulder, a narrow band of double curves between very elaborate line decorations; at elbow, a slightly different double-curve motif with equally elaborate line decorations.

Cuffs: Similar to shoulder bands.

Outer borders: Red around coat, collar, and cuffs.

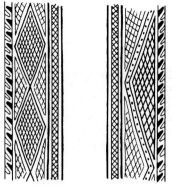

Front borders

Sleeve band at shoulder

Sleeve band at elbow

10. Canadian Ethnology Service, Canadian Museum of Civilization, Hull-Ottawa (III B 632)

Man's painted caribou-skin coat
Montagnais-Naskapi, Quebec, most likely
1765–1775

See colour plates page 48

This coat, like No. 9, comes from the Drummond family and was purchased by the Canadian Museum of Civilization from Lord Strange. The acquisition was made possible by a contribution from the Government of Canada, under the terms of the Cultural Property Export and Import Act, Department of Communications.

The flare of the skirt is extreme and the quality and strength of the painting superb, both suggesting that the coat was collected by Colin Drummond between 1765 and 1775, rather than by his son in the early part of the 19th century. This fairly firm period of origin helps in dating other coats (Nos. 5–15) to the same time or possibly a little earlier. Like this coat they are all characterized by bold, vigorous painting and in many cases rather unorthodox renderings of the double-curve motif.

Quality: Superb. Excellent medium-weight skins; very strong, skilled painting.

Condition: Good. Some loss of paint.

Cutting: Flare of 1:2.3.

Size: Length, 101 cm. Back of neck to wrist, 82 cm.

Sewing: Entirely with sinew, 27 stitches per 5 cm.

Colours: Yellow for layout and background crosshatching; red, probably vermilion, for drawing motifs; strong bright green for details. This unusual colour scheme repeats that of No. 7.

Tools: A 3-prong, *A*, with a wide striated central line, with yellow for layout. Four single prongs, *B* and *C* with red for drawing motifs, *D* with green, *E* for fine lines in all colours. Two stamps for dots, *F* with red, *G* with green.

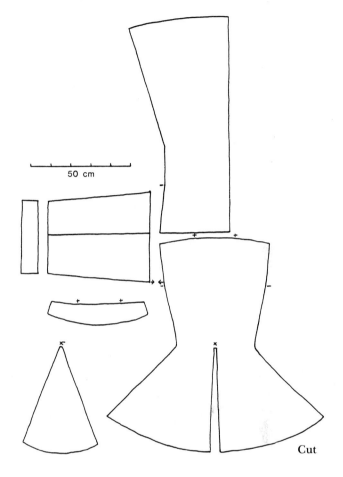

Cut

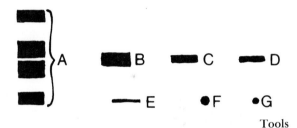

Tools

Bottom border: A most unusual design of large zigzags supporting circles and patterned with small wedge-shaped zigzags. The units are separated by "heart" motifs (see Hearts in Design Motifs section for comment).

Bottom border

Central gore form: Graduated compartments each contain a very strong and unusual double-curve variation with a small circle on either side of the central line and one suspended on a line of track from the centre of the double curve. The horizontal divides are zigzags, and the surrounds are parallel lines and a row of dots.

Centre-back extension: A continuation of motifs used in central gore form.

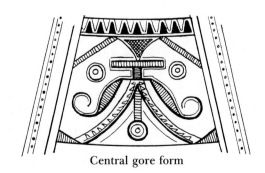

Central gore form

Shoulders: Crossed by parallel lines.

Collar: A double curve with single curves on either side, somewhat similar to collar of No. 8. Narrow bands of wedge-shaped zigzags are used as a break.

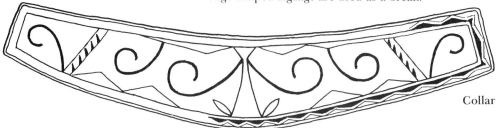

Collar

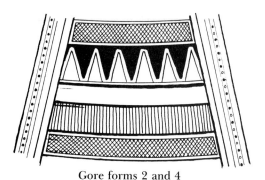

Gore forms 2 and 4

Gore forms 1 and 5: Similar to central gore form. The surrounds of parallel lines and dots come together at the waist in a blunt point, from the centre of which a single band of lines and dots extends to the shoulder.

Gore forms 2 and 4: Track variation and crosshatched bands alternating with rows of steep interlocking zigzags (No. 11 makes similar use of zigzags). At the waist the surrounds closer to the front terminate, while those closer to centre back continue unbroken to the shoulder.

Additional: A band similar to the extensions of the gore forms runs down from the shoulders just in front of the armholes, ending unattached to anything, at the waist. It is as though the maker intended to use seven gore forms and then found that there was space for only five.

Front borders: Similar wedge-shaped zigzags on left and right fronts, but the colours vary between the two sides, giving two different effects.

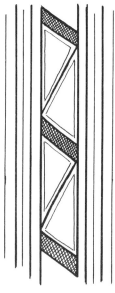

Front borders

Sleeves: At shoulder, a band with a diagonal cross variation; at elbow, a band of zigzags.

Cuffs: A simple double-curve motif.

Outer borders: Red, narrow, around coat and collar.

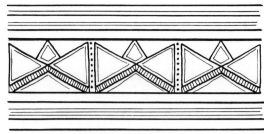

Sleeve band at shoulder

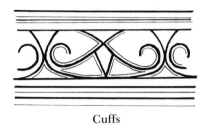

Cuffs

Sleeve band at elbow

11. Rijksmuseum voor Volkenkunde, Leiden (RMV 524 M6)

Man's painted caribou-skin coat
Montagnais-Naskapi, Quebec, probably mid
18th century

This coat was purchased in Paris in 1885; there is no further information about it.

The extreme shape of this coat provides strong proof that the cutting in no way fits with the normal economic use of an animal skin but is based rather on style following the visual effect of contemporary European men's clothing.

As with No. 10, double curves swelling into leaf forms are very important on this coat. In both cases these motifs are combined with a hanging circle and a "heart" motif. Both coats also have bands of interlocking zigzags in the side gore forms and make considerable use of smaller zigzags and single track. Both coats show a remarkable boldness in the drawing of the motifs, but the contrast between the worn and faded condition of No. 11 and the beautiful condition of No. 10 masks their close relationship.

Quality: Excellent. Good medium-weight skins; precise but fairly simple painting.

Condition: Not good. Skins stained and stiff; paint worn; collar missing. Red paint has run badly at tops of sleeves.

Cutting: An extreme flare of 1:2.8. Both back and front skins are exceptionally large.

Size: Length, 99 cm. Back of neck to wrist, 78.5 cm.

Sewing: Sinew, 26 stitches per 5 cm. Remnants of linen thread where collar has been removed; some mends, probably not original, also with linen.

Colours: Dark yellow for layout and crosshatching in background of many patterned areas; red, probably vermilion, for drawing motifs; medium blue; blue-black.

The use of blue is comparatively rare at this early date, but an imported blue pigment was available before the arrival of laundry blue, which dominates the colour scheme of so many of the coats from the late 19th and early 20th centuries.

Tools: When this coat was examined an accurate record was made of only one tool, a 2-prong, *A*, used with dark yellow for layout. There were also several single prongs.

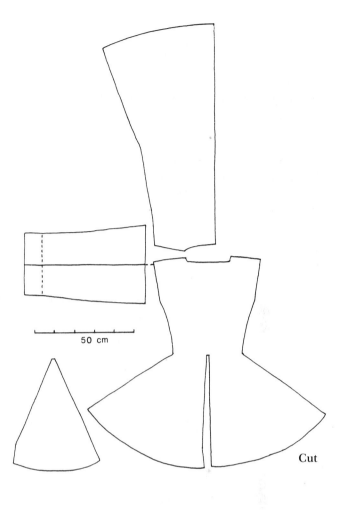

50 cm

Cut

Tool

Bottom border: Compartments each contain a double curve with the lines of the curves swelling into leaf forms.

Bottom border

Central gore form: Graduated compartments each contain a double-curve variation centred by a "heart" motif (see Hearts in Design Motifs section for comment). A circle hangs down from the centre of the double curve.

Centre-back extension: Repeats motifs of central gore form.

Central gore form

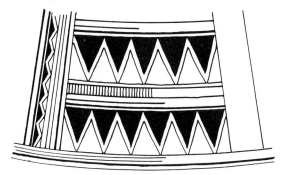

Gore forms 2 and 6

Front borders

Shoulders: Plain.

Collar: Missing.

Gore forms 1, 3, 5, and 7: Similar to central gore form. The surrounds of parallel lines, small zigzags, and rows of dots come together at the waist in a blunt point, from which a single band extends to the shoulder seam.

Gore forms 2 and 6: Crossed by parallel lines, single track, and steep interlocking zigzags similar to those used in same position on No. 10. The surrounds of parallel lines and small zigzags converge at the waist and continue without a break to the shoulder.

Front borders: Different from each other. On left, a band crossed by diagonal lines with triangles; on right, diagonal lines that break down into a curve.

Sleeves: Bands at shoulder and elbow; no notes were made of patterns used.

Cuffs: A double-curve variation similar to but simpler than those in gore forms.

Outer borders: Red around coat.

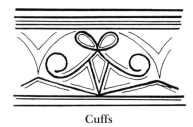

Cuffs

12. British Museum, London
(Q79 Am8)

Man's painted caribou-skin coat
Montagnais-Naskapi, Quebec-Labrador, probably
about 1770

This coat was discovered by Jonathan King, curator of the North American ethnographic collection at the British Museum; it was unnumbered and unlabelled in the museum's storage. When trying to trace it in the old records Mr. King found an early entry that reads "1771 April 12: The habit of the chief of the Nescopee Indians from Adair Esq." This coat may well fit in with that date and it seems most probable that it is the 1771 acquisition.

Although the condition is very poor, this is a very interesting coat; it is unusual in having nine patterned gore forms. The probability that it is the coat recorded in 1771 as having been given to the British Museum adds to its importance, and the question as to who this Mr. Adair might be led to enquiries. No suitable candidate was found among the employees of the Hudson's Bay Company,[6] and so far the only Adair found who might possibly be the donor is James Adair, whose book, *The History of the American Indians: Particularly those Nations adjoining to the Mississippi, East and West Florida, Georgia, South and North Carolina, and Virginia*, was published in London in 1775. Unfortunately, there is nothing in the book to indicate that Mr. Adair ever had any contact with areas north of Virginia. The timing is right—he may well have been in London about the time the gift was given. Perhaps he acquired the coat in trade. Regrettably, it is just one more example of the tantalizing and frustrating lack of evidence that characterizes research concerning just where and when these coats were made.

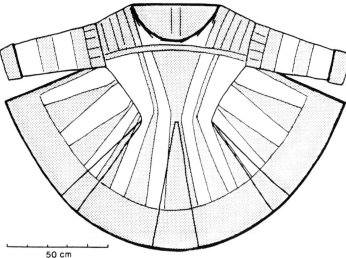

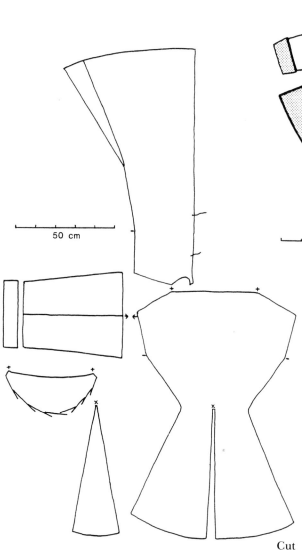

50 cm

50 cm

Cut

The condition of the coat is such that the photograph shows very little detail; this diagram shows the layout of the patterning and how it relates to the cutting of the garment.

Quality: Mixed. Skins badly flymarked; painting quite coarse, but with a most unusually elaborate layout of design with nine fully patterned gore forms.

Condition: Very sad. Skins soiled, stiff, and dark; paint very worn. The condition of the coat made it very difficult to produce a clear photograph, so a diagram has been added to show the pattern layout. The drawings, made while examining the coat, show the motifs.

Cutting: Flare of 1:2.2. The shoulders are unusually wide and the coat was obviously made for a larger-than-usual man. When the coat is compared with Nos. 13–14 the similarity of size and shape is startling, suggesting the possibility that all three coats were made for the same man.

Size: Length, 120 cm. Back of neck to wrist, 90.5 cm.

Sewing: Entirely with sinew, 28 stitches per 5 cm.

Colours: Yellow, now very dark, for layout and background crosshatching; red, probably vermilion, very thick and cracked, for drawing motifs; black and brown for details.

Tools: Two 2-prongs with yellow for layout, *A* in bottom border, *B* in gore forms; *B* also with red and brown. A 5-prong, *C*, with yellow across shoulders and some gore forms. Three single prongs, *D*, *E*, and *F*, with red. A fine single prong, *G*, with black and yellow. A small stamp, *H*, for black dots.

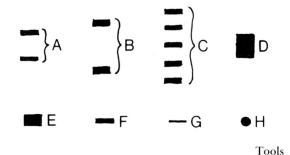

Tools

Bottom border: A band of double curves, each with a segment of a circle above its centre, bordered by scallops, dots, and a track variation.

Central gore form: A vertical line of ovals. This unusual pattern relates fairly closely to the motifs used in the same position on Nos. 13–14. A smaller version of the pattern is used in the side gore forms on Nos. 1 and 3. Here on No. 12 the vertical line of ovals supports double curves, whereas the earlier designs have paired leaves. The surround is a line of sharp, wedge-shaped zigzags which also echoes an earlier use (Nos. 2, 4).

Bottom border

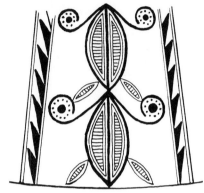

Central gore form

Centre-back extension: Zigzag surround of central gore form continues, enclosing plain horizontal parallel lines.

Shoulders: Crossed by parallel lines, above which, heavy and light vertical parallel lines run up to shoulder seams. There are similar lines on the tops of the sleeves. This type of shoulder treatment is repeated in various ways on Nos. 13–21.

Collar: A central lozenge band with double curves growing out from it. This type of design is repeated in many versions on contemporary and somewhat later coats.

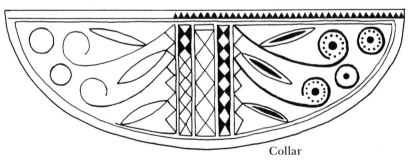

Collar

Gore forms 1 and 9: Graduated compartments, each with a double curve supporting a segment of a circle, similar to those in bottom border. The surrounds of all the side gore forms converge at the waist and, unlike those on many coats, continue unbroken into a band that extends to the shoulder.

Gore forms 1 and 9

Gore forms 2, 4, 6, and 8

Gore forms 3 and 7

Cuffs

Gore forms 2, 4, 6, and 8: Crossed alternately by parallel lines and rows of sharp zigzags. These are similar to the motif used in the same position on Nos. 10–11, but smaller. The condition of the coat makes it impossible to establish whether they interlock with zigzags of another colour.

Gore forms 3 and 7: Graduated compartments each contain lanceolate leaves that support a segment of a circle, as do the double curves in the bottom border and in gore forms 1 and 9.

Front borders: Narrow, with parallel lines and a single band of wedge-shaped zigzags.

Sleeves: At top, vertical parallel lines similar to those on the back shoulders. Below, a band with a double-curve variation. At elbow a band with parallel lines, zigzags, and a line of dots.

Cuffs: A band of inverted double curves.

Outer borders: Brown around coat and cuffs and across top of collar; red around bottom of collar.

Markings: A line of red paint was applied to shoulder seams after the basic painting was done.

13. Musée de la civilisation, Québec (75.1197)

Man's painted caribou-skin coat
Montagnais-Naskapi, Quebec-Labrador, probably late 18th century

This coat was transferred to the Musée de la civilisation from the Musée du Québec with no information concerning acquisition or source.

The cut is remarkably similar in size and shape to both Nos. 12 and 14, with the same unusual main motif in the back gore form. The measure of the average coat indicates that most of the hunters were around 170–175 cm (5 feet, 7–9 inches) tall, while these three coats seem to have been made for men who were around 183–185 cm (6 feet) tall and to have been cut for powerful shoulders. This, coupled with the unique pattern, although not providing proof, does suggest very strongly that the three coats have a similar area of origin, and that they were

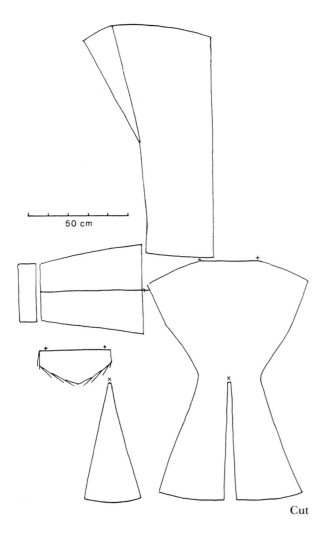

50 cm

Cut

made, if not for the same larger-than-usual man, at least for men in the same family. The British Museum coat (No. 12) has a probable history that would take it back to about 1770. Its pattern layout, with nine fully developed gore forms, fits with that early date, while Nos. 13–14, with the more normal seven gore forms, are probably somewhat later in date.

Quality: Good. Medium-weight skins; complex but rather coarse painting.

Condition: Good. Skins somewhat soiled; some loss of paint. The red is not stable and has run and smudged in some places.

Cutting: Flare of 1:2.2. As with No. 12, the back is unusually wide.

Size: Length, 115 cm. Back of neck to wrist, 90.5 cm.

Sewing: Entirely with sinew, 24 stitches per 5 cm. The collar is sewn on with running stitches on the outside (see Sewing section for comment).

Colours: Strong yellow for layout; red, probably vermilion, for drawing motifs; blue-green for some details; unusually strong medium blue. A similar blue is used on another comparatively early coat, No. 11; interestingly, the red on No. 11 is, like this one, not stable.

Tools: A 3-prong, *A*, and a 2-prong, *B*, both with yellow for layout. Probably at least one other 2-prong. Several single prongs, the weights of which were not noted. Two stamps, *C* for rings, *D* for dots.

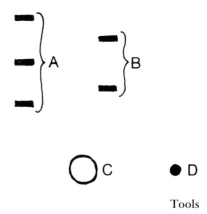

Tools

Bottom border: Repeated double curves above a series of large scallops; lines of ringed dots above and below main motifs.

Bottom border

Central gore form: A vertical line of ovals supports double curves, very similar to design used in central gore form of No. 12; the surround, as on No. 12, is a line of wedge-shaped zigzags.

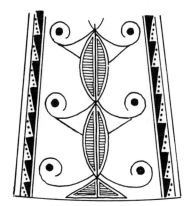

Central gore form

Centre-back extension: Crossed and surrounded by rows of ringed dots.

Shoulders: A band of ringed dots and parallel lines, above which vertical parallel lines run up to shoulder seams.

Collar: A central lozenge band with double-curve variations extending to either side. It is similar in type to the collar on No. 12, but simpler.

Collar

Gore forms 1 and 5: Similar to but slightly simpler than central gore form. Surrounds of wedge-shaped zigzags and dots converge at the waist where the zigzags stop and the two lines of dots continue in a single band to the shoulder.

Gore forms 2 and 4: Crossed by parallel lines and alternate rows of dots and small lozenges. Surrounds of ringed dots converge at the waist and from there a band of plain parallel lines extends to the shoulder.

Gore forms 2 and 4

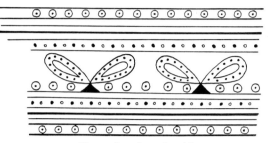

Sleeve band at shoulder

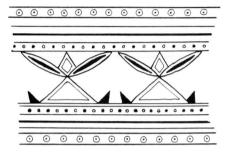

Sleeve band at elbow

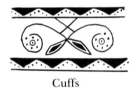

Cuffs

Front borders: A band of ringed dots and plain dots terminating below neck. From there a lozenge band extends to the armholes. Above the lozenge band vertical lozenge rows and parallel lines run up to the shoulder seams.

Sleeves: At shoulder, paired rounded leaves between rows of dots and ringed dots. At elbow, paired lanceolate leaves supported on a large triangle, which is flanked by small wedge shapes; this motif is used in the same position on No. 19.

Cuffs: Inverted double curves. The wearer would see the curve right way up; this probably ties in with the widespread practice of placing the pattern on moccasin toes to face the wearer rather than the observer.

Outer borders: Red around coat, cuffs, and tops of sleeves; brown around collar.

Markings: As with No. 12, a rough red band painted across shoulder seams after sewing was completed.

PUBLICATIONS: Musée de l'Homme/National Gallery of Canada, cat. no. 136 (colour plate with caption); Dickason, cat. no. 43 (photograph with caption).

14. Royal Artillery Institution, Woolwich, London (UN 828)

Man's painted caribou-skin coat
Montagnais-Naskapi, Quebec-Labrador, probably late 18th century

See colour plate page 49

This coat is part of a small collection of native artifacts that belonged to General Sir John Henry Lefroy (1817–1890), a very distinguished artillery officer in the British Army. As a young lieutenant, Lefroy was employed with an international project, recording magnetical observations. In 1842 he was transferred to the observatory in Toronto and during the following year he journeyed, by canoe and snowshoe, to the far Northwest, making frequent magnetical observations as he travelled out to Fort Chipewyan. This fascinating history does not explain how Lefroy came to own this coat and No. 39, which both come from the other end of the country. Lefroy landed at Quebec and after his arrival was also in Montreal briefly where he may well have seen painted caribou-skin coats in fashionable use, as shown in Figure 13. He remained in Canada until 1853, so he would have had ample time for collecting. We know that he was

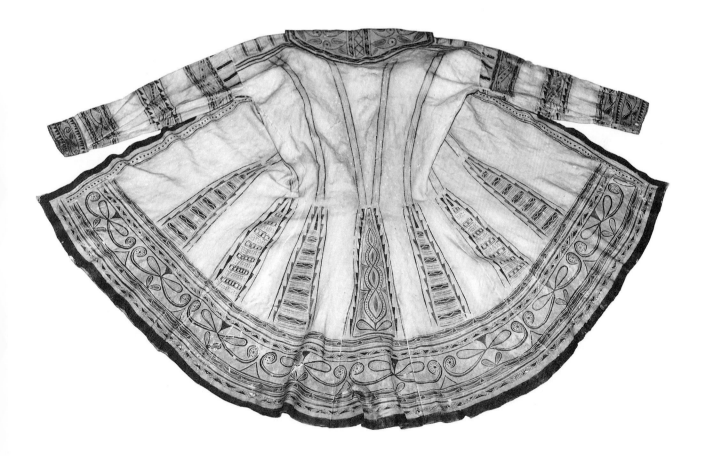

interested in owning native artifacts, for in a letter home in 1845 he wrote:

I wish you could see the trophy we have set up in what we magnificently term the lobby of our mansion, Snowshoes, two or three daggers in Indian-worked cases, my gun, ditto, Calumets, a Head dress of Grisley bears claws, and other things, the admiration of all beholders.[7]

It was hoped that the date of Lefroy's stay in Canada would provide a period within which the coats he collected might have been made. No. 39 probably does date from the 1840s, but No. 14 must have been an antique when Lefroy acquired it. From the evidence of its cut and decorative motifs it probably predates Lefroy's time in Canada by about fifty years.

The similarity of No. 14 to Nos. 12–13 is remarkable. All three coats are long and have wide shoulders; they are so close in size that a single owner is suggested. The tools used on the three coats, however, are not the same, so we cannot tie the making to one woman. No. 12 has a probable date of about 1770. In spite of the extraordinary similarity of size, shape, and design motifs, a less definite and more conservative dating of late 18th century has been given to Nos. 13–14. But in the back of my mind there remains the intriguing thought that three coats owned by the same unusually large man may have survived.

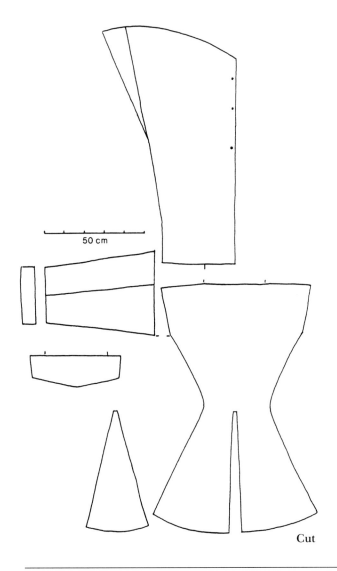

50 cm

Cut

Quality: Good. Back skin badly flymarked; painting elaborate and strong but not very precise.

Condition: Very good. Some soiling; some insect damage; one large hole at lower centre back.

Cutting: Flare of 1:2.25. As with Nos. 12–13, the shoulders are wide enough for a powerfully built man.

Size: Length, 120 cm. Back of neck to wrist, 91 cm.

Sewing: Entirely with sinew, 25 stitches per 5 cm. Both collar and cuffs have been attached with coarse running stitches on the outside (see Sewing section for comment).

Colours: Strong yellow for layout, crosshatching and solid filling of some of background; red, probably vermilion, for main drawing of motifs; blue-green, which is quite blue in central gore form and greener elsewhere, for some motifs; brown for some details and outer borders.

Tools: Two 3-prongs and two 2-prongs with yellow for layout, *A* in bottom and front borders, *B* in gore forms, *C* for outlining gore forms, *D* on shoulders and sleeves. Two 2-prongs with red, *E* for gore extensions and *F* on sleeves. A 2-prong, *G*, with brown across gore forms and on shoulders. Two single prongs with red, *H* for drawing motifs, *I* on shoulders. A fine single prong, *J*, with yellow for crosshatching. The very heavy brown line, *K*, on tops of sleeves was made by using a fine tool repeatedly. Two stamps for dots, a small one, *L*, with red and a larger one, *M*, with dark blue-green.

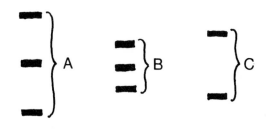

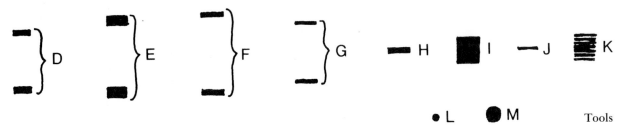

Tools

Bottom border: Repeated double curves with paired broad leaves below them; at juncture of the curve, larger similar leaves and a stemmed triangle. Narrow lines of scallops and lines of zigzags above and below main border.

Bottom border

Central gore form: A vertical row of graduated ovals appears to be growing up from a small pair of broad leaves. This pattern relates fairly closely to the use of ovals on Nos. 12–13; the surround, with its line of sharp, wedge-shaped zigzags that provide a feeling of growth, is also similar on Nos. 12–13.

Centre-back extension: Empty space enclosed by simple parallel lines that extend up under collar. There is a slight break at the waist between the gore form and the extension.

Shoulders: Crossed by horizontal parallel lines, above which heavy and light vertical parallel lines run up to shoulder seams. There are similar lines on the tops of the sleeves and on the fronts.

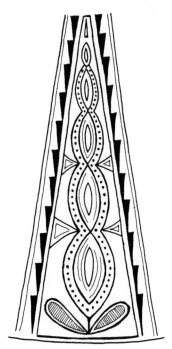

Central gore form

Collar: Pentagonal in form. A central lozenge band between narrower lozenge bands. Curves and broad leaves grow out from the centre and in from the corners. The whole is surrounded by a narrow border of interlocking zigzags.

Collar

Gore forms 1 and 7: Crossed alternately by parallel lines and narrow rows of interlocking zigzags. The surrounds are wedge-shaped zigzags and, like the surrounds of all the side gore forms, they converge at the waist, break, and then continue as simple parallel lines up to the shoulder bands.

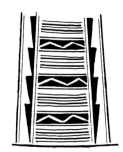
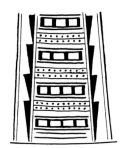

Gore forms 1, 3, 5, and 7   Gore forms 2 and 6

Sleeve band at shoulder

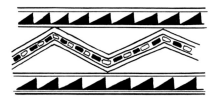

Sleeve band at elbow

Sleeve band at wrist

Gore forms 2 and 6: Crossed alternately by triple lines enclosing a double row of dots and lines of a bold track variation. The surrounds are wedge-shaped zigzags.

Gore forms 3 and 5: Similar to gore forms 1 and 7.

Front borders: Parallel lines enclose a single row of large dark blue-green dots.

Sleeves: At top, a short section with very heavy dark brown vertical parallel lines. Below that, a band with a track variation forming a large zigzag enclosed by rows of small lozenges. At elbow, a similar zigzag band enclosed by lines of small wedge-shaped zigzags. Most unusually, a third band encircles the sleeve just above cuff. It has a row of scallops surmounted by paired leaves and narrow lozenge bands above and below.

Cuffs: Double curves between narrow bands of zigzags.

Outer borders: Brown around coat and collar; narrow around collar.

Additional: Three brass hooks have been sewn to the inside border on the lower part of the right coat front (see diagrams for shape and placement). The hooks are made of brass wire which is round in section but has been flattened on the top face of the hook. Opposite the hooks on the left front of the coat are three thread loops, 9 mm wide, worked in buttonhole stitch in linen thread (Z,2S, evenly spun). These loops are on the face of the coat. Each loop and its surrounding area has been carefully coloured with red-brown paint to disguise it presence. At the Royal Artillery Institution in Woolwich there are many dated uniforms, some of which were examined in the hope that the brass hooks might be datable. Similar hooks were found on a uniform dating back to the 1790s, but they were also found on uniforms up to about 1880. The hooks were probably added to this coat to ensure proper closing of the garment in front, making it suitable for fancy dress or amateur theatricals. They could have been sewn on at any time up to the end of the 19th century.

Cuffs

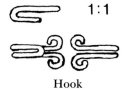

1:1

Hook

15. National Museums of Scotland, Edinburgh (L.402)

Man's painted caribou-skin coat
Montagnais-Naskapi, Quebec-Labrador, probably late 18th century

See colour plate page 49

This coat has no history except that it was lent to the museum by a Miss Wedderburn.

This is a handsome coat with a very strong use of vertical lines on the shoulders and sleeves. The diagonal cross used in gore forms 2 and 6 may well be a shortened form of double curve (see Diagonal Crosses in Design Motifs section for comment); if that is the case, the coat has a version of the frequently used arrangement of double curves and horizontal banding in alternate gore forms.

Although this coat does not have breaks between the gore forms and their extensions, as do some other coats, the heavy surrounding line, which terminates abruptly at the waist, provides a different kind of break and suggests that the coat was designed to be worn with a sash around the waist.

Quality: Good. Painting complex and careful; skins rather heavy and badly flymarked.

Condition: Good. Skins soft; minimal loss of paint.

Cutting: Flare of 1:2.2. Although this coat is considerably shorter than Nos. 12–14, the shoulders are equally wide, suggesting that the wearer must have been a powerful man.

Size: Length, 110 cm. Back of neck to wrist, 91 cm.

Sewing: Entirely with sinew, 19 stitches per 5 cm. There is a pair of thong ties, which do not appear to be original.

Colours: Yellow for layout and crosshatching in many background areas; red, probably vermilion, for drawing motifs; brown; pale blue-green for details.

Tools: A 2-prong, *A*, a 3-prong, *B*, and a 4-prong, *C*, all with yellow for layout. A 2-prong, *D*, with yellow and brown. An unusually heavy striated single prong, *E*, with brown to outline gore forms. Other narrower single prongs, the weights of which were not noted.

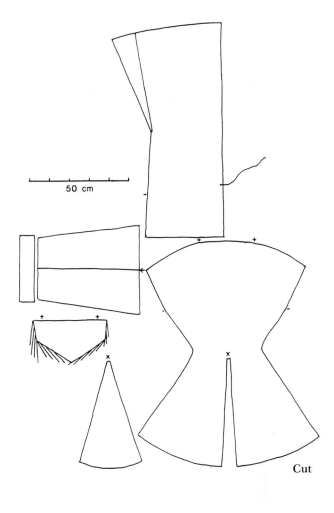

Cut

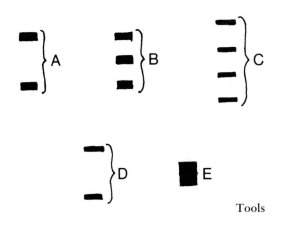

Tools

Bottom border: Double curves centred by a circle above a series of large scallops. The double-curve terminals enclose an unusual crosshatched ring around a single large dot.

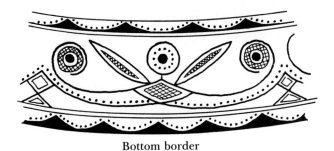

Bottom border

Central gore form

Central gore form: Graduated compartments each contain a double curve of rather flattened form. Surrounds are simply a couple of light lines and a very heavy dark brown one.

Centre-back extension: Crossed four times by a heavy red line.

Shoulders: Both back and front crossed by parallel lines above which heavy red vertical lines alternating with triple yellow lines extend to shoulder seams.

Collar: Pentagonal in shape with sparse, obliquely slashed fringe. It has a very handsome version of the central band and double-curve design used on Nos. 11–14 and a number of other coats.

Collar

Gore forms 1 and 7

Gore forms 2 and 6

Gore forms 1 and 7: Crossed by alternate parallel lines and bands of an unusual little motif of two adjoining wedge-shaped triangles. This motif occurs once again, in the bottom border of No. 34. The surrounds of all the side gore forms are parallel lines, one of which is very heavy. They terminate at the waist in a blunt point, from the centre of which simple parallel lines extend to the shoulder.

Gore forms 2 and 6: Graduated sections each contain a diagonal cross with paired lanceolate leaves. Different versions of diagonal crosses are used in this position on Nos. 18–19.

Gore forms 3 and 5: Crossed by alternate triple parallel lines and bands of small lozenges.

Gore forms 3 and 5

Front borders: Parallel lines and a row of wedge-shaped zigzags.

Sleeves: At top, vertical parallel lines; on upper arm, a band of double-curve motifs, fairly similar to those in bottom border; at elbow, a scallop variation.

Cuffs: A repeating double-curve motif with a row of wedge-shaped zigzags above and below.

Outer borders: Dark brown around coat and collar.

Markings: Red and rough on back of shoulder seams and top of armhole seams; applied before sewing was done.

Sleeve band at shoulder

Sleeve band at elbow

Cuffs

16. Canadian Ethnology Service, Canadian Museum of Civilization, Hull-Ottawa (III B 642)

Man's painted caribou-skin coat
Montagnais-Naskapi, Quebec-Labrador, probably late 18th century

See colour plates page 50

The history of this coat is not useful: it was purchased from a dealer, who got it from a picker, who had found it at a small-town auction sale in the United States.

The design themes are fairly similar to those of Nos. 12–15. The branching leaves used in the central gore form differ from the strange oval motifs on Nos. 12–14, but the basic central line is similar. The strength of the drawing, the feeling of growth, and the use of wedge-shaped zigzags for the surrounds are all the same.

The obvious break between the top of each gore form and its line extension to the shoulders is a strong indication that this coat was made to be worn with a sash around the waist.

This is not the most skilfully designed or the most carefully painted coat in the series, but the richness and exuberance of pattern and colour are remarkably satisfying.

Quality: Good. Lightweight skins; elaborate bold painting.

Condition: Good.

Cutting: Flare of 1:1.9.

Size: Length, 105 cm. Back of neck to wrist, 79 cm.

Sewing: Entirely with sinew, with an irregular count of about 24 stitches per 5 cm. Collar sewn to back of neck with coarse running stitches on outside (see Sewing section for comment).

Colours: Strong yellow for layout, crosshatching, and solid filling-in of some background areas; red for drawing most of motifs; grey-blue; brown.

Tools: A 3-prong, *A,* and a 2-prong, *B,* with yellow for layout. A 3-prong, *C,* with red in gore forms. A 2-prong, *D,* with brown. Several single prongs including *E* with red, *F* with brown, *G* with yellow. Stamps for dots, *H* with blue, *I* with red. A ring, *J,* with red.

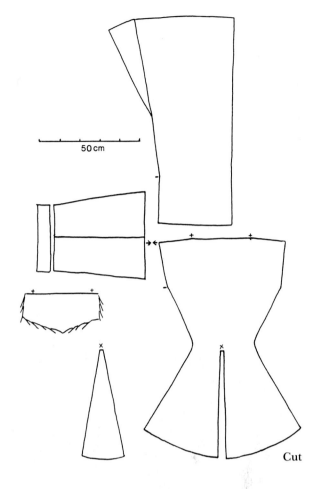

Cut

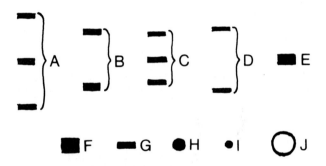

Tools

Bottom border: Double curves and quatrefoil leaves with very strong line decorations above and below.

Central gore form: Paired rounded leaves grow up and out from a central line. The surrounds of wedge-shaped zigzags add considerably to the feeling of upward growth.

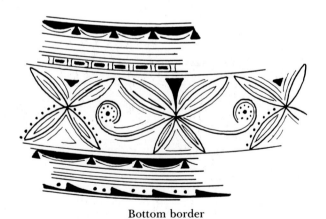

Bottom border

Central gore form

Centre-back extension: After a break at the waist, the extension is crossed by parallel lines and rows of zigzags. The surrounds are simple parallel lines.

Shoulders: Both back and front crossed by a band of parallel lines, above which groups of vertical parallel lines run up to shoulder seams.

Collar: Pentagonal in form. Same type of design as Nos. 13–15. Double curves extend out from a central line and rounded leaves fill in the spaces.

Collar

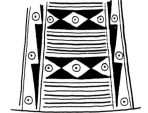

Gore forms 1, 3, 5, and 7

Gore forms 2 and 6

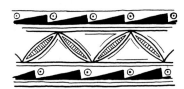

Sleeve band below shoulder

Cuffs

Gore forms 1, 3, 5, and 7: Crossed by alternate groups of parallel lines and lozenge bands. All side gore forms have surrounds with wedge-shaped zigzags and ringed dots. They break completely at the waist and a simple band of parallel lines extends from the break to the shoulder.

Gore forms 2 and 6: Crossed by alternate groups of parallel lines and rows of ringed dots. On the right-hand side of the coat the lines are very slanted and are way off where they should meet the line of the bottom border.

Front borders: Two rows of wedge-shaped zigzags with dots.

Sleeves: At shoulder, groups of vertical parallel lines; below this a wide band with leaves forming a zigzag. At elbow, a band of simple parallel lines.

Cuffs: Inverted double curves with a row of lozenges above and below.

Outer borders: Brown around coat and collar.

Markings: Rough and red on shoulder and armhole seams; applied after sewing was done.

17. Museum für Völkerkunde, Berlin (IV B 12730)

Man's painted caribou-skin coat
Montagnais-Naskapi, Quebec-Labrador, probably about 1800

See colour plate page 51

This coat was bought from the Speyer Collection; there is no further information about it.

The bottom border with its double curves and paired, wedge-shaped triangles ties very closely to the border on No. 18, one of the few coats with a fairly firm history, which suggests a date between 1820 and 1830. On that evidence this coat has been dated a little later than might otherwise have been the case. The simplicity of design and the lack of precision in the painting probably also fit better with an early 19th-century date than with an earlier one.[8]

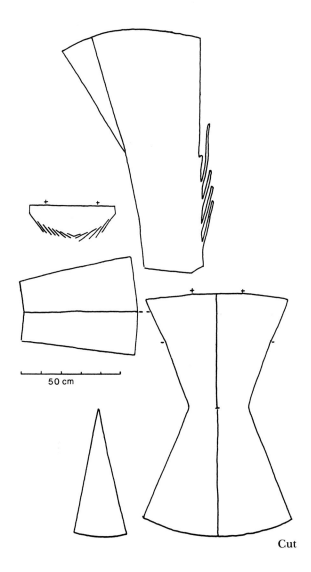

50 cm

Cut

Quality: Fair. Medium-weight skins; simple, rather coarse painting.

Condition: Good but soiled. Skins slightly torn; some paint gone, probably eaten by insects.

Cutting: Flare of 1:2.3. The cut is unusual in that the back of the coat is in two pieces with a centre seam into which a back gusset with a sharp point has been inserted. The centre fronts have been slashed upwards to make a long fringe, the tags of which meet fairly well and could have been used as five pairs of ties.

Size: Length, 117 cm. Back of neck to wrist, 90 cm.

Sewing: Entirely with sinew, 25 stitches per 5 cm. Collar attached with running stitches on outside (see Sewing section for comment).

Colours: Yellow for layout; red, probably vermilion, for drawing motifs; brown for outlining gore forms, for some details, and for entire collar.

Tools: A 2-prong, *A*, with yellow for layout and also with brown. A 3-prong, *B*, with yellow. Several single prongs, including *C* and *D* with red and *E* with both red and brown. A stamp, *F*, for red and brown dots.

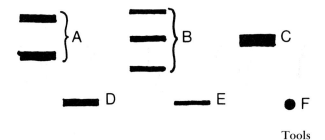

Tools

Bottom border: Above large scallops double curves are centred and separated by paired, wedge-shaped triangles, possibly leaves. The terminals of the curves have the unusual filling of a straight-armed cross with a dot in each quarter. The double-curve motif without the crosses is repeated very closely in the bottom border of No. 18.

Bottom border

Central gore form: Crossed by bands of small zigzags alternating with double lines of dots. The surrounds are simple lines.

Centre-back extension: The simple surrounds of the central gore form continue upwards to enclose a space, which is empty except for a single narrow brown line applied over the centre-back seam.

Shoulders: Both back and front crossed by parallel lines; above them repeated groups of vertical parallel lines run up to shoulder seams.

Collar: A very simple design of plain brown vertical lines within a border. Lower edge of collar is slashed obliquely to make a sparse fringe.

Gore forms 1, 3, 5, and 7: Crossed by alternate rows of dots and a track variation. The surrounds of all the side gore forms are simple lines and a heavy brown outline that come together in a blunt point at the waist; only the lines closest to centre back continue to the shoulder band. The brown outline turns to edge the shoulder bands.

Gore forms 2 and 6: Crossed by double rows of dots alternating with a heavy red line.

Front borders: Simple parallel lines.

Sleeves: Encircled by three bands of parallel lines enclosing a row of dots; no cuffs.

Outer borders: Brown around coat and collar.

Markings: Rough and brown on shoulder and armhole seams; narrow brown line on centre-back seam; all applied after sewing.

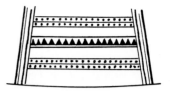

Central gore form

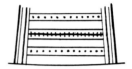

Gore forms 1, 3, 5, and 7

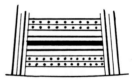

Gore forms 2 and 6

Sleeve bands

18. Museum für Völkerkunde und Schweizerisches Museum für Volkskunde, Basel (IV a 41)

Man's painted caribou-skin coat
Montagnais-Naskapi, Quebec-Labrador, probably 1820–1830

See colour plate page 51

This coat was given to the museum in 1844 by Lukas Vischer, who probably collected it while travelling in North America between 1820 and 1830.

All the coats that have vertical lines on the shoulders have been placed in a sequence. Three more probably earlier examples, Nos. 19–21, are described following this one because they connect in another way with the group that follows them. This coat has a fairly firm history that most likely places it between 1820 and 1830 and is probably the actual end of this series, which started with No. 12 some sixty year earlier.[9]

Some of the coats with this type of shoulder decoration use the vertical lines on both back and front shoulders and on the tops of the sleeves, while others use them in only one or two of these places. Most, but not No. 18, combine the vertical lines with rough markings applied to shoulder or armhole seams after sewing. The vertical lines were applied before sewing and no attempt seems to have been made to match them up on the adjoining parts of the coat. The rough markings on the seams, however, give the feeling that they are joining one section of skin to another. The two types of line use probably have different ideas behind them.

The vertical lines occur only in a very minor way after the early 19th century. They are found on the sleeve tops of two coats collected by Lucien Turner between 1882 and 1884, both in the National Museum of Natural History, Smithsonian Institu-

tion, Washington, D.C. (90241, No. 40 in this series, and 90245, which is quite similar and so has not been included in this catalogue). There is also an extraordinary survival of this type of decoration on the shoulders of No. 60, which was made about 1926, to be worn at a "mokoshan" feast. The rough markings, however, continued in common use as long as the painted hunting coats were made.

Quality: Good. Medium-weight skins; well-designed but comparatively coarsely executed painting in a limited colour range.

Condition: Good. Skins slightly soiled.

Cutting: Flare of 1:2.15.

Size: Length, 100 cm. Back of neck to wrist, 84 cm.

Sewing: Entirely with sinew, 27 stitches per 5 cm. Tags of sinew sewing at bottom of some seams (see Sewing section for comment).

Colours: Unusually limited. Yellow for basic layout and background crosshatching; dark brown for drawing motifs; dark blue for a few details.

Tools: A 3-prong, *A*, and a 2-prong, *B*, with yellow for layout. A 2-prong, *C*, with brown across gore forms. Several single prongs, the weights of which were not noted.

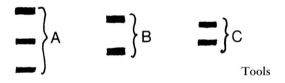

Tools

Bottom border: Repeated double curves similar to those in bottom border of No. 17, with track variation and rows of dots above and below.

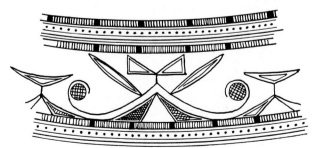

Bottom border

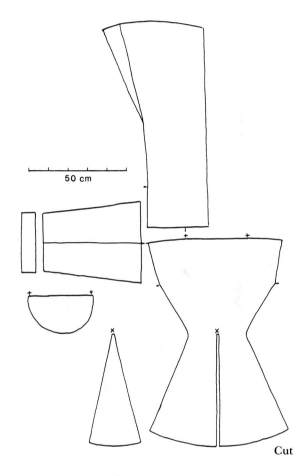

Cut

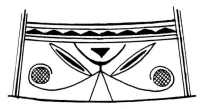

Central gore form

Central gore form: Graduated sections each contain a double curve. At the waist the motif reduces to crossed leaves similar to the main motif of gore forms 3 and 5. The horizontal divides are zigzags and the surrounds simple parallel lines.

Centre-back extension: Crossed by triple parallel lines.

Shoulders: Horizontal bands of parallel lines on both back and front; above them a very short section of vertical lines running up to shoulder seams.

Collar: Yet another example of the type with double curves growing out from a central vertical band.

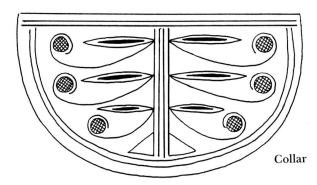

Collar

Gore forms 1 and 7: Crossed by alternate rows of dots and small lozenges. All side gore forms have surrounds of simple, narrow parallel lines that converge at the waist and continue without a break to the shoulder band.

Gore forms 2 and 6

Gore forms 2 and 6: Graduated sections each contain leaves that form a diagonal cross similar to motifs used in the same position on Nos. 15–16 and 19.

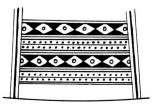

Gore forms 3 and 5

Gore forms 3 and 5: Similar to gore forms 1 and 7, but here each lozenge contains a ringed dot.

Front borders: A row of dots and track variation similar to those used in bottom border.

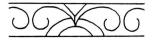

Sleeve bands

Sleeves: At top, repeating vertical lines. Bands of decoration just below shoulder, at elbow, and just above cuff, all with simple inverted double curves.

Cuffs: A band of small plain diagonal crosses similar to those used on collar of No. 20.

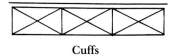

Cuffs

Outer borders: Brown around coat, collar, and cuffs.

19. Museum für Völkerkunde, Frankfurt am Main (NS 4287)

Boy's painted caribou-skin coat
Montagnais-Naskapi, Quebec-Labrador, probably late 18th century

See colour plate page 51

This small coat was bought from Umlauff in Hamburg and was in the Frankfurt museum by 1906.

This coat would fit only a quite young boy. The design themes relate closely to those of No. 16, which has similar double curves in the bottom border and considerable use of wedge-shaped zigzags in the surrounds. Here the strong line of large triangles in the central gore form is different, but it supports rounded leaves similar to those on No. 16. Both coats have an unusual break at the top of all the gore forms.

Although on the basis of its patterning this coat could be placed earlier in the sequence, it has been placed here where it seems to be the start of another group of coats (Nos. 19–23, 28, 31–39), all of which have a rather strange technical feature: the side seams were sewn up *after* the painting was done (see Sewing section for comment). Most of the coats in this group date from the early to mid 19th century.

Quality: Excellent. Good skins; bold, precise painting.

Condition: Good. Skins soft and flexible but somewhat soiled.

Cutting: Flare of 1:2.4.

Size: Length, 83 cm. Back of neck to wrist, 59 cm.

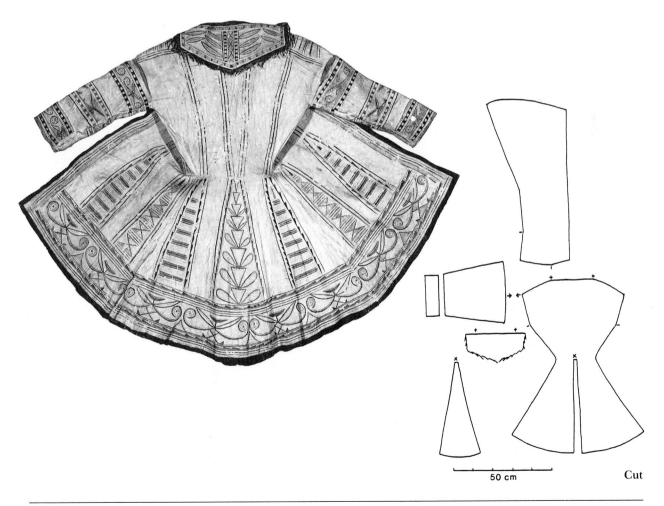

50 cm

Cut

Sewing: Entirely with sinew, 31 stitches per 5 cm. Side seams sewn up *after* painting. This practice, which on the face of it would seem very inefficient, is quite common and occurs on many of the coats in this group (see Sewing section for comment).

Colours: Yellow for layout and background crosshatching; red, probably vermilion, for drawing motifs; pale blue for fillings, details, and dots; brown for details and outer bands.

Tools: A 3-prong, *A*, and two 2-prongs, *B* and *C*, with yellow for layout. A 3-prong, *D*, and a 2-prong, *E*, with brown. Single prongs *F* and *G* with red, *H* with brown. Two small stamps, *I* with blue, *J* with both brown and red.

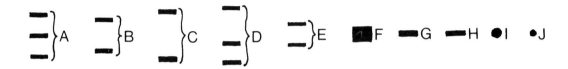

Tools

Bottom border: Strongly drawn double curves with wedge-shaped zigzags above and below.

Central gore form: Reminiscent of Nos. 12–14 and 16 with motifs growing up from a central line and surrounds of wedge-shaped zigzags. Here the design has a graduated series of triangles supporting paired leaves.

Bottom border

Central gore form

Centre-back extension: As with No. 16 the surrounds of the central gore form break at the waist and continue as narrow bands of plain parallel lines, which on this coat enclose empty space.

Shoulders: Both back and front crossed by a band of parallel lines above which short vertical lines run up to shoulder seams.

Collar: Pentagonal in form, obliquely slashed fringe. Centred by a line of small lozenges and track variation with leaves, instead of the usual double curves, on either side.

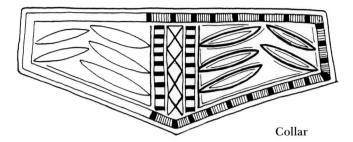

Collar

Gore forms 1 and 7: Crossed by triple yellow parallel lines alternating with a heavy red line. The surrounds are red wedge-shaped zigzags. All side gore forms break at the waist; just above the break a narrow band of parallel lines extends to the shoulder band.

Gore forms 2 and 6: Graduated compartments each contain a diagonal cross, a plainer version of motifs used in same area on Nos. 15 and 18.

Gore forms 3 and 5: Similar to gore forms 1 and 7 but with brown rather than red surrounds.

Front borders: Parallel lines and a closely spaced single track, which turns just below neck and extends to armholes.

Sleeves: At shoulder, a band of double curves enclosed between lines of heavy brown track. At elbow, a band of paired leaves between similar track in red. The elbow-band motif is similar to one used in the same position on No. 13.

Cuffs: A band of double curves with a repetition of the heavy track in brown.

Outer borders: Brown around collar and coat.

Markings: Rough and red, painted across shoulder and armhole seams after sewing.

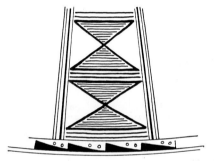

Gore forms 2 and 6

Sleeve band at shoulder

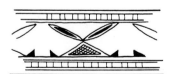

Sleeve band at elbow

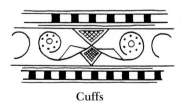

Cuffs

20. British Museum, London
(1954 w Am 5 964)

Man's painted caribou-skin coat
Montagnais-Naskapi, Quebec-Labrador, probably
about 1800

See colour plate page 52

The coat has a label "Stevens, Dec. 1898 20/4-99."
There is no further information.

The design layout is most unusual. No other
coat with a band around the waist has as yet been
recorded.

Quality: Good. Medium-weight skins with very few fly
marks; careful painting.

Condition: Sound but soiled. Some insect damage; some
loss of paint.

Cutting: Flare of 1:1.9.

Size: Length, 100 cm. Back of neck to wrist, 81 cm.

Sewing: Entirely with sinew; rather irregular with 20–24 stitches per 5 cm. The side seams were sewn *after* painting (see Sewing section for comment).

Colours: Yellow for layout and fine background cross-hatching; red, probably vermilion, for drawing motifs; dark brown and green for some details.

Tools: A 3-prong, *A*, with yellow for layout. A 2-prong, *B*, with red and with dark brown. A 5-prong, *C*, with yellow for vertical lines on shoulders. Several single prongs, the weights of which were not noted.

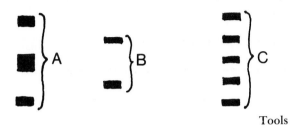

Tools

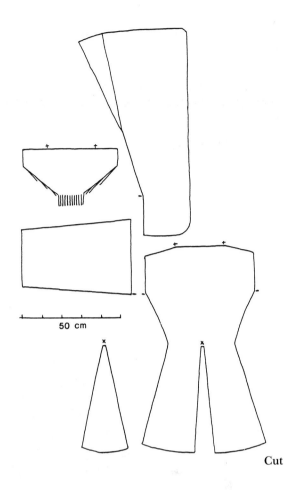

50 cm

Cut

Bottom border: Two parallel lines enclosing a row of dots form large zigzags that have triangles and pointed ovals at the angles. Above, a row of zigzags and a row of dots; below, a track variation and another row of dots.

Bottom border

Central gore form: Graduated compartments each contain a double-curve motif with a stiff triple leaf below and a very large triangle above. The horizontal divides are a track variation and a line of small zigzags; the surrounds are simple parallel lines.

Centre-back extension: The surrounds of the central gore form converge at the waist in the usual way and then spread out again but only for a distance of about 10 cm, where they are cut short by a most unusual band of parallel lines and rows of dots that encircles the coat. Above this band the back is undecorated.

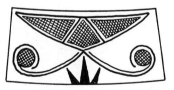

Central gore form

Shoulders: Both back and front crossed by a band of zig-zags and dots. As with Nos. 12–19 and 21, short vertical lines fill the small space between the shoulder bands and the shoulder seams.

Collar: On either side, a very handsome double-curve variation with pendant ovoids. A most unusual zigzag bar on top of the central double curve is crossed by the central vertical line. At the bottom there is an extension decorated with a line of plain diagonal crosses similar to the motif used on the cuffs of No. 18. The lower edge of the extension is slashed in a short straight fringe.

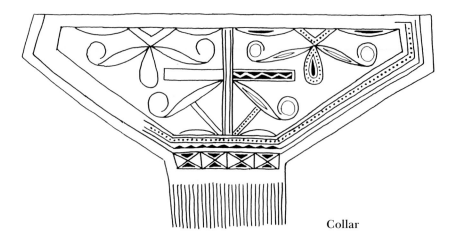

Collar

Gore forms 1 and 3

Gore forms 1 and 3: Graduated compartments each contain a double curve that supports the same type of ovoid used in the bottom border and hung from the double curves on the collar. The design is similar to that used in the central gore form of No. 21. The surrounds are simple parallel lines that come together at the waist in a blunt point, from the centre of which a single band of lines extends up to be cut short by the band that encircles the coat about 10 cm above the waist.

Additional: On either side of the three gore forms vertical bands run from the bottom border to the band above the waist. All four bands have parallel lines, a row of dots, and a line of zigzags. A similar use of vertical lines is made on Nos. 21 and 23–24.

Front borders: Plain parallel lines.

Sleeves: At shoulder, diagonal crosses and zigzags; at elbow, zigzags between two rows of dots; at wrist, a track variation; no cuffs.

Outer borders: Red around collar and bottom of coat; brown at wrist.

21. Museum für Völkerkunde, Vienna (P. XXIV-1965)

Boy's painted caribou-skin coat
Montagnais-Naskapi, Quebec-Labrador, probably about 1800

This coat was acquired by the museum from the Speyer Collection with the information that it had previously been part of a pre-1850 collection in the British Isles.

Considering the rarity of these early coats it is surprising how many have survived that, like this one and Nos. 5, 9, 19, and 23, are not for fully grown men, but still have fully developed and very rich designs.

Quality: Good. Medium-weight, unblemished, but pieced skins; fairly simple but precise painting.

Condition: Good. Somewhat soiled.

Cutting: Flare of 1:2.3.

Size: Length, 80 cm. Back of neck to wrist, 57 cm.

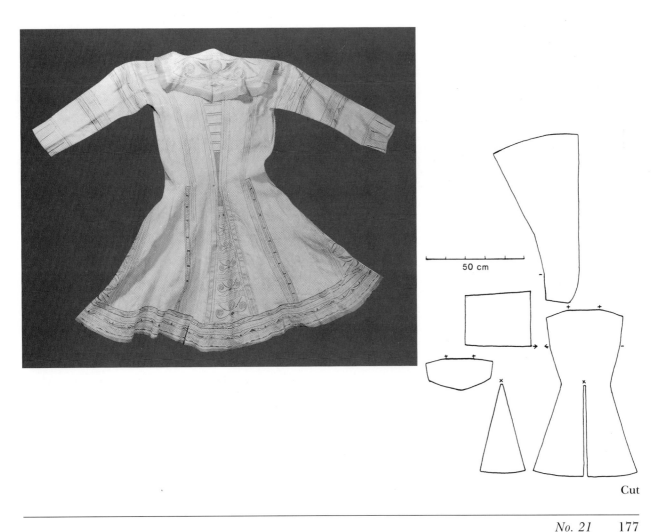

50 cm

Cut

Sewing: Entirely with sinew, 27 stitches per 5 cm. The side seams were sewn up *after* the painting was done (see Sewing section for comment).

Colours: Yellow for layout; red, probably vermilion, for drawing many of the motifs; brown and dark green for details.

Tools: A 3-prong, *A*, with wide striated central line, with yellow for layout. A 3-prong, *B*, with yellow for long vertical lines and also on collar, wrists, and shoulders. A 2-prong, *C*, with brown and red in border and on sleeves. Several single prongs including *D*. A small stamp, *E*, for dots.

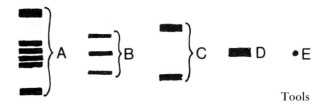

Tools

Bottom border

Central gore form

Bottom border: A small-scale design with two narrow rows of scallops, rows of dots, and at the bottom a scalloped line.

Central gore form: Graduated compartments each contain a double curve that supports paired leaves and an ovoid; the motif is quite similar to the one in the side gore forms of No. 20. The horizontal divides and surrounds are simple lines of various thicknesses.

Centre-back extension: Crossed by parallel lines.

Shoulders: A band of lines, above which short vertical parallel lines run up to shoulder seams as with Nos. 12–20. These vertical lines seem to be almost a remnant of this tradition of shoulder decoration, for there are no vertical lines on the fronts or the sleeve tops.

Collar: One large double curve supports a circle that encloses a ring of dots surrounding a crosshatched circle. The terminals of the double curve also have a crosshatched circle inside a ring of dots.

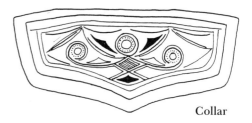

Collar

Gore forms 1 and 3: Graduated compartments each contain leaves that form a diagonal cross somewhat similar to the motifs used in the same position on Nos. 15 and 18–19. The surrounds are triple lines that come together at the waist in a blunt point, from the centre of which a triple line extends to the shoulder.

Additional: Besides the three actual gore forms there are four bands of lines that run from the bottom border to the shoulder band; similar lines are used on Nos. 20 and 23–24.

The bands on either side of the front borders consist of simple parallel lines. Beside this band, below the waist and towards the front, there is an additional band of straight lines enclosing a scalloped line.

The bands between the gore forms are similar to those on the fronts but have, below the waist, the addition of a track variation.

Front borders: Simple lines that turn in a curve below neck and extend to armholes.

Sleeves: At shoulder, a repetition of the scallop variation used in bottom border; at elbow, a line of small plain scallops; at wrist, short vertical parallel lines running up to a narrow band of horizontal lines; no cuffs.

Outer borders: Red around coat and collar, across shoulders, and around top edges of sleeves.

PUBLICATION: Feest, pp. 39–40.

Gore forms 1 and 3

Lines between gore forms

22. Pitt Rivers Museum, Oxford (1906)

Man's painted caribou-skin coat
Montagnais-Naskapi, Quebec-Labrador, probably
about 1800

See colour plate page 52

The only information known about the history of
this coat is that it was given to the museum by Mrs.
S. W. Silver in 1906.

It is a very handsome and interesting coat with
a great richness and variety in the line decorations
used to frame the double-curve motifs. The collar is
unusually elaborate and very beautifully drawn. A
similar although considerably simpler collar is used
on No. 23. It is interesting to note that the fronts on
No. 23 are cut with irregular lines similar to the
fronts of this coat; also, both have similar vertical
lines at the wrist and no cuffs.

Quality: Good. Lightweight skins with some fly holes; skilful and exact painting.

Condition: Good.

Cutting: Flare of 1:1.8. There is a band collar as well as the falling one. The fronts were cut with the spinal line of the skin at the sides rather than the centre, which probably explains the unusually irregular front edges, particularly at the top.

Size: Length, 99 cm. Back of neck to wrist, 83 cm.

Sewing: Entirely with sinew, 25 stitches per 5 cm. Side seams sewn up *after* painting was completed (see Sewing section for comment).

Colours: Light whitish yellow for layout; red, probably vermilion, for drawing motifs; dark and light blue; yellow-green. All the colours are quite muted and all are used for hatching and crosshatching in the background of most of the patterned areas.

Tools: A 3-prong, *A*, with yellow for layout and cross banding on gore forms. A narrow 2-prong, *B*, also with yellow, often used double. Several single prongs including two very fine ones, *C* and *D*.

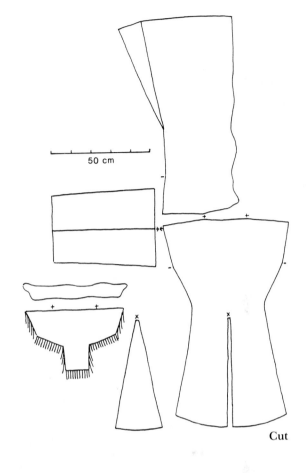

Cut

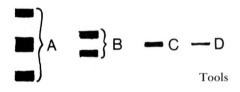

Tools

Bottom border: Repeated double curves with quite strong hatching and crosshatching in blue in background. Above and below there are numerous line decorations including an interesting dot variation that alternates a long dash with a group of four dots.

Bottom border

Central gore form

Central gore form: Graduated sections each contain a rather flattened double curve supporting a circle. The surrounds are parallel lines and a row of dots.

Centre-back extension: Crossed by simple horizontal lines and rows of dots.

Shoulders: Crossed by a band with a row of dots. Short vertical parallel lines extend from the band towards the shoulder seam. This is possibly a decorative version of the vertical line treatment of shoulders previously described (Nos. 12–21), but the lines do not run into the shoulder seam as on those coats.

Collar: There are two collars. The stand-up band collar has simple line decoration. The falling collar is magnificent with double curves, a quartered circle to either side (compare with Nos. 25, 27), and a tail filled with scallops. The collar is fringed all around. The fringe is cut obliquely in the usual way on the side edges, but on the bottom edge of the collar and the tail the fringe is cut straight with alternate segments removed.

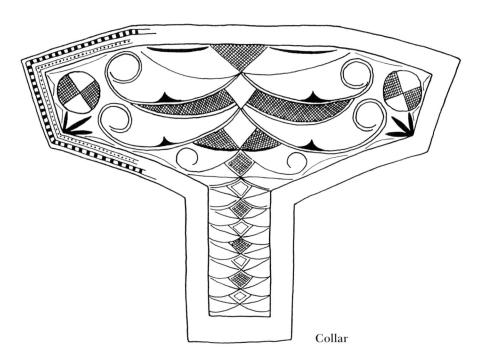

Collar

Gore forms 1, 3, 5, and 7: Horizontal rows of small lozenges alternate with 4-fold lines. The simple line surrounds of all side gore forms come together at the waist in a blunt point, from the centre of which a single band of lines extends to the shoulder.

Gore forms 2 and 6: Graduated sections each contain a double-curve motif.

Front borders: Plain parallel lines turn in a curve just below neck and extend to armholes.

Sleeves: At shoulder, lozenges, single track, and a line of alternating dashes and four dots similar to the line in the bottom border. At elbow, a track variation and rows of dots. At wrist, a band of vertical lines. No cuffs.

Outer borders: Red around coat, falling collar, wrists, and tops of sleeves and across shoulders and band collar.

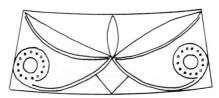

Gore forms 2 and 6

23. Newfoundland Museum, St. John's (III-B:208)

Small man's or boy's painted caribou-skin coat
Naskapi, Quebec-Labrador, probably about 1800

This coat was purchased by the Newfoundland Museum with the assistance of the Government of Canada, under the Cultural Property Export and Import Act, Department of Communications. It was bought from Alika Podolinsky Webber, who acquired the coat from Ian Satow, grandson of Gordon Antoine Neilson, who owned material collected by his ancestor the Honourable John Neilson (1776–1848). In 1942 this coat was being used to wrap a plate that was once owned by Marquette and that was given in 1798 to John Neilson by Père Carot, a Jesuit priest. The supposition is that the coat was given to Neilson with the plate. From the cut and decoration of the coat, and particularly from the evidence of a button sewn onto the right front, a late 18th- to early 19th-century date is most probable.

The skin of this coat is most unusual. It was not prepared in the usual way, which results in a white skin. Instead it was smoked, resulting in a darker colour. With smoking, the skin remains soft if it gets wet, but the dark skin does not show the painting to advantage. Possibly that is why these special coats were normally made of skins that were as white as they could be made.

Quality: Good. Lightweight, smoked skins with some fly marks; precise painting.

Condition: Fairly good. Skins supple but soiled; paint somewhat worn.

Cutting: Flare of 1:1.9. Front edges jagged with uneven, lapel-like extensions. These suggest that although the fronts are as usual made from one skin split down the centre, the fronts were cut with the spinal line of the skin at the sides of the coat and the outer edges of the skin, which are apt to be uneven, at the centre front of the coat, as was done with No. 22. The position of the fly marks, however, suggest otherwise; the uneven front edges must therefore be deliberate. A short slash was made for a buttonhole in the left extension of the front, and a round, white metal button was sewn to the right. The button probably dates between 1760 and 1790.[10]

Size: Length, 91 cm. Back of neck to wrist, 86 cm.

This length suggests a wearer of somewhat less that 150 cm (5 feet) tall. The measurement from back of neck to wrist is comparable to other men's coats, but the size of the sleeve at the shoulder is quite small (35 cm), indicating that the wearer was either very thin or not a full-grown man.

Sewing: Sinew, 23–25 stitches per 5 cm. Button sewn on and buttonhole strengthened with linen thread. Side seams sewn *after* painting. Tags of sinew sewing at bottom of two seams (see Sewing section for comment on both these features).

Colours: Yellow for layout and some crosshatching; red, probably vermilion, for drawing motifs; brown for lozenges; black for details; blue, now very faded, for crosshatching used below double curves, in their terminals, and in lozenges of bottom border.

Tools: Two slightly different 3-prongs, *A* and *B*, both with a central striated line, with yellow for layout. A 6-prong, *C*, also with yellow. Two single prongs, *D* and *E*, with brown, red, and blue. Two stamps for dots, *F* and *G*, with red and brown.

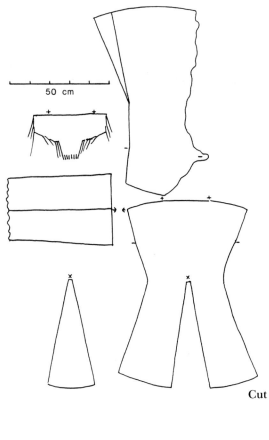

50 cm

Cut

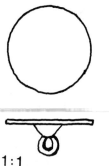

1:1

Metal button on right front

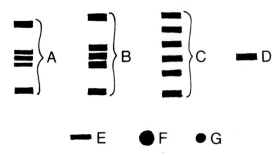

Tools

Bottom border

Bottom border: A row of lozenges; a line of small scallops and a row of dots above; a crosshatched line, a row of alternating dash and four dots, a line of small scallops, single track, and track variation below. As with No. 22, the elaborate line decorations almost overpower the main border motif.

Central gore form: Graduated compartments each contain a double curve surmounted by paired leaves and a circle. The horizontal divides are small zigzags and dots and the surrounds are parallel lines with a row of dots.

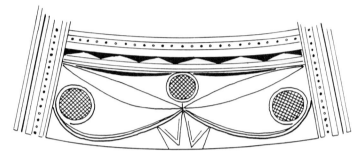

Central gore form

Centre-back extension: Crossed by 6-fold lines alternating with a single vermilion or brown line.

Shoulders: Crossed by a band of parallel lines, dots, and track variation.

Collar: Similar in shape to No. 22 but not as extreme. The main design is a beautifully drawn, doubled double curve; the entire collar is surrounded by a line of single track, and there is a fringe, cut obliquely at the sides and short and straight at the bottom.

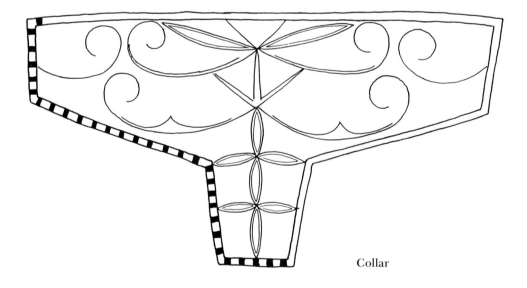

Collar

Gore forms 1 and 5: Similar to central gore form with horizontal divides of simple parallel lines. The surrounds of all the side gore forms are parallel lines that come together at the waist in a blunt point, from the centre of which a single band of lines extends to the shoulder.

Gore forms 2 and 4: Crossed by 6-fold yellow lines alternating with a single vermilion or brown line similar to design of centre-back extension.

Additional: Two triple lines run from bottom border to shoulder band between front borders and gore forms 1 and 5. Below the waist, towards the front edges, the lines are widened by the addition of a row of dots. Such lines are used on other coats of about this same period (Nos. 20–21, 24).

Front borders: A triple yellow line that turns in a curve below neck and, with the addition of a row of dots, extends to armholes.

Sleeves: At shoulder, a band with parallel lines, rows of dots, scallops, and single track. At elbow, a band of parallel lines with two rows of dots. At wrist, a wide band of vertical parallel lines below a triple yellow line and a row of dots. No cuffs. Nos. 21–22 have similar treatment of the wrists.

Outer borders: Red around bottom, across shoulders, around tops of sleeves, and around wrists; now very worn.

24. Horniman Museum, London
(635 F 36)

Man's painted caribou-skin coat
Montagnais or Cree?, Quebec, probably
about 1800

There is no information as to how this coat reached
the museum.

The design is most unusual. At first sight there
appear to be no parallels for the strong simple
design on the collar and the four-petalled motifs
used in the gore forms. With further consideration
it does not seem to be stretching relationships too
far to allow the possibility that the collar design, with
its great sweeping double-curve motif and rather

special cross, may be the expression one hundred
years later of the same thought that motivated the
intricate pattern on the collar of No. 1. Although the
motifs used in the gore forms are very irregularly
drawn they do have four petals and so may have
their origin in the quadrate type of pattern layout.
Further, lozenges, although used frequently in many
less important ways, are rare as the main motif of
the bottom border; they are used in this way on
No. 23 and on No. 46, a later coat that appears to
have ties to the West. It is unfortunate that this coat
is in such poor condition, for it is a rare and very
interesting piece and perhaps provides another
example of the more southern and western Montagnais or Cree coats from a date in between Nos. 1–4
and the later Nos. 43–46 and 50–51 collected by
Lucien Turner and Robert Flaherty.

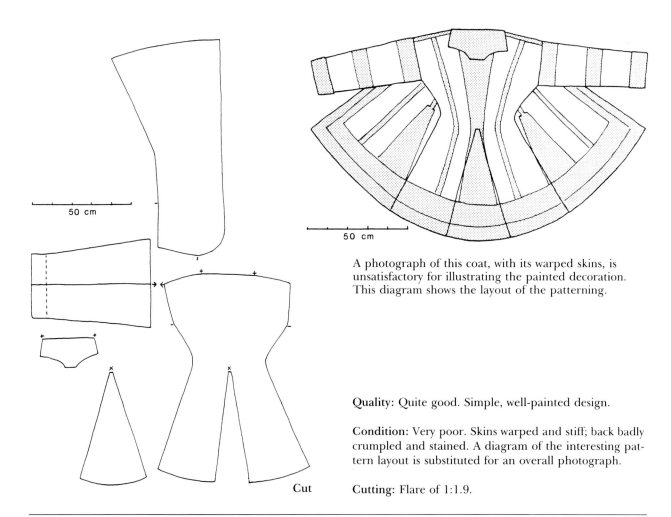

50 cm

50 cm

A photograph of this coat, with its warped skins, is
unsatisfactory for illustrating the painted decoration.
This diagram shows the layout of the patterning.

Quality: Quite good. Simple, well-painted design.

Condition: Very poor. Skins warped and stiff; back badly
crumpled and stained. A diagram of the interesting pattern layout is substituted for an overall photograph.

Cutting: Flare of 1:1.9.

Cut

Size: Length, 99 cm. Back of neck to wrist, 84 cm.

Sewing: Entirely with sinew, quite fine with 30 stitches per 5 cm.

Colours: Yellow for layout; red, probably vermilion, for drawing most motifs; brown and green for details.

Tools: A 3-prong, *A*, with yellow for layout. A 2-prong, *B*, with yellow across gore forms. Several single prongs, the weights of which were not noted.

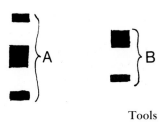

Tools

Bottom border: A lozenge band with simple parallel lines above and below. The drawing of all the patterned sections is simple but exceptionally strong.

Central gore form: Graduated sections contain four-petalled motifs. The horizontal divides and surrounds are simple parallel lines.

Centre-back extension: Crossed by groups of parallel lines.

Shoulders: Crossed by a band of parallel lines.

Collar: A large double curve above a most unusual central cross that has four leaves in the centre and large ovals at the ends of the arms.

Gore forms 1 and 3: Graduated compartments each contain four-petalled motifs similar to those in the central gore form. The surrounds are simple parallel lines that come together at the waist in a blunt point, from the centre of which a single band of lines extends to the shoulder.

Additional: Four narrow vertical bands of simple lines extend from the bottom border to the shoulder band on either side of the gore forms, similar to the bands on Nos. 20–21 and 23.

Front borders: A band of parallel lines.

Sleeves: Bands of parallel lines and rows of dots at shoulder, at elbow, and on turnback that forms cuff.

Outer borders: Red around coat.

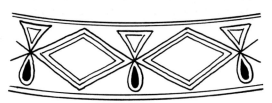

Bottom border

Central gore form

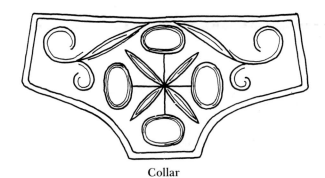

Collar

25. Musée de la civilisation, Québec (68.2875)

Man's painted caribou-skin coat
Montagnais-Naskapi, Quebec-Labrador, probably about 1800

See colour plate page 53

This coat was transferred to the Musée de la civilisation from the Musée du Québec. It was the gift of Mrs. A. D. Mann; there is no further information.

Two things about the design of this coat are remarkable: the collar pattern is extraordinarily complex but very carelessly executed in comparison to the rest of the painting, and the triangular extensions used above and to the sides of gore forms 2 and 4 are, as far as is known, unique additions to the normal layout of pattern.

Quality: Good. Heavy skins; well-executed but rather simple and coarse painting.

Condition: Fair. Skins supple, somewhat soiled; some loss of paint; holes at top left front and right underarm, two of the six buttons missing.

Cutting: Flare of 1:1.8.

Size: Length, 112 cm. Back of neck to wrist, 87 cm.

Sewing: Mostly with sinew, 19 stitches per 5 cm. Linen thread used to piece the skin on right front and also to attach buttons. The buttons are metal, flat, round, and white and were sewn on the right front of the coat. Slits were made opposite to them on the left front. The buttons probably date from the late 18th century (see No. 23 for comparable button and note). It is likely that they were added by a second owner of the coat.

Colours: Yellow for layout; red for drawing all motifs; brown for a few details on sleeves. This limited colour scheme and the lack of crosshatching in the background give an unusually open and simple effect.

Tools: A 3-prong, *A*, with striated lines, and a 4-prong, *B*, both with yellow for layout. A similar 4-prong, which appears to have slightly narrower lines, with red. Several single prongs, the weights of which were not noted.

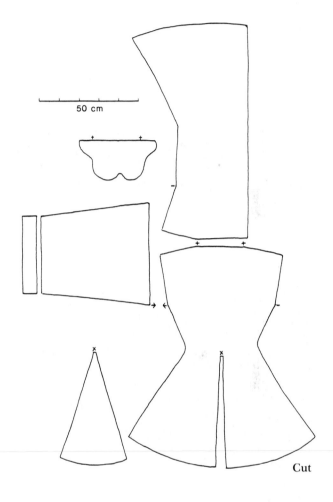

50 cm

Cut

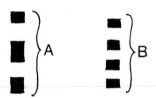

Tools

Bottom border: Compartments each contain a very simple double curve. Bands of plain parallel lines between compartments, between arms of double curves, and above and below band of motifs.

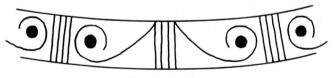

Bottom border

Central gore form: Graduated compartments each contain a double curve. The surrounds are parallel lines edged by strong zigzags.

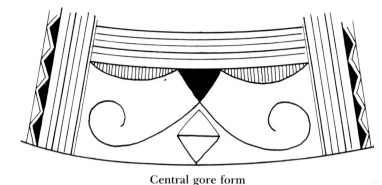

Central gore form

Centre-back extension: Continues patterning of central gore form.

Shoulders: Plain.

Collar: A complicated, broken-up double-curve variation, more carelessly painted than rest of coat. Mixed up in the confusion is a quartered circle on either side near the bottom, which compares with a similar use of this motif on the collars of Nos. 22 and 27.

Collar

Gore forms 1 and 5: Similar to central gore form but with simple line surrounds that meet at the waist in a blunt point, from the centre of which a narrow band of lines extends to the shoulder.

Gore forms 2 and 4: Graduated compartments each contain a circle hanging from a double curve. Joined to the front of each of these gore forms is a most unusual triangular extension, which is crossed by closely set lines. This triangle narrows to the waist and then widens again, extending up to the shoulder at the front and the back of each armhole. No parallel for this type of layout has as yet been recorded.

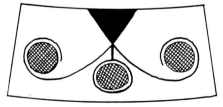

Gore forms 2 and 4

Front borders: Parallel lines enclose repeated slim triangles on left side and a single track on right side.

Sleeves: At shoulder, a band of parallel lines and a zigzag. At elbow, a band of smaller zigzags and lines.

Cuffs: A repeat of zigzag theme in leaf form.

Outer borders: Red around coat and collar.

Cuffs

Front border, left

26. Deutsches Ledermuseum/ Schuhmuseum, Offenbach am Main (11569)

Man's painted caribou-skin coat
Montagnais-Naskapi, Quebec-Labrador, probably about 1800

See colour plate page 53

The museum purchased this coat from the Speyer Collection; there is no further information.

The truncated sleeves give almost a feminine appearance, but in every other way this is a very handsome and completely traditional man's hunting coat.

With the usual layout of sleeve decoration it is unusual for there to be a red band below the top band of decoration, but it could be that the lower part of the sleeve was covered with painted patterning as with Nos. 8 and 32, in which case the red band would fit less obtrusively into the decorative scheme.

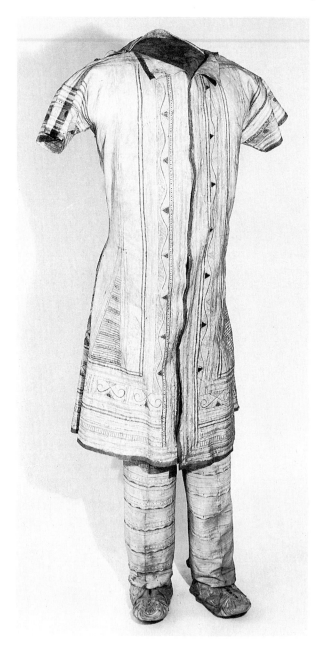

Quality: Excellent. Medium-weight skins, the front one considerably flymarked; precise and fairly complex painting.

Condition: Good, except that the sleeves have been cut off above elbow.

Cutting: A considerable flare of 1:2.5.

Size: Length, 101 cm. Width of shoulders, 57 cm. (With the sleeves cut off it was impossible to take the usual back-of-neck-to-wrist measurement.)

Sewing: Entirely with sinew, 23 stitches per 5 cm. Small patches have been applied under each arm.

Colours: Yellow for layout; paler yellow on sleeves and for background crosshatching; red, probably vermilion, for drawing most motifs; black for details.

Tools: Two 3-prongs, *A*, with wide striated central line, and *B*, both with yellow for layout. A 2-prong, *C*, and a 4-prong, *D*, with red. Several single prongs, the weights of which were not noted.

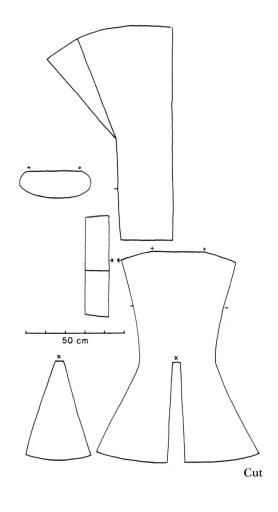

50 cm

Cut

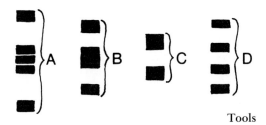

Tools

Bottom border: Compartments each contain a double curve. Above are simple parallel lines; below are many more lines and a single track.

Central gore form: Graduated compartments each contain a double curve supported and surmounted by triangles as in the bottom border. The horizontal divides are rows of dots and the surrounds are parallel lines in yellow and then in red.

Bottom border

Central gore form

Centre-back extension: A continuation of central gore form.

Shoulders: Both back and front crossed by simple parallel lines.

Collar: A large central double curve with paired leaves, surmounted by a double-curve variation. Below is an inverted double curve. There are paired leaves in the corners.

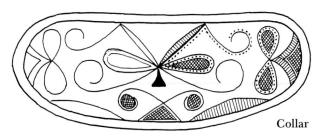

Collar

Gore forms 1, 3, 5, and 7: Crossed alternately by a 4-fold line and a single track. The surrounds are simple parallel lines that come together at the waist in a blunt point, from the centre of which a single group of lines extends to the shoulder.

Gore forms 2 and 6: Similar to central gore form but with surrounds of red double line only. The surrounds come together at the waist and then both continue to the shoulder, one on either side of the armhole.

Front borders: Rounded zigzags with triangles.

Sleeves: At shoulder, parallel lines and rows of dots enclose a band of inverted double curves. Below this is a wide red band similar to the outer borders on many coats. Below the red band the sleeves are cut right off. The red band looks so like a finish that some researchers have thought the sleeves to be complete, but examination shows that the seams have been cut through at this point and no attempt was made to finish them off (see Sewing section for description of usual seam finish).

Outer borders: Red around coat.

Markings: Rough red line applied to armhole seams after sewing.

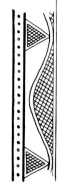

Front borders

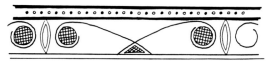

Sleeve band at shoulder

PUBLICATION: Deutsches Ledermuseum, colour pl. 1, cat. no. 4-20.

27. Museum für Völkerkunde, Berlin (IV B 12822)

Boy's painted caribou-skin coat, with narrow fur bandings
Montagnais-Naskapi, Quebec-Labrador, probably early 19th century

This coat was purchased from the Speyer Collection with the information that it came from an old French mission in the St. Augustine area of Quebec.

As there are no painted outer borders under the fur bandings this coat appears to have been made with the original intention of adding the fur, which suggests strongly that the coat was made to order for a European customer. The fairly coarse sewing done entirely with linen thread strengthens this possibility.

There is a truly extraordinary number of angled lines on this coat. There are zigzags in the bottom and front borders, in four of the gore forms, and on all the sleeve bands. Chevrons carrying zigzags are the main motif of the back gore form and its extension. Even on the collar, with its beautifully drawn double curves, zigzags fill the side spaces and decorate the lines.

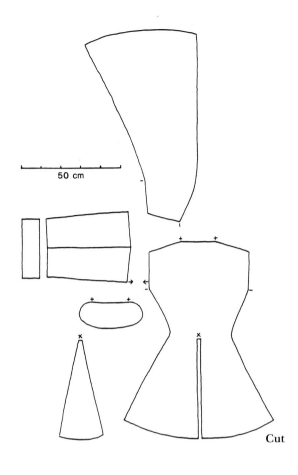

50 cm

Cut

Quality: Good. Excellent, fairly heavy skins; simple but careful painting.

Condition: Quite good. Skins flexible and sound but soiled, stained at underarm; painting in good condition; pelage of bandings completely gone.

Cutting: Flare of 1:2.2. Fur borders, probably hare, about 1 cm wide, attached around coat, collar, and cuffs.

Size: Length, 95 cm. Back of neck to wrist, 67 cm.

Sewing: Entirely with linen thread, Z,2S, used double, 18 stitches per 5 cm. Original mends in skin done with sinew. Fur edging hemmed down both inside and out with linen thread, 11 stitches per 5 cm.

Colours: Yellow for layout; red, probably vermilion, for much of drawing of motifs; green-black for details.

Tools: A 4-prong, *A*, with yellow for layout. A 2-prong, *B*, with red in gore forms. A 3-prong, *C*, with wide striated central line, with red and yellow on sleeves. Several single prongs including *D* used with red, and *E* with red, yellow, and black.

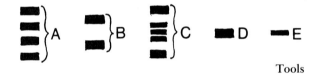

Tools

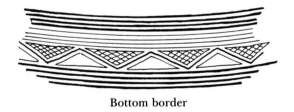

Bottom border

Bottom border: A row of zigzags with coarse crosshatching in red filling all upper spaces and in yellow filling lower spaces. Simple parallel lines above and below.

Central gore form: Filled with chevrons of graduated size made of parallel lines, small zigzags, and hatched lines in regular repeat. Surrounds are simple parallel lines.

Centre-back extension: A continuation of design of central gore form.

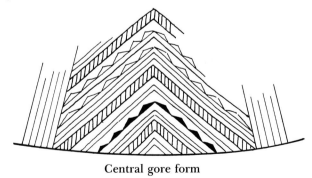

Central gore form

Shoulders: Both back and front crossed by bands of parallel lines.

Collar: A double double curve in centre. In each arm of the lower double curve is a circle divided by a cross. A similar use of quartered circles is found on Nos. 22 and 25.

Collar

Gore forms 1, 3, 5, and 7: Crossed by small zigzags and wide single track. All side gore forms have surrounds of simple parallel lines that meet in a blunt point at the waist, from the centre of which a single group of lines extends to the shoulder.

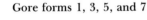
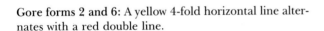
Gore forms 1, 3, 5, and 7

Gore forms 2 and 6: A yellow 4-fold horizontal line alternates with a red double line.

Front borders: Same as bottom border.

Sleeves: Similar bands of large and small zigzags at shoulder and elbow.

Cuffs: A band of zigzags between lines of small zigzags.

Outer borders: None.

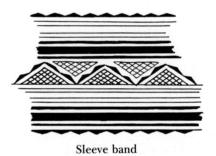
Sleeve band

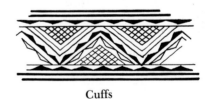
Cuffs

28. Canadian Ethnology Service, Canadian Museum of Civilization, Hull-Ottawa (III B 633)

Man's painted caribou-skin coat
Montagnais-Naskapi, Quebec-Labrador, probably 1810–1815

This coat was purchased from Lord Strange. Its acquisition was made possible by a contribution from the Government of Canada under the terms of the Cultural Property Export and Import Act, Department of Communications. The coat is from the same family as Nos. 9–10 and it is possible that like those coats it was collected by Colin Drummond between 1765 and 1776. But the less extreme flare of the skirts and the fact that the side seams were sewn after the painting was done makes it more likely that this coat dates from the time of the military service of Colin's son, Sir Gordon Drummond, either 1808–1811 or 1815–1816.

The likelihood of a date after 1800 is strengthened by the type of leaf sprays that extend from the centre of the collar. They do not fit with the leaf forms used on the earlier coats but seem rather to relate to the weeping willows that were so popular in European decorative art during the early years of the 19th century.[11]

Quality: Excellent. Good, fairly heavy skins; careful painting; superb beaded fringes.

Condition: Fairly good. Skins somewhat warped and soiled; some loss of paint.

Cutting: Flare of 1:1.8. The fronts have the spinal line of the skin at the side seams; slits used when stretching the skin remain at the front edges.

Size: Length, 103 cm. Back of neck to wrist, 88 cm.

Sewing: Entirely with sinew, 22 stitches per 5 cm. Fringed bands sewn into original shoulder, armhole, and sleeve seams of coat. Side seams sewn *after* painting (see Sewing section for comment).

Colours: Yellow for layout and background crosshatching; red, probably vermilion, for drawing motifs; a little pale blue; dark green for crosshatching; a small amount of brown.

Tools: A 3-prong, *A*, with yellow for layout. A 7-prong, *B*, with yellow in gore forms. A 2-prong, *C*, with red in borders. Three single prongs, *D* with red, *E* with red and brown, *F* for crosshatching. A stamp, *G*, for dots.

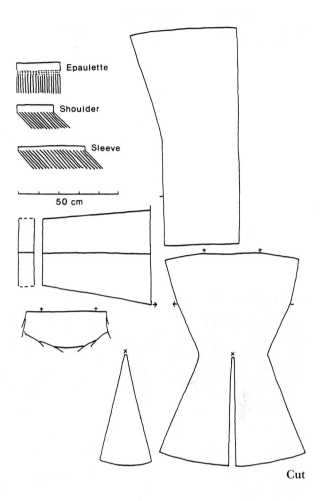

Cut

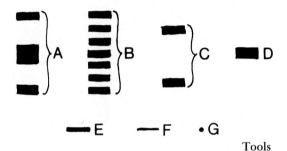

Tools

Bottom border: Double curves with paired leaves. Above main design, two lines of zigzags and one of dots; below it, a wide track variation and rows of dots.

Bottom border

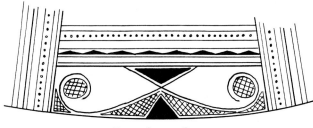

Central gore form

Central gore form: Graduated compartments each contain a double curve. The horizontal divides are zigzags and a row of dots; the surrounds are parallel lines and a row of dots.

Centre-back extension: Crossed by 7-fold lines alternating with zigzags.

Shoulders: Crossed by same bold track variation of bottom border, parallel lines, and rows of dots.

Collar: A large central double curve supported by a diagonal cross and surmounted by paired leaves, leaf sprays, and a floating circle. Edge slashed diagonally into a very sparse fringe.

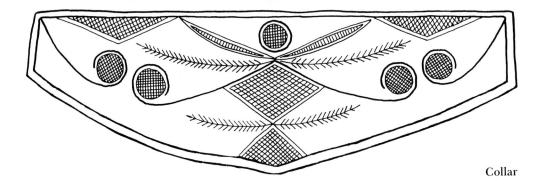

Collar

Gore forms 1, 3, 5, and 7: A 7-fold yellow horizontal line alternates with a double red and brown line. The surrounds of all side gore forms have parallel lines and rows of dots that come together in a blunt point at the waist, from the centre of which one group of lines with dots continues to the shoulder.

Gore forms 2 and 6: Similar to central gore form.

Front borders: Parallel lines, a single track, and rows of dots. The borders turn below the neck and extend to the armholes.

Sleeves: At shoulder, a zigzag pattern between parallel lines. At elbow, rather unusual scallops and a track variation with rows of dots.

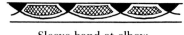

Sleeve band at elbow

Cuffs: A band of lozenges between dots and parallel lines.

Outer borders: Red around coat, collar, and cuffs, partly around tops of sleeves; narrow across back shoulders.

Fringes: Fringes of slashed skin, quill-wrapped and beaded, and of excellent workmanship, sewn into the seams of the shoulders, across the tops of the sleeves to form epaulettes, and into the upper part of the sleeves. The unslashed bands from which the fringes hang are painted like the outer borders of the coat, but the slashed fringes are not.

The shoulder fringe has very fine diagonal slashing wrapped with white quill and threaded with yellow, white, green, and black beads and finished with a red wool tassel, now almost gone. The sleeve fringe is similar.

The epaulettes are slashed vertically into a long fringe that is used as a warp for ten rows of bead weaving;[12] the wefts are of sinew. The beads are blue and white. Below the weaving the fringe is wrapped with white quill, then threaded with opaque brown, white, and blue beads, then again quill-wrapped, terminating with a red wool tassel.

Detail of epaulette.

29. British Museum, London (2613)

Man's painted caribou-skin coat
Montagnais-Naskapi, Quebec-Labrador, probably
early 19th century

There is no history of any kind.

Parallel lines play an important part in the decoration of all the coats as a natural result of the multipronged tools used in the painting. This handsome coat is, however, very rare in that the painted design uses lines only (see also Nos. 42, 47). One cannot help but wonder if the hunter's dream was just of multiple lines, presenting his wife with an unusual problem. If that is the case, she rose magnificently to the challenge with the making of this very elegant garment.

Quality: Good. Simple but well-painted design; beautiful quill-wrapped fringes on shoulders and sleeves.

Condition: Good. Some soiling.

Cutting: Flare of just over 1:2. The shape of the collar is unusually irregular. On the fronts the spinal line of the skin is placed at the sides.

Size: Length, 104 cm. Back of neck to wrist, 89.5 cm.

Sewing: Sinew, 20 stitches per 5 cm. Fringes inserted with original sewing of corresponding seams.

    A pocket was added inside on top of the left side seam. The fabric is hemp tabby with warp Z singles, 13 per cm, and heavier weft Z singles, 10 per cm. The pocket is sewn with handspun linen thread, Z,2S. Entry to the pocket is only from the inside of the coat.

Colours: Whitish yellow for layout; red, probably vermilion; brown.

Tools: A 3-prong, *A*, with very wide striated central line, for layout. A 7-prong, *B*, with yellow in gore forms and on sleeves. A 5-prong, *C*, with red. At least one single prong, *D*, with red, sometimes used to make two lines side by side.

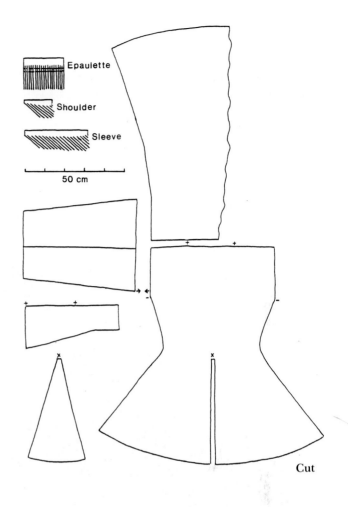

Epaulette

Shoulder

Sleeve

50 cm

Cut

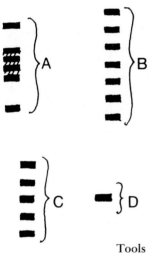

Tools

Bottom border: Two repeats of triple lines in yellow alternate with paired red lines.

Central gore form: A 7-fold horizontal line in yellow alternates with a 5-fold line in red. Surrounds of triple yellow lines.

Centre-back extension: Repeats pattern of central gore form.

Detail of epaulette.

Shoulders: Both back and front crossed by bands of parallel lines similar to those in bottom border.

Collar: Undecorated.

Gore forms 1, 3, 5, and 7: A 7-fold horizontal line in yellow alternates with a single red line. Surrounds of triple lines in yellow converge at the waist and continue side by side to the shoulder.

Gore forms 2 and 6: Crossed by lines similar to those in central gore form. Triple-line surrounds come together in a blunt point at the waist, from the centre of which a single triple line extends to the shoulder.

Front borders: One repeat of bottom border continues up front edges.

Sleeves: Completely covered by horizontal yellow 7-fold lines, used twice, alternating with a single red line. At wrist there are two triple lines in yellow. No cuffs.

Outer borders: Brown around bottom of coat and wrists.

Fringes: Fringes of slashed, quill-wrapped skin sewn into seams of shoulders, across the tops of sleeves to form epaulettes, and into upper part of sleeves. The solid bands at the tops of the fringes are painted brown but the fringes themselves are not.

The shoulder-seam fringes are slashed obliquely, wrapped with white and yellow quills, threaded with opaque brown beads, and finished with a red wool tassel (Z,2S), now much worn.

The epaulette fringes are slashed straight and are wrapped with white and yellow quills, followed by a line of blue translucent beads, another quill-wrapped section, another line of blue beads, and a white quill-wrapped section, with the end of the fringe left plain. The beads are attached between the fringes with sinew, which passes alternately through a bead and then a piece of fringe (see Figure 30).

In the upper sleeve seams the fringes are obliquely slashed and wrapped at the top with white and yellow quills.

PUBLICATION: King, fig. 40, p. 41.

30. Art Gallery and Museum, Kelvingrove, Glasgow (A 6533)

Man's painted caribou-skin coat
Montagnais-Naskapi, Quebec-Labrador, probably early 19th century

This coat came to Kelvingrove from the Grierson Museum, Dumfrieshire, which was opened in 1895 and closed in 1965. There is no further information.

Double curves are obviously the main theme of the coat; less obvious are the rounded leaves that form a sort of heart motif above many of the double curves and may possibly be equally significant (see Hearts in Design Motifs section for comment).

It should be noted that the zigzags in the bottom and front borders, although small, are painted with two meticulously interlocking colours in the same way as the larger zigzags used on some of the earlier coats.

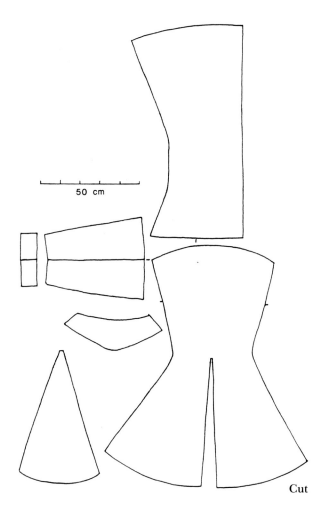

Cut

Quality: Uneven. Heavy skins with many fly marks and holes; painting good.

Condition: Quite good. Some loss of paint.

Cutting: Flare of 1:2.2.

Size: Length, 119 cm. Back of neck to wrist, 81 cm.

Sewing: Entirely with sinew, 20 stitches per 5 cm.

Colours: Yellow for layout and background crosshatching; red, probably vermilion, for drawing motifs; brown; black.

Tools: One 3-prong, *A*, with wide striated centre line, with yellow for layout. One 2-prong, *B*, with red. Several single prongs, the weights of which were not noted.

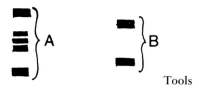

Tools

Bottom border: Repeated double curves with lines of zig-zags and rows of dots above and below.

Bottom border

Central gore form: Graduated compartments each contain a double curve that supports a pair of rounded leaves. The horizontal divides are parallel lines and two rows of dots. The surrounds are parallel lines and a row of dots.

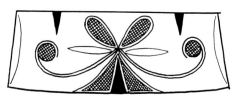

Central gore form

Centre-back extension: Repeats motifs of central gore form.

Shoulders: Crossed by a band of parallel lines.

Collar: Covered by simple vertical lines.

Gore forms 1, 3, 5, and 7: Crossed alternately by parallel lines and an unusual motif, pointed ovals lying on their sides. The simple parallel line surrounds of all the side gore forms meet at the waist in a blunt point, from the centre of which a single band of lines extends to the shoulder.

Gore forms 2 and 6: Graduated compartments each contain a double-curve motif somewhat similar to the one in the central gore form.

Front borders: A wide line of zigzags enclosed by smaller zigzags and rows of dots. These borders terminate where a wide band of parallel lines crosses the shoulders.

Sleeves: At shoulder, a band of zigzag variation with a strange small leaf spray. At elbow, a band of lozenges.

Cuffs: A band of zigzag variation made of leaf forms.

Outer borders: Red and narrow around coat, collar, and cuffs.

Gore forms 1, 3, 5, and 7

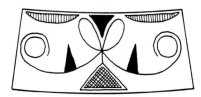

Gore forms 2 and 6

Sleeve band at shoulder

31. Royal Ontario Museum, Toronto (32113)

Man's painted caribou-skin coat
Montagnais-Naskapi, Quebec-Labrador, probably
about 1805

See colour plates page 54

This coat came to the Royal Ontario Museum when the collections of the old Ontario Provincial Museum were transferred in the early 1930s. It had been acquired from C. G. Gladman and was catalogued in 1912. It is possible that the coat was originally collected by Mr. Gladman's father, an employee of the Hudson's Bay Company who was at Fort George on James Bay about 1862. From the style of the coat is seems much more probable that it was collected by Mr. Gladman's grandfather who was agent-in-chief of the Hudson's Bay Company in 1805.

In the cutting, the sewing, the colours, the motifs used, the layout of design areas, the technique of painting, and the order of making up, this coat is so similar to No. 32 that one cannot help but wonder if they were made in the same family or even by the same woman. The measurements vary slightly but it is possible that they could have been made for the same man.

Quality: Excellent. Good, lightweight skins; careful painting.

Condition: Good. Skins somewhat soiled; paint worn in places.

Cutting: Flare of 1:1.9.

Size: Length, 108 cm. Back of neck to wrist, 85.5 cm.

Sewing: Entirely with sinew, 26 stitches per 5 cm. The sides seams were sewn *after* the painting was done (see Sewing section for comment). Two pairs of thong ties have been inserted through the front edges of the coat in the manner shown in the diagram.

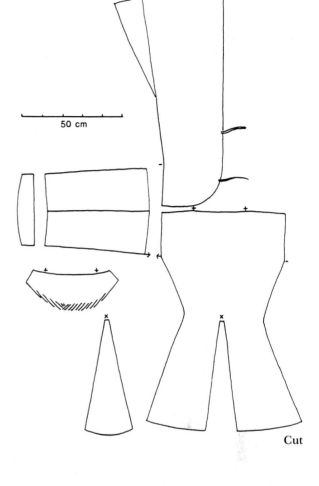

50 cm

Cut

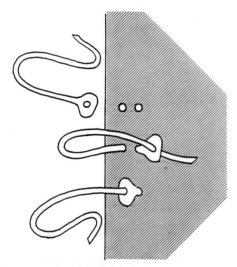

Thong ties on front opening

Colours: Yellow for layout and background filling, both solid and crosshatching; vermilion for drawing most motifs; reddish brown; black shading to dark green.

Tools: A 3-prong, *A,* for layout with yellow. A 7-prong, *B,* with yellow across gore forms. A 2-prong, *C,* with red. Several single prongs, including *D* and *E,* with red and black. Three stamps for dots, *F, G,* and *H.*

Tools

Central gore form

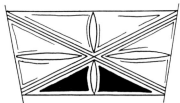

Centre-back extension

Bottom border: Double curves surmounted by a circle filled by a ring of dots around a larger dot; similar fillings in terminals of double curves both here and in central gore form. Above there is a row of dots and below a row of dots and a secondary border of small scallops between rows of dots.

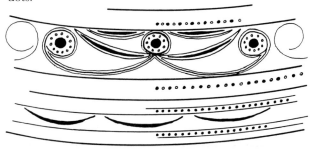

Bottom border

Central gore form: Graduated compartments each contain a double curve similar to those in the bottom border. The motif reduces to a fancy curved diagonal cross and then to a plain diagonal cross at the waist. The horizontal divides are a double row of small zigzags and the surrounds are simple parallel lines.

Centre-back extension: Graduated compartments each contain a diagonal cross with a leaf form in each section.

Shoulders: Crossed by a handsome hexagonal lozenge variation and rows of dots.

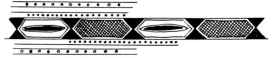

Shoulders

Collar: In centre, two double curves, and in each corner, additional single curves. All lines of the curves are strengthened by rows of dots. On either side at centre there is a small cross made up of four triangles radiating from a central point. There is a sparse, obliquely slashed fringe.

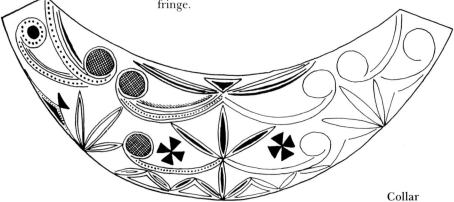

Collar

Gore forms 1 and 7: Crossed by parallel lines alternating with a heavy line between rows of dots. The surrounds of all the side gore forms are parallel lines that converge at the waist in a blunt point, from the centre of which a single band of lines extends to the shoulder.

Gore forms 2 and 6: Similar to central gore form.

Gore forms 3 and 5: Crossed by parallel lines alternating with a row of small diagonal crosses.

Front borders: Simple parallel lines that turn in a curve below neck and extend to armholes.

Sleeves: At shoulder, a zigzag band between two rows of dots. At elbow, a band with scallops and rows of dots.

Cuffs: Similar to elbow band.

Outer borders: Red around coat, tops of sleeves, collar, and cuffs, and across both back and front of shoulders.

PUBLICATION: Rogers, [1969a]. Excellent colour photographs illustrate details of the painting on this coat.

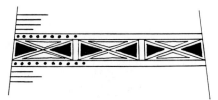

Gore forms 3 and 5

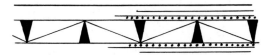

Sleeve band a shoulder

Sleeve band at elbow

32. Royal Ontario Museum, Toronto (36435)

Man's painted caribou-skin coat
Montagnais-Naskapi, Quebec-Labrador, probably about 1805–1810

See colour plates page 55

This coat was transferred to the Royal Ontario Museum from the old Ontario Provincial Museum in the early 1930s. It had been acquired from Mrs. Lucinda McLean of Kingsville, Ontario, and was catalogued in 1916 as "Buckskin coat (painted)." There is no further information.

The name of the donor, Lucinda McLean, raised hopes that this coat might have been collected by John McLean, author of *Notes of a Twenty-five Years' Service in the Hudson's Bay Territory*. McLean was sent to York Factory by the Hudson's Bay Company in 1837 and then on to Fort Chimo until 1842. He is famous not only for the book but for an amazing journey of discovery he made in 1838 over the height of land to Hamilton Inlet. During those years he would have had ample opportunity to collect native material, but research in census and other records has provided no clue that might attach Lucinda McLean's coat to him, and from the evidence of cut and style it may well date from quite a few years earlier than McLean's term of office in Quebec-Labrador.

This coat is very closely related to No. 31 and, like it, has many subtleties in the way the main and supporting motifs have been varied and repeated. An additional and unique design element here is the use of realism in the stylized bird and fish of the back medallions.

Quality: Excellent. Soft, lightweight skins with a number of fly holes; complex and precise painting.

Condition: Not very good. Skins crumpled, stiff, and stained; only slight loss of paint.

Cutting: Flare of 1:2. The front skin has been used with its spinal line at the sides of the coat. Each sleeve is made from three pieces.

Size: Length, 102 cm. Back of neck to wrist, 83 cm.

Sewing: Sinew, 26 stitches per 5 cm. Cuffs sewn back with linen thread. The side seams were sewn up *after* the painting was done (see Sewing section for comment).

Colours: Yellow for layout and for solid filling of some background areas; vermilion for drawing most motifs; brown; green.

Tools: A 3-prong, *A*, with yellow for layout. A 5-prong, *B*, with yellow for vertical lines on sleeves. Several single prongs, including *C* and *D* with red and brown, and *E* with red, green, and brown for fine crosshatching in motifs. Two stamps, *F* and *G*, for dots.

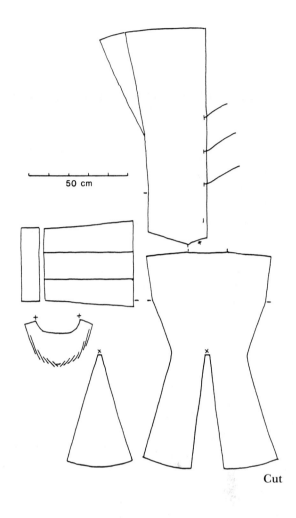

Cut

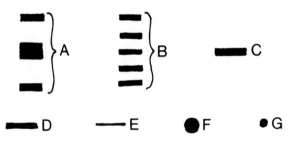

Tools

Bottom border: Double curves sitting in long shallow scallops with double lines of small zigzags above and below. At bottom, a narrow secondary border of small scallops.

Central gore form: Graduated compartments each contain a very complex double-curve variation. The horizontal divides have two lines of small zigzags; the surrounds are simple parallel lines.

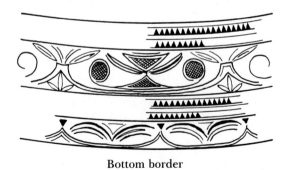

Bottom border

Central gore form

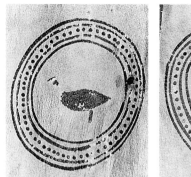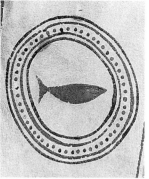

Details of medallions on back.

Centre-back extension: Graduated compartments each contain a simple diagonal cross that may be an echo of the double-curve thought (see Diagonal Crosses in Design Motifs section for comment).

Additional: To either side of the centre-back extension there is a slightly lopsided circle of lines and dots. The one on the right contains a simple drawing of a fish and the other a standing bird, now rather worn, but probably a goose. The realism of these small drawings is unique.

Shoulders: Crossed by a band of dots with a track variation.

Collar: A large double curve in the centre, with two single curves running into the centre above, and a double-curve motif to each side below. The lines of the curves are strengthened by rows of dots. There is an obliquely slashed fringe.

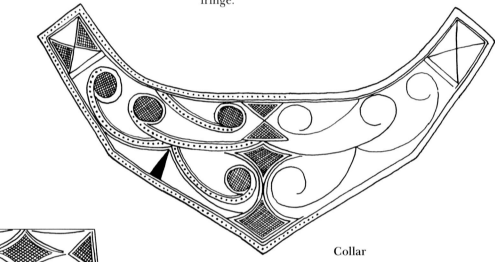

Collar

Gore forms 1 and 7

Gore forms 2 and 6

Gore forms 3 and 5

Gore forms 1 and 7: Graduated compartments each contain lozenges and triangles. The horizontal divides are two lines of zigzags. The surrounds of all the side gore forms are simple parallel lines that come together at the waist in a blunt point, from the centre of which a single band of lines extends to the shoulder.

Gore forms 2 and 6: Graduated compartments each contain a double curve surmounted by a large lozenge. The horizontal divides are two lines of zigzags.

Gore forms 3 and 5: Graduated compartments each contain a slightly different double curve and lozenge from those used in gore forms 2 and 6. The horizontal divides differ slightly also, with a single row of zigzags and a line of single track.

Front borders: Parallel lines and rows of dots which turn in a curve below neck and extend to armholes.

Sleeves: At shoulder, a band of double curves. Below it the upper arm is covered by vertical parallel lines and rows of dots that terminate at the elbow with a band of scallop variation. The vertical line covering of the sleeve is unusual at this period but relates to earlier coats (Nos. 2–3, 8).

Cuffs: A band of double curves.

Outer borders: Red around coat, cuffs, and collar, and across both back and front of shoulders and top edges of sleeves.

Sleeve band at shoulder

Sleeve band at elbow

Cuffs

33. Newfoundland Museum, St. John's (III-B:127)

Boy's painted caribou-skin coat
Montagnais-Naskapi, Quebec-Labrador, probably about 1825

In 1965 this coat was given to the Newfoundland Museum by James R. Simms, the great-grandson of the Honourable James Simms, Newfoundland's first attorney general, in whose house Shananditti, the last surviving Beothuk, lived for a time before her death in 1828. Traditionally, the coat was thought to be Beothuk and to have been made by Shananditti. It is definitely Naskapi and not for a woman but, as it may well date from her time and as it is a small size, it is possible that it was given to her to wear while she was in Simms's house.

This possible history, which suggests a date of about 1825, adds considerably to the importance of this attractive coat. The painting is well designed and well executed with a most unusual collar and interesting main motifs, but much of the richness is due to the lavish use of dots and rows of small meticulously interlocked zigzags.

Quality: Excellent. Fine lightweight skins; careful painting.

Condition: Fair. Skins soft and supple; very considerable loss of paint; evidence of insect damage on inner surface.

Cutting: Flare of 1:1.9.

Size: Length, 86 cm. Back of neck to wrist, 73 cm.

Sewing: Entirely with sinew, fine, 30 stitches per 5 cm. The side seams were sewn *after* the painting was done (see Sewing section for comment).

Colours: Yellow for layout and for solid filling in some background areas; vermilion for drawing pattern motifs; two shades of brown, one dark, one paler with a green cast.

Tools: A 3-prong, *A*, with yellow for layout. A 2-prong, *B*, also with yellow across gore forms. A single prong, *C*. Several other single prongs, the weights of which were not noted. A stamp, *D*, for dots.

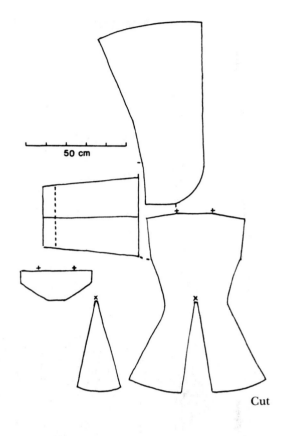

Cut

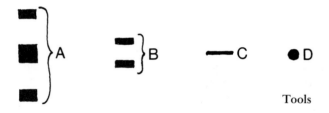

Tools

Bottom border

Bottom border: Sections each contain a double curve surmounted by a pointed ovoid; rows of dots and zigzags above and below.

Central gore form: Graduated compartments each contain a doubled double curve. The horizontal divides are parallel lines with a row of dots; the surrounds are simple parallel lines.

Central gore form

Centre-back extension: Graduated compartments each contain a simple diagonal cross.

Shoulders: Both back and front crossed by a band of zigzags and dots.

Collar: A very unusual pattern centred by a large, rather fancy double curve supporting paired leaves and a pointed ovoid. Below it a large triangle and a miniature double curve. There is a triangle like the central one at either side. As with No. 32 there is a simple diagonal cross in each corner.

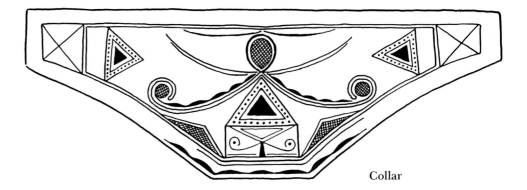

Collar

Gore forms 1, 3, 5, and 7

Gore forms 2 and 6

Gore forms 1, 3, 5, and 7: Crossed by small interlocking zigzags alternating with crosshatched lines between rows of dots. The surrounds of all the side gore forms are simple parallel lines that come together at the waist in a blunt point, from the centre of which a single band of lines extends to the shoulder.

Gore forms 2 and 6: Graduated compartments contain double-curve motifs surmounted by a most unusual large single scallop. Use of this motif has been noted on only one other coat, No. 38, where it occurs in the bottom border as well as in the side gore forms.

Front borders: A row of dots and parallel lines.

Sleeves: At shoulder, a band with parallel lines, dots, and scallops. At elbow, two rows of dots with zigzags between them. These bands are unfinished on the underside of the sleeves, a common practice on later coats.

Cuffs: A band of parallel lines, zigzags, and a row of dots.

Outer borders: Red around collar and coat, across top edges of sleeves, and on shoulders; brown around cuffs.

PUBLICATION: Such, p. 42 (photograph with caption).

34. Canadian Ethnology Service, Canadian Museum of Civilization, Hull-Ottawa (III B 259)

Man's painted caribou-skin coat, with narrow fur bandings
Montagnais-Naskapi, Quebec-Labrador, probably early to mid 19th century

This coat was purchased from F. E. Wright in 1939. There is no further information. It is fairly similar to Nos. 31–32, but it is not of as good quality and the condition is poor, which makes the connection less obvious.

Because the usual painted red outer borders are present but hidden under the fur trim, it seems probable that the coat was made in the normal way for a native wearer and was later adapted to non-native taste with the addition of the fancy fur edgings.

Quality: Fair. Back skin badly flymarked; painting well done and precise.

Condition: Very poor. Skins soiled; paint badly worn; fur edgings very soiled and worn.

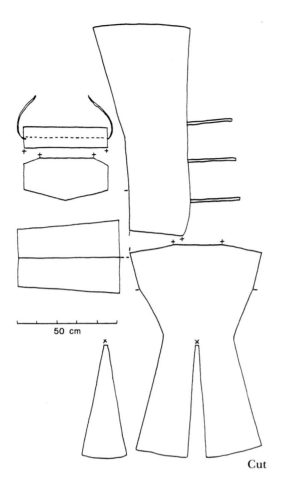

50 cm

Cut

Cutting: Flare of about 1:1.75. There is a second, stand-up band collar and much-pieced, narrow bands of fur, possibly mink, for edging the coat.

Size: Length, 102 cm. Back of neck to wrist, 84 cm.

Sewing: Basically with sinew, 18 stitches per 5 cm. The side seams have been sewn *after* painting (see Sewing section for comment). Three pairs of flat skin ties are sewn rather clumsily to the inside of the fronts. The stand-up band collar has thong ties and is undoubtedly part of the original making of the coat, for the two collars have been attached to the coat with sinew, all three thicknesses together. The fur bandings, probably a late addition, are sewn on with linen thread around the coat, the collar, and the wrists.

Colours: Yellow for layout and fine background cross-hatching; vermilion for drawing motifs; brown; grey-green.

Tools: A striated 3-prong, *A,* and a second 3-prong, *B,* both with yellow for layout. A 4-prong, *C,* with yellow across gore forms. A narrow 2-prong, *D,* with red and brown. Several single prongs, including *E* and *F,* both with red. A small stamp, *G,* for red, brown, and green dots.

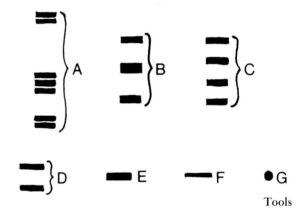

Tools

Bottom border: Repeated double curves. A triple track and a row of dots above; a row of dots below. Below that is a narrow secondary border with an unusual line decoration of paired wedge-shaped triangles, a motif that has only been noted on one other coat, No. 15.

Bottom border

Central gore form: Graduated compartments each contain a double-curve motif. The horizontal divides are two rows of single track; the surrounds are parallel lines and a row of dots.

Centre-back extension: Graduated compartments. The two just above the waist each contain a plain diagonal cross. The three wider compartments higher on the back contain a fancier version of the diagonal cross motif.

Shoulders: Crossed by parallel lines and single track.

Collar: Double curves grow out from a central vertical line of lozenges. Single curves extend towards the centre from the ends of the collar. The arrangement of the design is similar to the collars on Nos. 12–16 and 18–19. The stand-up band collar has simple vertical lines and is attached right around the neck.

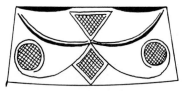

Central gore form

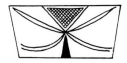

Centre-back extension

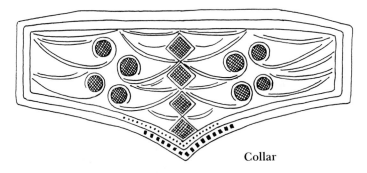

Collar

Gore forms 1, 3, 5, and 7: Horizontal parallel lines alternate with rows of dots. The surrounds of all the side gore forms are simple parallel lines that come together at the waist in a blunt point, from the centre of which a single band of lines extends to the shoulder.

Gore forms 2 and 6: Similar to central gore form.

Front borders: Simple parallel lines that turn in a curve below neck and, with the addition of a single track, extend to armholes.

Sleeves: An unusual number of four bands of decoration. At shoulder, zigzags and parallel lines; at upper arm, parallel lines and single track; at lower arm, parallel lines; at wrist, parallel lines and zigzags; no cuffs.

Outer borders: Red around coat, top edge of sleeves, and wrists, and across shoulders and neck edge of both collars.

PUBLICATION: Patterson, fig. 5, p. 26.

35. National Museums of Scotland, Edinburgh (1970.1001)

Man's painted caribou-skin coat
Montagnais-Naskapi, Quebec-Labrador, probably about 1820

See colour plate page 56

This coat was found in the wardrobe of the Royal Lyceum Theatre in Edinburgh by a new wardrobe mistress, Miss Lorraine Mackay. She recognized that it was something special that should not be used as stage costume, and it was transferred to the museum. How it came to the theatre is not known.

With its unusual length and its second, stand-up collar this magnificent coat shows strongly the influence of European styles of about 1820. A water-colour by J. Crawford Young (Figure 13), shows four Quebec men in their winter outfits, one of which has the typical painted designs of a Montagnais-Naskapi caribou-skin coat. It has both a stand-up and a falling

collar and long full skirts that cover the man's boot tops, as the skirts of this coat would.

A number of coats show evidence of having been altered to make them more to the taste of a second and non-native wearer: Nos. 23 and 25 have buttons added, Nos. 27 and 34 fur edgings, No. 29 a pocket, and Nos. 36 and 39 warm wool linings. The extreme length of this coat suggests that it was most likely made specially to fill the order of a Euro-Canadian customer. Although the main motifs and most of the subsidiary ones fit right in with the normal range of motifs used on these coats, the leaf sprays on the back shoulders may show European influence.

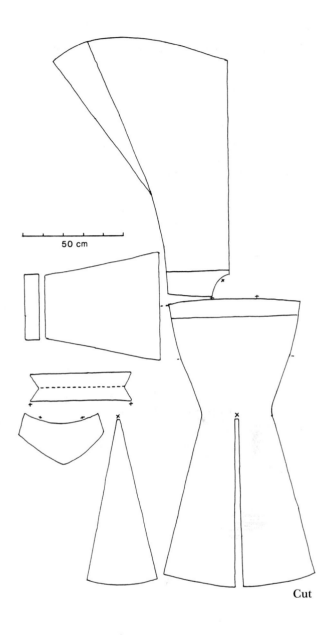

50 cm

Cut

Quality: Excellent. Good, lightweight skins; extremely complex, careful painting.

Condition: Not very good. Soiled; some tears; considerable loss of paint.

Cutting: The pieces were cut in the usual way except for the extreme length, which necessitated piecing to extend both back and front skins. The flare is considerable, 1:2.5, but if the coat was of average length, the flare would be about 1:2, as with other coats of early 19th-century date.

Size: Length, 138 cm. Back of neck to wrist, 89 cm.

Sewing: Sinew, 28 stitches per 5 cm. There is a brass hook and a thread loop for fastening at the neck. The side seams have been sewn *after* the painting was done. Several of the seams have sinew sewing tags (see Sewing section for comment).

Colours: Yellow for layout and background crosshatching, which is so fine that it almost appears to be solid. Red for drawing motifs; brown; black; a few details in green.

Tools: A 3-prong, *A*, with yellow for layout. A 2-prong, *B*, with red in bottom border. Several single prongs, the weights of which were not noted. Two small stamps, *C* for rings, and *D* for dots.

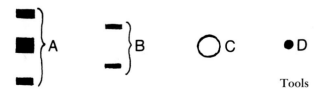

Tools

Bottom border: Double curves with two rows of ringed dots enclosing a most unusual hatched "barber-pole" line above and more dots, lozenges, and zigzags below.

Bottom border

Central gore form: Graduated compartments each contain a double-curve variation with a strange large zigzag above it. The horizontal divides are small lozenges; the surrounds are parallel lines and a row of dots.

Centre-back extension: Repeats motif of central gore form. The top compartment has in addition an arrangement of leaf sprays that is almost hidden under the collar.

Shoulders: Crossed by parallel lines and rows of ringed dots.

Collar: There are two collars. The stand-up band collar has double curves on the outside, and the inside is completely covered by line decorations of zigzags, lozenges, dots, and a "barber pole." The falling collar is very handsome with two double curves above a large lozenge that contains a cross formed by four leaves. In the corners there are leaf sprays.

Central gore form

Band collar, outside

Band collar, inside

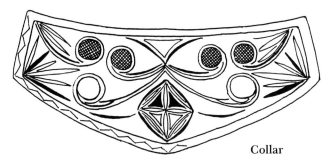

Collar

Gore forms 1 and 7: Graduated compartments each contain two double curves above a leaf spray. Horizontal divides of lozenge lines are used on all the side gore forms as are surrounds of parallel lines and rows of dots. The surrounds come together at the waist in a blunt point, from the centre of which a single band of lines extends to the shoulder.

Gore forms 1 and 7

Gore forms 2 and 6: Similar to central gore form.

Gore forms 3 and 5: Graduated compartments each contain a double-curve variation combined with lanceolate leaves.

Front borders: Parallel lines that, with the addition of a lozenge and a zigzag band, continue around neck front and across shoulders.

Sleeves: At shoulder, a double-curve motif with the curves widened into a black leaf form. At elbow, double curves with a leaf spray.

Cuffs: Double-curve motifs enclosed between lines of "barber-pole" pattern.

Outer borders: Red and narrow around coat and collar and across front shoulders.

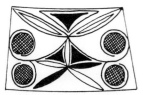

Gore forms 3 and 5

Sleeve band at shoulder

Sleeve band at elbow

36. City of Bristol Museum and Art Gallery, Bristol (E.6140)

Man's painted caribou-skin coat, with narrow fur bandings
Montagnais-Naskapi, Quebec-Labrador, probably 1820–1830

It is thought that this coat is from a collection made by a Dr. Goldwyer of Bristol, which was given to the museum by his widow in 1845, but there is another possibility. When Harold Burnham visited Bristol in the 1960s, he went into some of the early records and found a note dated 1832, which stated that a Naskapi coat had been given by Wm. Lee. Either of these sources would fit with the probable date of this coat.[13]

The coat was probably made originally as a normal hunting coat and then passed to a non-native owner who had it altered, trimmed with fur, and lined to make a warm winter coat. We know from the number of these beautiful coats that have survived in Great Britain and in Europe that they were a desirable souvenir of a visit to North America, but the fact that this coat has been warmly lined with wool shows that the former owner was not just a summer tourist but probably passed a least one winter in Canada.

Quality: Good. Medium-weight skins; excellent fairly simple painting.

Condition: Good. Somewhat soiled; paint worn; pelage on fur additions completely lost.

Cutting: Originally quite standard with a flare of 1:2. Changes were made to adjust the cut to the taste of a Euro-Canadian owner. The armholes were rounded and small triangular gussets inserted on either side of the neck. These may be original, but as the shoulder line has been changed, cutting right through the patterning, they were probably added at the same time as the lining and the fur trimmings, which include a stand-up collar, facings at the top of the fronts, and cuffs, all probably hare.

Size: Length, 110 cm. Back of neck to wrist, 79 cm.

Sewing: Basic coat with sinew. A count of the stitches was not taken because of the lining. The side seams were sewn *after* the painting was done (see Sewing section for comment). A lining of scarlet worsted 2/2 twill in the body and glazed brown tabby in the sleeves was added. Alterations and additions were made with linen thread.

Colours: Strong yellow for layout and background cross-hatching; brown for drawing motifs; vermilion for a few details.

Tools: Two 3-prongs, *A* and *B*, with yellow for layout. A 2-prong, *C*, with both red and brown. Several single prongs, the weights of which were not noted.

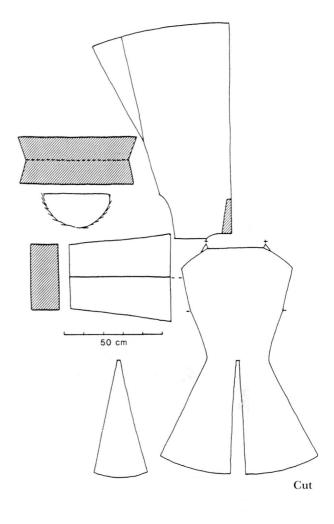

Cut

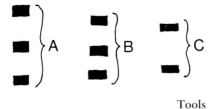

Tools

Bottom border: Double curves supported on a diagonal cross and surmounted by a rather rounded stemmed triangle and a pair of curved lines; parallel lines and a row of zigzags above and below.

Bottom border

Central gore form

Central gore form: Graduated compartments each contain a double curve supporting a circle. Horizontal divides are small zigzags; surrounds are simple parallel lines.

Centre-back extension: Surrounds of parallel lines enclose empty space.

Shoulders: Crossed by a band of parallel lines, which was cut into during alterations.

Collar: Design layout similar to Nos. 12–16 and 18–19, with double curves growing out from a central band. In this case the central band consists of two converging rows of small zigzags. An added wide stand-up collar is made of a folded band of fur. There is a sparse, obliquely slashed fringe.

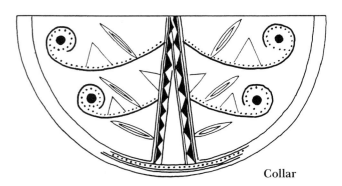

Collar

Gore forms 1, 3, 5, and 7: Crossed by parallel lines alternating with a double row of dots. Surrounds of all side gore forms are simple parallel lines and come together at the waist in a blunt point, from the centre of which a single band of lines extends to the shoulder.

Gore forms 2 and 6: Similar to central gore form.

Front borders: A simple zigzag. A small bit of fur was applied as a finish to the front just below the neck.

Sleeve band at shoulder

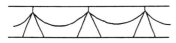

Sleeve band at elbow

Sleeves: At shoulder, a band of inverted double curves similar to motif used on sleeve bands of No. 18. At elbow, a band with a scallop variation.

Cuffs: Wide bands of fur.

Outer borders: Brown around coat and collar and across top edges of sleeves.

Markings: At centre back there is an unusual rough red vertical mark, applied after sewing, as though to join the back gusset to the coat back.

37. National Museums of Scotland, Edinburgh (1881.37.44)

Man's painted caribou-skin coat
Montagnais-Naskapi, Quebec-Labrador, probably
early to mid 19th century

This coat was acquired by the museum in 1881. An old and not very useful catalogue entry, supposedly for this piece, reads: "Nascappie Deerskin leather with stamped ornament in red, yellow, brown and dark green. From the 'Wood Indians' interior of Labrador. L.31in. Bought 5s 6d." The colours listed are those used on this coat, but the measurement does not agree with the actual length of 101 cm, which is just under 40 inches. Perhaps the "L.31in." should have read "41," but even if the entry is for this coat, "Wood Indians" does not help much with the provenance.

With the collar missing we can see that, as on many other coats, the painting is left unfinished on the part of the skin that was hidden by the collar. This does not seem to have anything to do with the quality of a coat: it happens on some with poor work as well as on others that are meticulously and elaborately painted. The delicate and precise decoration on this coat is quite remarkable and yet unfinished where it would have been hidden.

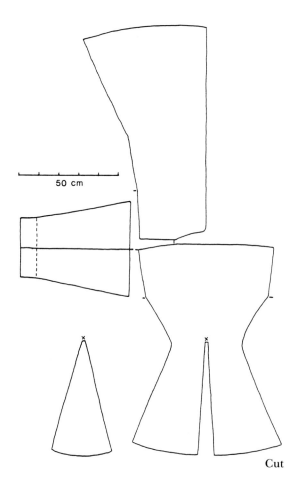

50 cm

Cut

Quality: Good. Medium-weight skins; precise and rather delicate painting.

Condition: Good. Somewhat soiled; some insect damage and loss of paint; collar missing.

Cutting: Flare of 1:1.9.

Size: Length, 101 cm. Back of neck to wrist, 79.5 cm.

Sewing: Entirely with sinew, 25 stitches per 5 cm. Side seams were sewn *after* painting was done (see Sewing section for comment).

Colours: Yellow for layout and fine background cross-hatching; vermilion for much of drawing of motifs; dark brown; green.

Tools: A 3-prong, *A*, with wide central striated line; a 4-prong, *B;* and a second 3-prong, *C;* all with yellow for layout. A 2-prong, *D*, with yellow and red. A narrow 2-prong, *E*, with brown. Several fine single prongs, the weights of which were not noted.

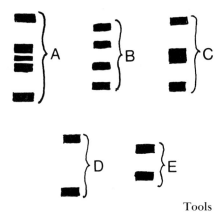

Tools

Bottom border: A band of large scallops with stiff triple leaves; parallel lines, rows of dots, and zigzags above and below.

Bottom border

Central gore form: Graduated compartments each contain a double-curve motif supporting a circle. Horizontal divides are rows of zigzags; surrounds are parallel lines and a row of dots.

Centre-back extension: Graduated compartments each contain a simple diagonal cross.

Shoulders: A band of shallow scallops between rows of dots.

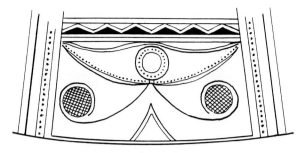

Central gore form

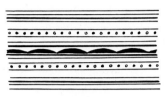

Shoulders

Collar: Missing.

Gore forms 1, 3, 5, and 7: Crossed by small hexagonal lozenge variations, rows of dots, and track variation. The surrounds of all the side gore forms are parallel lines and a row of dots that come together at the waist in a blunt point, from the centre of which a single band of parallel lines extends to the shoulder.

Gore forms 2 and 6: Similar to central gore form.

Front borders: Similar to back shoulder band, turning at neck and extending to armholes, making front shoulder bands.

Sleeves: At shoulder, a band of zigzags, wedge-shaped zigzags, and rows of dots; at elbow, a band with rows of dots.

Cuffs: Similar to shoulder bands and front borders.

Outer borders: Red around coat, top edges of sleeves, and cuffs, and across shoulders.

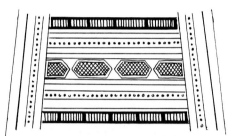

Gore forms 1, 3, 5, and 7

38. National Museums of Scotland, Edinburgh (1870 No. 45)

Man's painted caribou-skin coat
Montagnais-Naskapi, Quebec-Labrador, probably early to mid 19th century

See colour plate page 56

The history is, as usual, not very helpful. Since the catalogue number starts with 1870, it may be presumed that the museum acquired the coat in that year. It was bought from a Mr. J. Robbie for one pound. The old catalogue entry reads: "Indian Chief's robe or coat of deerskin elaborately ornamented. North American." Written in is "Hudson Bay."

This is an exceptional coat. The painting is complex and very fine. The inclusion of a Christian type of cross, the extravagant use of leaf sprays, and the gussets inserted at the neck edge show very strong European influence and suggest that this coat was made for a non-native wearer. The use of linen thread for some of the sewing strengthens that feeling, but apart from the gussets and a slight shaping of the neck, the cutting and layout of the design are traditional.

A strange thing that should be noted is that at the bottom corner of both side gussets there is a little section on the inside of the skin with quite finished painting. There are two similar small sections of painting on the inside beside the seams on one sleeve. All are painted in the same colours and weight as the surface patterning. Could they have been a trial? At present there is no explanation, and no other occurrences of the kind have been noted.

Painting on inside of side gore form.

Quality: Excellent. Very lightweight and supple skins; superb painting.

Condition: Generally good. Painting excellent. The coat has been partially cleaned.

Cutting: Flare of 1:2.

Size: Length, 105 cm. Back of neck to wrist, 80 cm.

Sewing: A mixture of sinew, 18 stitches per 5 cm, and linen thread, with a much finer count of 38 stitches per 5 cm. Stitch marks down the front edges and around the cuffs probably indicate that a fur edging was removed. Side seams were sewn *after* painting was done (see Sewing section for comment).

Colours: Dark and light yellow for layout and for solid filling of some of background; pinkish red and dark blue-black for drawing motifs; brown and green for details; red-brown for borders.

Tools: A 3-prong, *A*, with yellow for layout. Several single prongs, the weights of which were not noted.

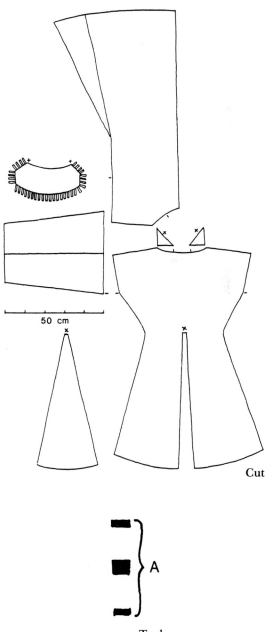

50 cm

Cut

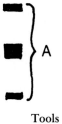

A

Tools

Bottom border

Central gore form

Bottom border: Compartments each contain a double curve combined with an unusual large single scallop. Use of this scallop motif has been noted on only one other coat, No. 33, where it too occurs above a double curve, but in the side gore forms. Line decorations are single track and scallops above the main border; below is a line in which a group of four dots alternates with a leaflike dash, and a line of scallops with dots.

Central gore form: Graduated compartments each contain a double-curve variation and a straight, Christian-type cross in the centre above another large single scallop. The horizontal divides are single track; the surrounds are single track and a line of alternating four dots and a dash.

Centre-back extension: Graduated compartments each contain leaves on a diagonal cross.

Shoulders: Crossed by a band with wedge-shaped zigzags, single track, scallops, dots, and dashes.

Collar: Two complex double-curve variations in the centre with a central lozenge between them. There are many other curves as well as scallops, dotted lines, and leaf sprays. There is a fringe cut straight with alternate segments cut right away.

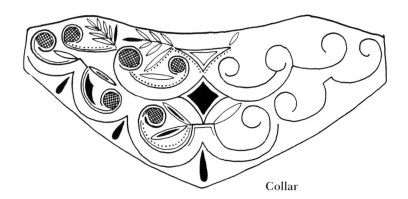

Collar

Gore forms 1 and 7

Gore forms 1 and 7: Graduated compartments each contain two fragmented double curves. To the sides very small crosses made up of four triangles have been fitted in unobtrusively. The surrounds of all the side gore forms are wide and strong, with parallel lines, single track, a line of alternating four dots and a dash, and scallops. A most unusual detail of design is that with gore forms 1, 7, 2, and 6 the front surround differs from the back surround. They meet at the waist, where the front surround ends and the back surround continues on without a break to the shoulder.

Gore forms 2 and 6: Graduated compartments each contain double-curve variations and rather indefinite Christian-type crosses. As with the other design areas, sprays of leaves are used in the background.

Gore forms 3 and 5: Graduated compartments each contain double-curve variations and a repeat of the large scallop motif in the bottom border.

Gore forms 2 and 6

Gore forms 3 and 5

Front borders: A band of parallel lines, small lozenges, and a line with alternating four dots and a dash. The bands turn below the neck, follow around the neck curve, and then extend to the armholes.

Sleeves: At shoulder, a wide band of parallel lines, two rows of the dot-dash pattern, and a line of track variation. At elbow, a narrower band of the dot-dash pattern and a line of track. At wrist, a band of the dot-dash pattern and a zigzag variation. No cuffs.

Outer borders: Red-brown around coat, across top edges of sleeves and front and back of shoulders, and on collar fringe.

39. Newfoundland Museum, St. John's (anonymous loan)

Man's painted caribou-skin coat
Montagnais-Naskapi, Quebec-Labrador, probably about 1840

This coat was collected by General Sir John Henry Lefroy, the same man who owned No. 14. He was the author of *In Search of the Magnetic North*, an account of his travels in Canada during the 1840s. This coat is owned by one of his descendants; it was formerly on loan to the British Museum and was recently transferred to the Newfoundland Museum.

Many caribou-skin coats have survived because they were bought by people from Great Britain and Europe and were taken home as souvenirs of a trip or a tour of duty in North America. So it is not surprising that a fair proportion of the surviving coats, including this one, show evidence of having been altered to suit the needs and tastes of a second owner. This coat was given a warm bright lining that adds considerable colour to an otherwise unusually sombre coat. It is handsome and the painting is well executed, but it does seems to lack the verve of many of the other examples. With the reduced size and flattened form of the double curves, and with the weight of a multitude of rather stiff dots, some of the life that is characteristic of double-curve designs seems to have vanished. One wonders if the formality of the design appealed to Sir John.

Quality: Excellent. Good skins, medium lightweight; skilful painting.

Condition: Good. Quite soiled; some insect damage; only slight loss of paint.

Cutting: A modest flare of 1:1.6.

Size: Length, 95 cm. Back of neck to wrist, 83.5 cm.

Sewing: Entirely with *linen* thread (Z,2S), 20 stitches per 5 cm, both for basic coat and for addition of lining. Side seams were sewn up *after* painting (See Sewing section for comment).

Wool tassels on a beaded string hang from the top sleeve seam.

The coat is fully lined with bright yellow wool tabby with lightly raised nap (warp S singles, 14 per cm; weft S singles, 20 per cm). The cuffs are red wool broadcloth (warp and weft both Z singles, 24 per cm). The hem of the lining is trimmed with narrow purple and yellow braid and a line of zigzag stitching.

Colours: Yellow for layout and background crosshatching; red, probably vermilion, for much of drawing of motifs; dark blue-black; brown; a few details in green.

Tools: A 3-prong, *A*, with yellow for layout. A 6-prong, *B*, with yellow across gore forms. Several single prongs, the weights of which were not noted.

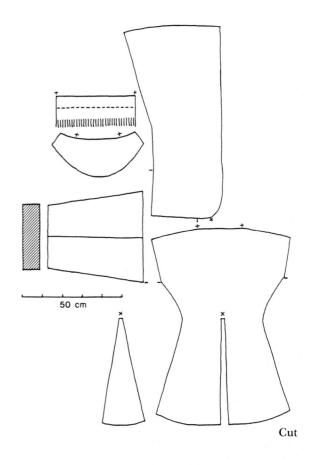

Cut

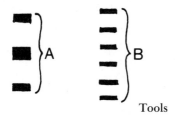

Tools

Bottom border: Quite small, flattened double curves outlined by dots; multiple line decorations including rows of dots, zigzags with dots, track, and scallops above and below.

Central gore form: Graduated compartments each contain a double curve supported by a stiff triple leaf and surmounted by paired leaves and a circle. The horizontal divides are a line of zigzags and a line of single track; the surrounds are simple parallel lines.

Bottom border

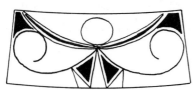

Central gore form

Centre-back extension: Crossed by groups of parallel lines.

Shoulders: Crossed by parallel lines and a row of dots.

Collar: Double curves and a double-curve variation as well as single curves, all outlined by lines of red and black dots.

There is an additional band collar, fringed at the bottom, which may be part of the original making of the coat, but the loose, scribbly painting is definitely an addition by a non-native hand. The red appears to be held in fish roe, but the green and purple lines were probably drawn with a pen.

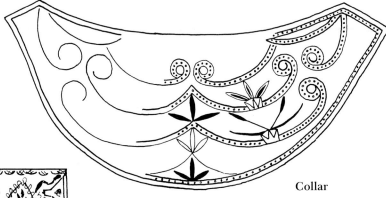

Collar

Band collar

Gore forms 1, 3, 5, and 7: Crossed by 6-fold lines alternating with single rows of dots in black and red. Surrounds of all side gore forms are simple parallel lines that come together at the waist in a blunt point, from the centre of which a single group of lines extends to the shoulder.

Gore forms 2 and 6: Similar to central gore form.

Front borders: Simple parallel lines.

Sleeves: Bands of parallel lines and rows of dots at shoulder, elbow, and wrist.

Cuffs: Red wool cloth.

Outer borders: Red around collar, coat, and top edges of sleeves and across front and back of shoulders.

PUBLICATION: King, fig. 39, p. 41 (black and white photograph with caption).

40. National Museum of Natural History, Smithsonian Institution, Washington, D.C. (90241)

Man's painted caribou-skin coat
Naskapi, northern Quebec, 1882–1884

This coat and Nos. 41–46 were collected at Fort Chimo by Lucien Turner. In 1882 Turner was sent as a meteorologist from the Smithsonian Institution in Washington to Fort Chimo on Ungava Bay in northern Quebec, where he stayed until 1884. Not very much is known about Turner himself, but he must have had wide-ranging interests and great abil-

ity, for he was a very acute observer and recorder of everything around him during his stay in the north. His observations were published after his return to Washington, under the title "Ethnology of the Ungava District, Hudson Bay Territory," as part of the *Eleventh Annual Report of the Bureau of Ethnology, Smithsonian Institution, 1889–1890,* and has since been reprinted in book form.

That he was also an able collector for the Smithsonian is evidenced by the valuable material he deposited in that institution. This coat and Nos. 41–46 are part of that collection, and, besides being fascinating pieces in themselves, they are documented examples of Naskapi painted coats, something that is very rare. Although the collecting was

done in the Fort Chimo district, it should be noted that Fort Chimo was a meeting place for people from both east and west. In this collection there are two distinct types of motifs used in the painting. This coat and No. 41, and possibly No. 42, probably came from the east, while Nos. 43–46 very likely arrived at Fort Chimo from the west.

About forty years stretch between No. 39 and the Turner coats, and there are no known examples to fill that void. It is obvious that considerable deterioration took place during the period. The skins of these later coats are still well prepared and the cutting and sewing fairly well done in the traditional way, but the painting is much coarser and the areas of decoration more limited, probably as a result of changes in the way of life, one of which was that less woman-power was available. A new colour scheme also takes over around this time, with the introduction by trade of a strong blue obtained from cakes of pigment made for blueing linens when doing laundry — Rekitt's Blue.

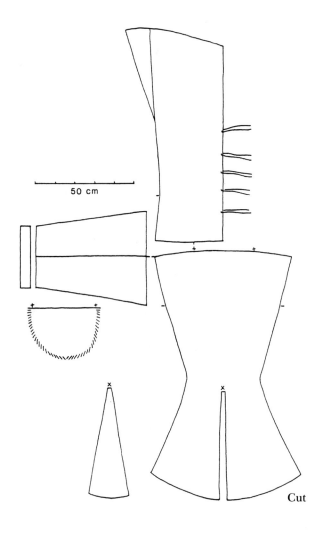

50 cm

Cut

Quality: Good. Medium-weight skins; quite complex but very coarse painting.

Condition: Good but soiled.

Cutting: Flare of 1:1.9. The back was cut longer than the fronts, causing considerable distortion.

Size: Length, 120 cm. Back of neck to wrist, 89 cm.

Sewing: Entirely with sinew, 17 stitches per 5 cm. Five thong ties on left front with small holes opposite them on right front.

Colours: Pale yellow for layout; strong red for drawing of much of pattern; laundry blue; brown.

Tools: A 3-prong, *A*, and a 2-prong, *B*, both with yellow for layout. A 2-prong, *C*, with brown in bottom border. A 3-prong, *D*, with yellow on collar. A very heavy single prong, *E*, with red. Lighter single prongs with red and fine ones with blue and yellow for crosshatching; their weights were not noted.

A B C D E

Tools

Bottom border: Double curves with crosses consisting of four small triangles in terminals; a row of lozenges and a line of single track above and below.

Central gore form: Graduated sections contain triangles and paired leaves. Surrounds are simple parallel lines that do not quite meet at the waist, where they stop abruptly.

Centre-back: Undecorated; no shoulder band.

Collar: A wide central band of parallel lines with small curves and leaves on either side, an obvious descendant of the popular earlier type in which double curves grow out from a central band (Nos. 12–16, 18–19). The collar is surrounded by many parallel lines and a short straight-cut fringe.

Bottom border

Central gore form

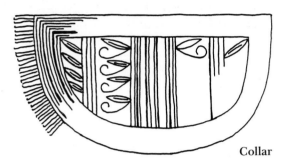

Collar

Gore forms 1 and 5: Two lower sections each contain two triangles, one above the other; the third (top) section is filled with a short vertical lozenge band. On all side gore forms horizontal divides are lozenge bands; surrounds of simple parallel lines terminate in a unfinished blunt point at the waist.

Gore forms 2 and 4: Two lower sections each contain double pairs of leaves; the third (top) section is filled with a short vertical lozenge band.

Front borders: Simple parallel lines that turn sharply below neck and extend partway to armholes.

Sleeves: On front face only, three horizontal bands of small lozenges similar to those in gore forms. Above the upper band there are three short vertical groups of parallel lines running up to the shoulder, a rare survival of the type of shoulder decoration used on Nos. 12–21. Similar lines are used on another of the coats collected by Turner, Smithsonian Institution no. 90245. It is quite similar to this one in design and so has not been included in this series.

Cuffs: A band of fairly large plain lozenges.

Outer borders: Brown around coat; red around collar.

Gore forms 1 and 5

Gore forms 2 and 4

41. National Museum of Natural History, Smithsonian Institution, Washington, D.C. (74455)

Man's painted caribou-skin coat, furred on inside and sewn closed in front
Naskapi, northern Quebec, 1882–1884

Lucien Turner collected Nos. 40–46 during his stay at Fort Chimo.

Caribou fur has excellent insulating properties; furred painted coats were undoubtedly made for the winter hunt as far back as painted coats were made. Caribou fur sheds very easily, and probably the idea of taking a fur coat back to Europe as a souvenir — the way so many early coats were saved — had little appeal. No examples older than the ones collected by Turner are known, but McLean records their use during the 1830s (see No. 54).

Quality: Good. Heavy skins with few fly marks; painting bold but precise.

Condition: Good but somewhat soiled.

Cutting: Flare of 1:1.65. At the centre bottom of each front there is a small pointed projection (see Cutting section for comment). Furred coats were made the same way as dehaired ones. The front skin was divided down the spine, the two halves were attached by side seams to the back skin, the painting was done, and then, with winter coats, the front was sewn closed again. This coat has a flap extension on one front that would have protected the wearer's chin. The inserted back gusset adds no fullness at all (see History section, p. 13, for comment).

Size: Length, 107 cm. Back of neck to wrist, 96 cm.

Sewing: Entirely with sinew, 14 stitches per 5 cm. All seams are as usual worked on the inside, even though it is the fur side.

Colours: Yellow for layout; strong red; laundry blue; brown.

Tools: A 3-prong, *A*, with yellow for layout. A 2-prong, *B*, with brown in bottom border. Three single prongs, *C* with red, *D* with blue, and *E* with blue and with yellow, for background crosshatching.

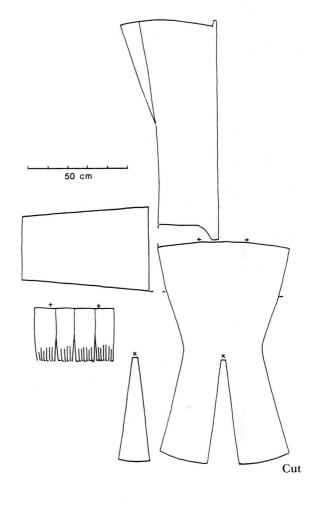

50 cm

Cut

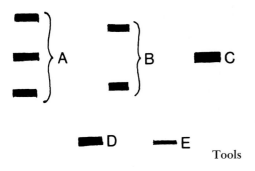

Tools

Bottom border: Double curves; above and below, a line of scallops that have small triangles between them, giving almost the appearance of a festoon.

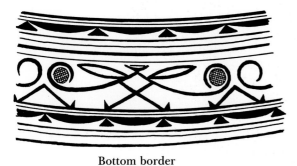

Bottom border

Central gore form: Crossed by three single lines. Surrounds of single lines follow the edge of the back gusset almost exactly and converge without quite meeting at the top of the gusset.

Shoulders: Crossed by a triple line.

Collar: Furred on outside; coarse slashed fringe.

Gore forms 1 and 3: Crossed by three single lines with single-line surrounds that come to a sharp point at waist.

Front borders: Simple parallel lines that turn sharply below neck and extend almost to armholes.

Sleeves: On front face only, four groups of triple horizontal lines; no cuffs.

Outer borders: Brown; narrow down fronts, wider around bottom.

Markings: Red, rough; applied after sewing to shoulder seams and across tops of sleeves at armholes.

PUBLICATION: Turner, Lucien M., figs. 75–76, pp. 123–124.

42. National Museum of Natural History, Smithsonian Institution, Washington, D.C. (90240)

Man's painted caribou-skin coat, furred on inside and sewn closed in front
Naskapi, northern Quebec, 1882–1884

Lucien Turner collected Nos. 40–46 during his stay at Fort Chimo.

   The survival of painted winter hunting coats is rare; this coat, although plain, is a beautiful example. Two other coats in this catalogue, Nos. 29 and 47, also have decoration of lines only. The rarity of this type may be due to the chances of survival, which are often not as favourable for plain simple things as for special productions.

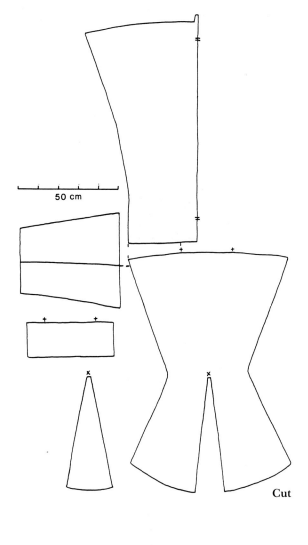

50 cm

Cut

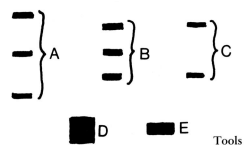

A   B   C

D   E   Tools

Quality: Skins with many fly marks and mends; painting very simple but good.

Condition: Good. Fur shedding.

Cutting: Flare of 1:1.7. There are two small triangular projections at the bottom on either side of the centre-front seam (see Cutting section for comment).

Size: Length, 116 cm. Back of neck to wrist, 87 cm.

Sewing: Entirely with sinew, 18 stitches per 5 cm. All seams are as usual worked on the inside, even though it is the furred side.

Colours: Yellow for layout; red; brown.

Tools: A 3-prong, *A*, with yellow for layout. A 3-prong, *B*, with red on sleeves. A 2-prong, *C*, with brown in bottom border. Much of the character of the design comes from the use of two very heavy single prongs, *D* and *E*, with red. Other single prongs were used, the weights of which were not noted.

Bottom border: Entirely parallel lines.

Central gore form: Crossed by three single lines. The single-line surrounds follow the cut edge of the back gusset, finishing as it does, in a blunt point at the waist.

Collar: Furred on outside, with a sparse slashed fringe.

Gore forms 1 and 3: Crossed by three single lines. The single-line surrounds meet at the waist in a sharp point.

Front borders: A single track between parallel lines, turning sharply below neck, extending partway to armholes.

Sleeves: Crossed on front face only by three groups of parallel lines; no cuffs.

Outer borders: Brown; narrow down fronts, wider around bottom.

Markings: Red, rough; applied after sewing on shoulder seams, across top of sleeves at armholes, and on upper part of top sleeve seams.

43. National Museum of Natural History, Smithsonian Institution, Washington, D.C. (74448)

Man's painted caribou-skin coat
Possibly Cree, northwestern Quebec, 1882–1884

Lucien Turner collected Nos. 40–46 during his stay at Fort Chimo.

    The layout of this coat is standard but the motifs, none of which are double curves, and the coarseness of the painting are unusual. They have obvious relationship to only three other coats collected by

Turner, Nos. 44–46, and two collected by Robert Flaherty about thirty years later, Nos. 50–51. There is a less obvious relationship to the early, very finely painted Montagnais coats with motifs based on the quadrate form of birch-bark bites, Nos. 1–4. The central gore form, which is broken into two halves, and the side gore forms, with a central stem on which leaves grow, also relate to Nos. 1–4. Probably 175 years lie between the two groups, and there is a world of difference in the skill of the painters, but it seems likely that these later coats represent a very decadent survival of that early style, and that they reached Turner at Fort Chimo through native people on the western side of the Quebec-Labrador peninsula.

Quality: Fair. Medium-weight skins; very coarse painting.

Condition: Good but soiled.

Cutting: Flare of 1:2.

Size: Length, 124 cm. Back of neck to wrist, 98 cm.

Sewing: Entirely with sinew, 20 stitches per 5 cm.

Colours: All very strong. Yellow for layout; red; a light blue, probably laundry blue; brown.

Tools: There were no multiple-prong tools; at least three single prongs were used: *A* with yellow for layout, *B* with red for drawing motifs, and *C* with blue. It is interesting that with this coat and No. 46, which was also painted without multiple-prong tools, the tradition of doing the layout with double or triple lines has been retained.

Bottom border: A bold repeating pattern of a lozenge containing a four-petalled motif with "hearts" between (see Hearts in Design Motifs section for comment); a track variation above and below.

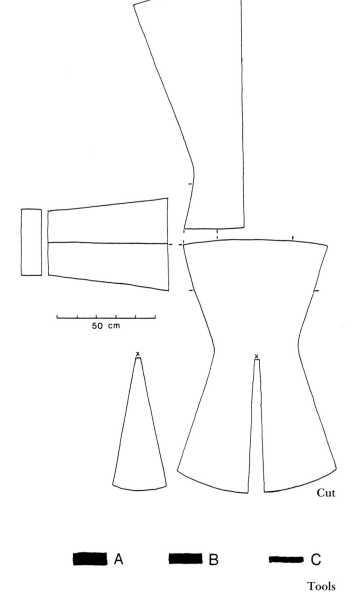

50 cm

Cut

A   B   C

Tools

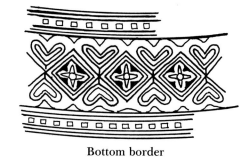

Bottom border

Central gore form: Divided in half vertically with very irregular rectangles on either side. The surrounds are narrow parallel lines and coincide with the cut edge of the back gusset, terminating with the gusset in a blunt point at the waist.

Centre-back extension: A straight narrow line of track variation running to neck.

Collar: Missing.

Gore forms 1 and 3: Paired leaves grow up from a central line. The surrounds are single lines and come to a sharp point at the waist.

Front borders: Lozenges between double lines, turning below neck and extending partway to armholes.

Sleeves: Three bands of parallel lines.

Cuffs: A line of lozenges, similar to front borders, with zigzag variation above.

Outer borders: Brown on fronts; red around bottom, cuffs, and armhole edges of sleeves and across shoulders.

Markings: Only a rough red line painted on side seams above waist after sewing.

PUBLICATION: Turner, Lucien M., figs. 67–68, pp. 117–118.

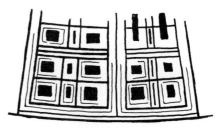

Central gore form

Gore forms 1 and 3

Cuffs

44. National Museum of Natural History, Smithsonian Institution, Washington, D.C. (90243)

Man's painted caribou-skin coat
Probably Cree, northwestern Quebec, 1882–1884

Lucien Turner collected Nos. 40–46 during his stay at Fort Chimo.

Nos. 43–46 and 50–51 seem to be from a design tradition other than that dominated by typical Naskapi double curves. It is likely that they all come from the Hudson Bay area and represent a survival of the earlier Montagnais type (Nos. 1–4).

Quality: Fair. Medium-weight skins, somewhat flymarked; painting bold and quite rough.

Condition: Good but soiled.

Cutting: Flare of 1:1.75.

Size: Length, 106 cm. Back of neck to wrist, 89 cm.

Sewing: Entirely with sinew, 17 stitches per 5 cm.

Colours: Strong yellow; red; dark laundry blue; brown.

Tools: A 2-prong, *A*, with yellow for layout. A 2-prong, *B*, with red. Several single prongs, the weights of which were not noted.

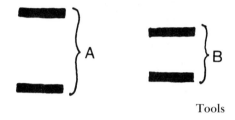

Tools

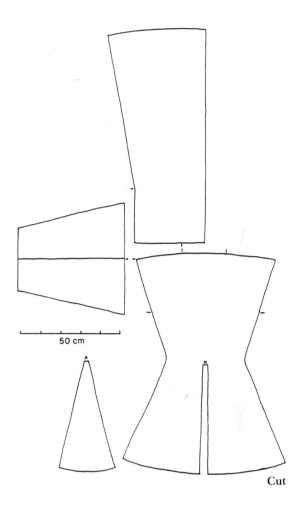

50 cm

Cut

Bottom border: A repeating motif of a quatrefoil leaf with a circle in the centre; lines of small lozenges above and below.

Bottom border

Central gore form: Graduated compartments each contain very crudely drawn diagonal crosses and lozenges. Rows of dots are used both for horizontal divides and for surrounds, which follow the line of the back gusset and terminate with the gusset in a blunt point at the waist.

Central gore form

Gore forms 1 and 3

Centre-back extension: A narrow vertical line of single track.

Shoulders: Crossed by a row of dots.

Collar: None. It may be missing or may never have existed.

Gore forms 1 and 3: Graduated compartments divided by a central vertical line, on either side of which are rectangles within rectangles outlined by dots. The single-line surrounds terminate in a sharp point at the waist.

Front borders: A line of track, turning below neck and extending partway to armholes.

Sleeves: Three bands, each with a row of dots enclosed by single lines; no cuffs.

Outer borders: Brown around coat.

Markings: Rough, red; applied before sewing across top edges of sleeves and both edges of lower sleeve seams.

45. National Museum of Natural History, Smithsonian Institution, Washington, D.C. (90242)

Man's painted caribou-skin coat
Probably Cree, northwestern Quebec, 1882–1884

Lucien Turner collected Nos. 40–46 during his stay at Fort Chimo.

This coat belongs with the group that probably comes from the western part of the area, Nos. 43–46 and 50–51. It has a very unorthodox double curve as its main motif. In the central gore form the leaves are quadrate, and in the side gore forms there is a strong feeling of growth; both of these design elements are characteristic of the group.

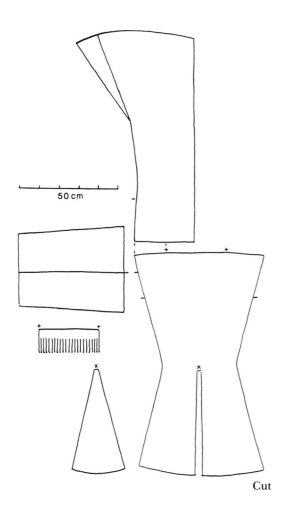

Cut

Quality: Quite poor. Medium-weight skins, badly fly-marked; painting strong but crude.

Condition: Good, but somewhat soiled. The blue colour has run.

Cutting: Flare of 1:2.

Size: Length, 107 cm. Back of neck to wrist, 85 cm.

Sewing: Entirely with sinew, 23 stitches per 5 cm.

Colours: Very strong yellow for layout and coarse background crosshatching; red; blue, which is not fast; brown.

Tools: One 2-prong, *A*, with yellow for layout. Three single prongs, *B* and *C* with red, *D* with yellow and blue. One stamp, *E*, with blue for dots.

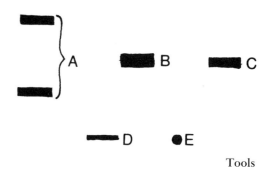

Tools

Bottom border: A repeating, bold, very strange double-curve variation that encloses a rough cross made from four triangles; a line of small lozenges above and below.

Bottom border

Central gore form: Divided vertically and horizontally by rows of dots into compartments, each of which contains a quatrefoil leaf. The surrounds are also rows of dots that follow the line of the back gusset exactly and finish with the gusset in a blunt point at the waist.

Centre-back extension: A narrow vertical band of small zigzags between parallel lines.

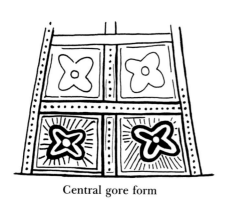

Central gore form

Shoulders: Crossed by zigzags and parallel lines, similar to centre-back extension.

Collar: A plain band of skin with a straight slashed fringe.

Gore forms 1 and 3: Leaflike double curves grow out from a central vertical line. The pattern in the gore form on the left side of the coat is somewhat more elaborate than that on the right. The single-line surrounds follow the edge of the side gusset exactly and terminate, as it does, in a sharp point at the waist.

Front borders: Bands of small lozenges similar to those in bottom border, turning below neck and extending almost to armholes.

Sleeves: Three narrow bands of parallel lines; no cuffs.

Outer borders: Brown around coat.

Markings: Red, rough; applied to top edges of sleeves and upper sleeve seams above elbow before sewing; narrower on side seams above waist, applied after sewing.

Gore forms 1 and 3

46. National Museum of Natural History, Smithsonian Institution, Washington, D.C. (74449)

Man's painted caribou-skin coat
Possibly Cree, northwestern Quebec, 1882–1884

Lucien Turner collected Nos. 40–46 during his stay at Fort Chimo.

This coat is unusually simple, with a minimum of decoration; there are no extensions to the shoulder, no painted collar, no front borders, and no sleeve bands or cuffs. Like Nos. 43–45, its design combines elements of quadrate patterning with a strong feeling of growth. It probably reached Fort Chimo from the west.

These coats collected by Turner have a technical feature that is shared with some coats of later date: the outlines of the central painted gore form coincide with the cut edge of the inserted back gusset, drawing attention to its presence. On the majority of coats the design of the gore form masks rather than emphasizes the fact that there is a cut gusset hidden beneath it.

Quality: Poor. Inexpert cutting; lightweight skins, badly flymarked; sparse clumsy painting.

Condition: Fairly good. Skins brittle and somewhat soiled.

Cutting: Flare of 1:1.6.

Size: Length, 95 cm. Back of neck to wrist, 83 cm.

Sewing: Entirely with sinew; quite coarse with only 14 stitches per 5 cm.

Colours: All strong. Yellow for layout; red; brown; green.

Tools: Two single prongs, *A* with yellow, red, and green; *B* with green only.

Tools

Bottom border: A line of bold lozenges with small triangles between them; simple parallel lines above and below.

Bottom border

Central gore form: Double curves grow up and out from a central line, quite similar to designs used on Nos. 43 and 45. The narrow surrounds of parallel lines follow the cut edge of the inserted back gusset and terminate with the gusset in a blunt point at the waist.

Collar: An undecorated irregular skin band.

Gore forms 1 and 3: A repetition of coarse chevrons made with alternately heavy and light lines. Surrounds of simple parallel lines terminate in a sharp point at the waist.

Outer borders: Brown around coat and wrists.

Markings: Fine brown lines applied after sewing to shoulder, armhole, sleeve, and side seams.

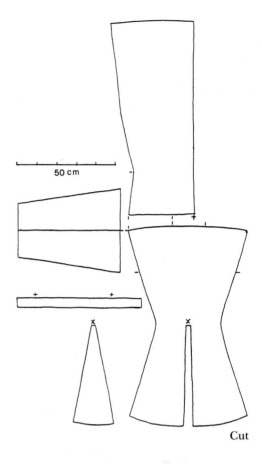

50 cm

Cut

Central gore form

Gore forms 1 and 3

47. Royal Ontario Museum, Toronto (HC.1916)

Man's painted caribou-skin coat
Naskapi, northern Quebec-Labrador, 1910–1912

Five coats, Nos. 47–51, were collected by Robert Flaherty during his journeys from Great Whale River on Hudson Bay across to Fort Chimo between 1910 and 1912. These coats were given to the Royal Ontario Museum by Sir William McKenzie.

In Flaherty's book *My Eskimo Friends: Nanook of the North*, the only mention made of the native peoples other than Inuit describes a stay at Fort Chimo in 1912:

On the heels of the ice came Indians in canoes from their "land of little sticks" — swampy Crees from the far southwest over towards Hudson Bay, and Nascopies from as far the other way, the Atlantic slope of Labrador. Unlike the prosaic and more sophisticated Crees, the Nascopies were a wild and primitive throng. Their whitish tan deerskin leggings and capotes were set off in the geometric Nascopie designs of vivid red and blue. Tall and lank and straight as the straightest tree, they strode with swinging hips, their heads held high — finely chiselled masks almost buried in their shoulder-long hair.[14]

Of the coats in the Royal Ontario Museum collected by Flaherty, Nos. 47–49 are most probably Naskapi, while Nos. 50–51 may well be Cree, although they do not seem either "prosaic" or "sophisticated," as the people themselves were described by Flaherty.

Quality: Good. Heavy skins, badly flymarked; painting very simple.

Condition: Good, but slightly soiled.

Cutting: Flare of 1:1.7. Five pairs of thongs are attached to the front edges, so that the right front overlaps the left slightly when fastened.

Size: Length, 127 cm. Back of neck to wrist, 89 cm.

Sewing: Basically sinew, 20 stitches per 5 cm; some black cotton thread.

Colour: Red-brown only.

Tools: A 3-prong, *A*, for layout. A single prong, *B*.

Bottom border: Two parallel triple lines.

Central gore form: Crossed by parallel triple lines, which are rather irregular, suggesting that they were made with the single-prong tool. The surrounds are also triple lines, the inner one of which follows the line of the inserted back gusset.

Centre-back extension: Crossed and surrounded by triple lines.

Shoulders: The triple-line surrounds of the central gore form and its extension turn sharply at either side of the point of the collar and extend across shoulders to armholes.

Collar: Triangular; undecorated except for band around edge.

Gore forms 1 and 3: Crossed by triple lines, similar to central gore form. The surrounds of triple lines meet at the waist and stop without being finished in any way.

Front borders: Triple lines, turning below neck and extending to armholes.

Sleeves: Three bands of triple lines; no cuffs.

Outer borders: Red-brown around coat, collar, and wrists.

Markings: Red-brown; applied before sewing to front and back of shoulders, across top of armholes, and across top of sleeve seams; a similar but narrower painted line applied to upper part of side seams after sewing.

Additional: There is a pair of leggings to match this coat.

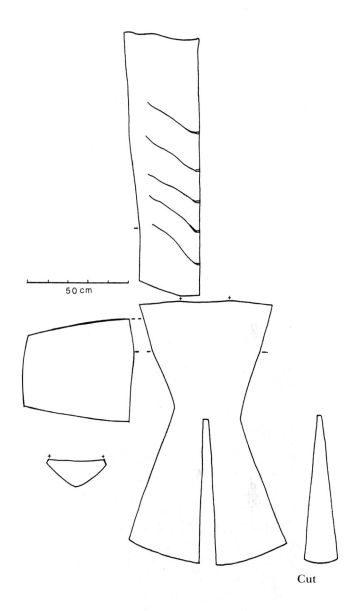

50 cm

Cut

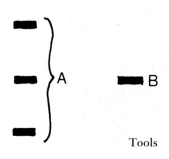

A   B

Tools

48. Royal Ontario Museum, Toronto (HC.2250)

Man's painted caribou-skin coat
Naskapi, northern Quebec-Labrador, 1910–1912

Five coats, Nos. 47–51, were collected by Robert Flaherty during his journeys from Great Whale River on Hudson Bay across to Fort Chimo between 1910 and 1912. All five were given to the Royal Ontario Museum by Sir William McKenzie.

   This coat seems to have been made for the same person as No. 47. They are similar in size, both are longer than usual, and the 3-prong tool used may be the same for both coats.

The decoration is unusually elaborate for the period and, as with No. 60, it may have been made to be worn at a special feast that the man was instructed, in a dream, to give before the caribou hunt. Perhaps the plainer coat, No. 47, was used for the actual hunt. Possibly both coats were made for Flaherty himself.

Quality: Good. Medium-weight skins; complex but rather clumsy painting.

Condition: Good. The medium must have been unusually weak because both the blue and the red have run and are smudged.

Cutting: Only a slight flare of 1:1.4. Seven pairs of thong ties are attached to the fronts.

Size: Length, 122 cm. Back of neck to wrist, 92 cm.

Sewing: Entirely with sinew, 18 stitches per 5 cm. An unusual addition is the loop sewn into the back of the neck to facilitate hanging.

Colours: Weak, pale pinkish yellow for layout; bright red used for drawing motifs; very bright laundry blue. Possibly the medium was not fish roe but something less satisfactory, such as egg white, which would account for the change from the usual strong yellow colour and the running and smudging of the red and blue pigments.

Tools: A 3-prong, *A*, with yellow for layout. A 2-prong, *B*, with blue in bottom border. At least three single prongs, *C*, *D*, and *E*, all with both red and blue.

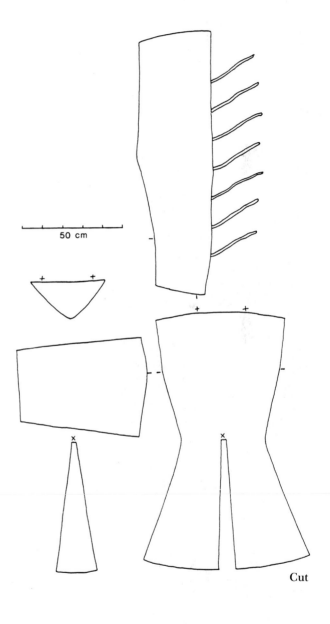

Cut

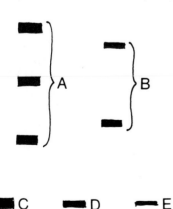

Tools

Bottom border: Repeating double curves with straight branches, each carrying a stemmed triangle between two wedge-shaped triangles; parallel lines and rows of scallops, with each scallop holding a small triangle, above and below.

Bottom border

Central gore form: Graduated compartments each contain a double-curve motif. Horizontal divides are double lines of scallops; surrounds are lines with small sprouts.

Waist: Large motif of concentric triangles on a stem on either side of centre back at waist. If the coat were closed with a sash, as is usual, these triangles would be covered, but with the thong ties the wearer probably did not use a sash.

Centre-back extension: Graduated compartments each contain a double-curve motif similar to those in central gore form, but inverted. The surrounds are double scallops.

Shoulders: The surrounds of the centre-back extension turn sharply to either side of the collar and stretch across shoulders to armholes.

Collar: A central double curve with branches, similar to those in bottom border.

Central gore form

Centre-back extension

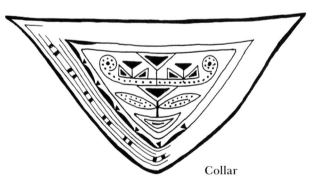

Collar

Gore forms 1 and 3

Gore forms 1 and 3: Graduated compartments each contain a stemmed triangle between paired leaves and wedges. The surrounds of single track come together at the waist and then spread out again.

Extensions of gore forms 1 and 3: Graduated compartments each contain a diagonal cross. The surrounds stretch up to the front and back shoulder bands on either side of the armhole.

Front borders: Simple parallel lines, turning below neck and extending to armholes.

Sleeves: At both shoulder and elbow, bands with a single track and scallops with a small triangle; at wrist, a wider band; no cuffs.

Outer borders: Red; wide around coat and wrists, narrower on collar.

Markings: Red; applied before sewing to back and front of shoulders, around tops of sleeves, and on top part of sleeve seams.

Extension of gore forms 1 and 3

Sleeve band at wrist

49. Royal Ontario Museum, Toronto (HC.2251)

Man's painted caribou-skin coat, furred on inside and sewn closed in front
Naskapi, northern Quebec or Labrador,
1910–1912

See colour plate page 57

Five coats, Nos. 47–51, were collected by Robert Flaherty during his journeys from Great Whale River on Hudson Bay across to Fort Chimo between 1910 and 1912. They were given to the Royal Ontario Museum by Sir William McKenzie.

In spite of a lapse of thirty years, this coat is very close in cut and decoration to No. 41. Another similarity is that the inserted back gusset adds no fullness at all.

Quality: Good. Medium-weight skins; careful painting.

Condition: Good. Skins soft; paint well preserved; torn at neck.

Cutting: A minimal flare of 1:1.3. At bottom of centre front on each side of the seam there is a small pointed extension (see Cutting section for comment).

Size: Length, 104 cm. Back of neck to wrist, 78 cm.

Sewing: Entirely with sinew, 17 stitches per 5 cm. The seams are sewn with overcast stitches on the inside, even though it is the fur side. There are small round patches applied at either underarm.

Colours: Yellow for layout and background crosshatching; red for drawing motifs; laundry blue; reddish brown for banding.

Tools: A 3-prong, *A,* and a 2-prong, *B,* both with yellow for layout. A narrow 2-prong, *C,* with red on sleeves and in gore forms. Two single prongs, *D* with red, *E* with blue and yellow.

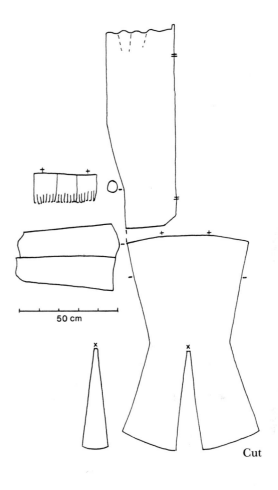

50 cm

Cut

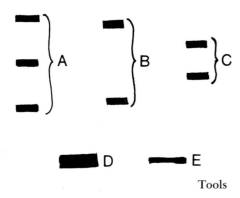

Tools

Bottom border: A double curve alternates with a diagonal cross, the lower arms of which enclose a small stemmed triangle; above and below, lines of scallops with small triangles and a double track.

Bottom border

Central gore form: Simply outlined and crossed three times by a double line in red. The surrounds closely follow the seamline of the inserted back gusset and terminate with the gusset in an unfinished blunt point.

Collar: Made of several pieces of fine skin, furred on outside; coarse slashed fringe. Other winter coats (Nos. 41, 52–53, 55) have similar collars, which, according to Lucien Turner, were made from the cheek skins of the caribou.[15]

Gore forms 1 and 3: Similar to central gore form, also terminating in an unfinished blunt point at waist.

Front borders: Parallel lines and a double track, turning below neck and extending partway to armholes.

Sleeves: Crossed by three bands of red double lines on front face only.

Outer borders: Reddish brown; narrow down fronts, wider around bottom.

Markings: Red, rough; applied after sewing to shoulder seams, tops of armhole seams, and top part of sleeve seams.

50. Royal Ontario Museum, Toronto (HC.2253)

Man's painted caribou-skin coat
Probably Cree, northern Quebec, 1910–1912

See colour plate page 57

Five coats, Nos. 47–51, were collected by Robert Flaherty during his journeys from Great Whale River to Fort Chimo between 1910 and 1912. They were given to the Royal Ontario Museum by Sir William McKenzie.

It is likely that this coat, with its strong feeling of growth and the quadrate basis of the leaves in the side gore forms, comes from the northwestern part of Quebec and has a Cree rather than a Naskapi origin. It is very close in style to No. 51 and ties in with four of the coats collected by Lucien Turner (Nos. 43–46). These six coats may be a last echo of the early Montagnais style of Nos. 1–4.

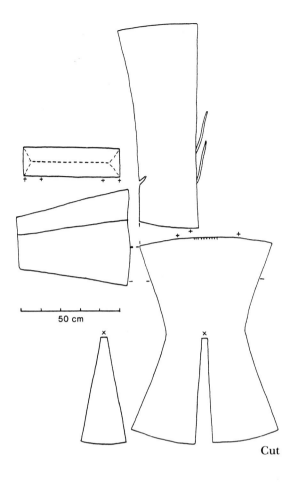

50 cm

Cut

Quality: Good. Medium-weight skins; fairly complex but rather coarse painting.

Condition: Not very good. Skins warped and soiled; painting considerably worn; fur collar badly torn, pelage gone.

Cutting: Flare of 1:1.75. There is a slight slash on either side at the underarm, probably to correct a miscalculation made in cutting out the sleeves. Two pairs of thong ties are sewn to the coat fronts.

Size: Length, 100 cm. Back of neck to wrist, 88 cm.

Sewing: Entirely with sinew, 24 stitches per 5 cm.

Colours: Very strong yellow for layout and for solid filling in some of background; red for drawing most of pattern; strong green.

Tools: All single prongs, A with yellow for layout, B with red, C with green and red. A stamp, D, with green for dots.

Tools

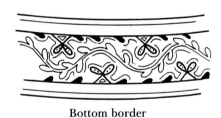

Bottom border

Bottom border: An undulating line, like a vine with small sprouts. The spaces created by the undulations are filled by pairs of motifs, possibly leaves. There are plain parallel lines above and below.

Central gore form: Curves and paired leaves grow up and out from a stem in the centre. The surrounds are parallel lines that follow the edge of the inserted back gusset accurately and terminate with the gusset in a blunt point at the waist.

Central gore form

Centre-back extension

Centre-back extension: A narrow vertical line with sprouts on either side.

Shoulders: Crossed by a horizontal band of small lozenges.

Collar: A folded band of hare fur, now completely missing its pelage.

Gore forms 1 and 3: Graduated compartments each contain a quatrefoil motif of leaves with jagged edges. The horizontal divides are small lozenges; the surrounds are simple lines that meet at the waist in a sharp point.

Gore forms 1 and 3

Front borders: An undulating line of dots coupled with upward-moving curves between parallel lines, strongly suggestive of growth. The parallel lines turn sharply, with the curves being replaced by small lozenges, and extend to armholes.

Sleeves: Three bands of simple parallel lines; no cuffs.

Outer borders: Red; narrow around coat, wrists, and tops of sleeves and across both back and front of shoulders.

Markings: Traces of red paint applied to side seams after sewing.

Shoulders

Front borders

51. Royal Ontario Museum, Toronto (HC.2254)

Man's painted caribou-skin coat
Probably Cree, northwestern Quebec, 1910–1912

Five coats, Nos. 47–51, were collected by Robert Flaherty during his journeys from Great Whale River to Fort Chimo between 1910 and 1912. They were given to the Royal Ontario Museum by Sir William McKenzie.

This coat does not have the same quadrate motifs or feeling of growth as No. 50, except for the sprouts on the surrounds of the side gore forms, but the quality of drawing and the colours are similar. It is most probable that this coat too is from western Quebec, close to Hudson Bay.

An intriguing and most unusual technical point is that much of the drawing has been done with a yellow line rather than the usual red. A similar use of yellow occurs on the coats in the very early group, Nos. 1–4, and is particularly noticeable on No. 4. Perhaps it is stretching connections too far, but, like the use of quadrate and growth motifs, this use of yellow may have moved up the western side of the province. The use of the circular sun motif in the central gore form strengthens that possibility.

Quality: Fair. Medium-weight skins with many fly marks; painting complex but crude.

Condition: Fair. Skins warped and soiled.

Cutting: Flare of 1:1.6. Three pairs of thong ties are sewn to the inside of the fronts.

Size: Length, 95.5 cm. Back of neck to wrist, 83 cm.

Sewing: Entirely with sinew, 23 stitches per 5 cm.

Colours: Yellow for layout and drawing of many motifs; red for some motifs and solid filling of background areas; green also for motifs and background.

Tools: Three single prongs, *A* with yellow, *B* with yellow and red, and *C* with green.

Tools

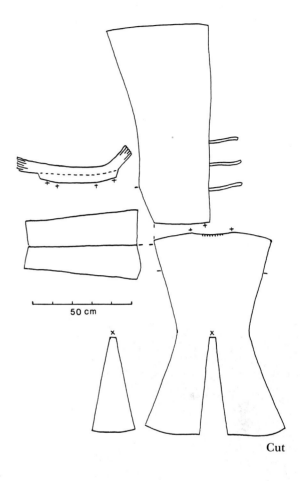

50 cm

Cut

Bottom border: A strong plain zigzag formed by a triple line with parallel lines above and below.

Bottom border

Central gore form: Graduated compartments each contain confused double-curve variations combined with circles and rayed circles. The motifs reduce to a diagonal-cross variation at the waist. The surrounds of parallel lines coincide with the edge of the inserted back gusset.

Central gore form

Gore forms 1 and 3

Centre-back extension: The parallel-line surrounds of the central gore form extend to the shoulder band and enclose six groups of triple horizontal lines.

Shoulders: Crossed by a band of track variation.

Collar: A plain band with the ends slashed into a coarse fringe.

Gore forms 1 and 3: Graduated compartments each contain confused zigzag variations and large dots. The surrounds of sprouting lines come together in a sharp point at the waist.

Front borders: A continuation of zigzags of bottom border. Below the neck the borders turn sharply, the zigzags changing to a row of lozenges, and extend to armholes.

Sleeves: Four encircling bands of simple parallel lines; no cuffs.

Outer borders: Red around coat and wrists.

Markings: Red; narrow on shoulder seams, armholes, tops of sleeve seams, and side seams above waist; wider across collar and neck; all applied after sewing.

52. Canadian Ethnology Service, Canadian Museum of Civilization, Hull-Ottawa (III B 574)

Man's painted caribou-skin coat, furred on inside and sewn closed in front
Naskapi, Labrador, probably Nain area, about 1908

This is an excellent example of the furred coats worn by the Naskapi men for the winter hunt. Survival of these coats is rare, but this one and No. 53 passed to a second owner, strangely enough a woman, and have been preserved.

The coat was purchased by the National Museum of Man (now the Canadian Museum of Civilization) with some other material, from Mrs. A. W. Wakefield, who supplied the following information:

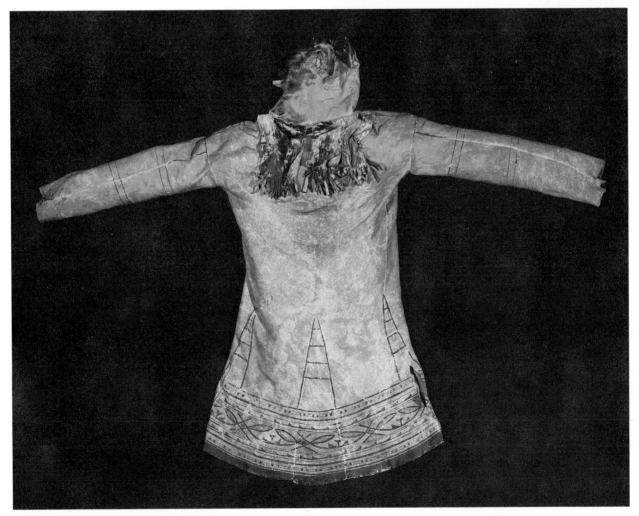

Made by Nascoppie Indian women, of cariboo skins and decorated with the traditional "Tree of Life" design. Bought for me by my husband, Dr. Wakefield, probably at Nain, Okak, — on one of his regular winter trips from Battle Harbour to Cape Chidley, in 1908–1909. I wore them on the coast during the winters of 1910 to 1914. They were all made by Indians north of Hamilton Inlet.

Dr. A. W. Wakefield was on the staff of the Grenfell Mission, which had its headquarters at St. Anthony, Newfoundland, and provided medical services to a long stretch of the Labrador coast.

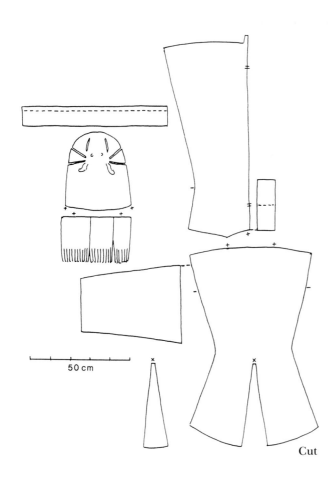

50 cm

Cut

Quality: Good. Very lightweight flexible skins; simple but well-designed painting.

Condition: Fair. Skins soiled; fur worn; some loss of paint.

Cutting: Flare of 1:1.5. A rectangle of skin is inserted into the front seam below the neck opening to give chin protection. At the bottom of the centre fronts there are short pointed extensions (see Cutting section for comment).
  The hood is made from a caribou head, fur side out, with small triangular darts taken in at either side to shape it to the wearer's head. The darts were cut so as to leave the cut-out triangles hanging loosely from their tips; no skin was discarded. The eyeholes were patched on the inside to close them; the ears and horn holes are open. A folded fur band with a drawstring through it was attached to the front.

Size: Length, 95 cm. Back of neck to wrist, 81.5 cm.

Sewing: Entirely with sinew, 18 stitches per 5 cm. The stitching was done as usual on the inside, even though it is the fur side.

Colours: Yellow for layout and background crosshatching; red for drawing motifs; laundry blue; brown.

Tools: A 3-prong, *A*, with yellow for layout. A 2-prong, *B*, with brown. At least four single prongs, *C, D,* and *E* with red, and *F* with blue and yellow for crosshatching.

Tools

Bottom border: The design, which at first appears to be a double-curve motif, is actually repeated interlocking scallops, each cradling a stemmed triangle between two wedge-shaped triangles, perhaps representing a blossom between two leaves. Above and below are lines of half scallops and double track.

On the diagram of the bottom border, the seams of the back gusset are marked with dotted lines. It is interesting to note that although the main border pattern does not relate to this spacing, the half-scallops both above and below it reverse from the centre of the gusset.

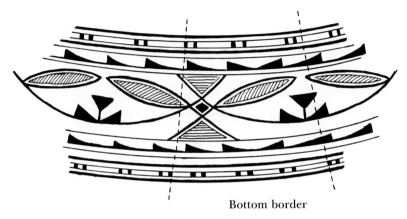

Bottom border

Central gore form: Crossed by four single lines. The surrounds are also single lines and follow the edge of the inserted back gusset closely. Both surrounds and gusset finish with a blunt point at the waist.

Collar: Made of several pieces of skin, furred on outside and slashed vertically into a sparse fringe.

Gore forms 1 and 3: Similar to central gore form but terminating at waist in a sharp point.

Front borders: Parallel lines enclosing a single track, turning below neck and extending partway to armholes.

Sleeves: Two pairs of parallel lines cross front face only; no cuffs.

Outer borders: Brown around coat, narrow in front, wider at bottom.

Markings: Red, rough, narrow; applied after sewing to shoulder seams, across tops of armholes, and on upper part of sleeve seams.

53. Royal Ontario Museum, Toronto (959.145)

Man's painted caribou-skin coat, furred on inside and sewn closed in front
Naskapi, Labrador, probably Nain area, about 1908

This coat was bought by the Royal Ontario Museum from Mrs. G. R. Younger, who was the daughter of Mrs. A. W. Wakefield, the owner of No. 52. The history is the same for both coats.

It is interesting that, because the coat tradition was so strong, these furred winter garments were not made like a parka, with the front a single piece. Instead the front skin was split in two as with the unfurred coats, both halves were seamed to the back, the painting was done, and then the fronts were sewn together again to make the coat warm enough to wear in the winter.

Quality: Good. Heavy furred skins; simple but well-done painting.

Condition: Fairly good in spite of the fact that the fur is shedding and the paint has been eaten by insects in some places.

Cutting: Flare of 1:1.6. A small triangular gusset was inserted at the top of the front seams to make passage of the head possible. The back gusset adds no fullness. At the bottom of the centre fronts there are short, pointed extensions (see Cutting section for comment).

The hood is made from a caribou head, fur side out, with a small triangle taken out on either side and seamed up to shape the skin to a human head. Probably the triangles of skin were originally left hanging as with No. 52, but they are now missing. The eyeholes are covered with small patches, the ear holes are open, and there are no horn holes. The front is edged with a band of fur threaded with a thong drawstring.

Size: Length, 107 cm. Back of neck to wrist, 80.5 cm.

Sewing: Entirely with sinew, 19 stitches per 5 cm, worked as usual on inside, even though it is the fur side.

Colours: Yellow for layout; two shades of red; laundry blue.

Tools: A 3-prong, *A*, with yellow for layout. A narrow 2-prong, *B*, with red for lines of track. Three single prongs, *C* and *D* with red, *E* with blue.

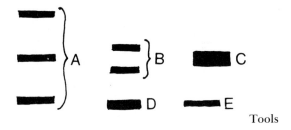

Tools

Bottom border: Large lozenges alternating with triangles, very similar to border designs on two earlier coats, Nos. 23–24; scallops and a line of double track above and below.

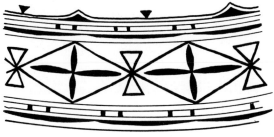

Bottom border

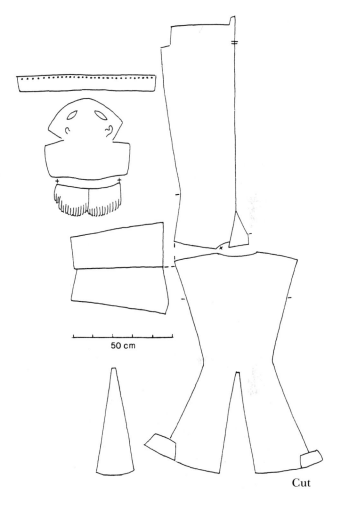

50 cm

Cut

Central gore form: Crossed by three double lines. The single-line surrounds follow the edge of the inserted back gusset exactly and terminate with it in a blunt point at the waist.

Collar: Furred on outside; coarse slashed fringe.

Gore forms 1 and 3: Crossed by three double lines; single-line surrounds meet in a point at waist.

Front borders: Parallel lines enclosing a scalloped line, turning below neck and extending about halfway to armholes.

Sleeves: Crossed by a single line just above elbow and another just below, on outer face only; no cuffs.

Outer borders: Red around coat; narrow down fronts, wider around bottom.

Markings: Red, rough; applied after sewing to shoulder seams, tops of armholes, and top part of upper sleeve seams. A short line crosses each shoulder seam at a right angle.

54. Canadian Ethnology Service, Canadian Museum of Civilization, Hull-Ottawa (III B 21)

Man's painted caribou-skin coat, furred on outside and closed in front
Naskapi, northern Labrador, 1921–1922

F. W. Waugh collected this coat in the interior, back of Nain, while doing fieldwork for the National Museum of Man (now the Canadian Museum of Civilization).

A rare and interesting piece, this is the only coat in this series that is furred on the outside and has a border design painted on the *inside*.[16] In the records of the Canadian Museum of Civilization, there is a note, presumably from Waugh, that this coat was worn fur side out with No. 55 (III B 20), which was worn fur side in. The two coats were collected together, but, as they both have hoods, it seems more likely that each of them would have been paired with a hoodless coat.

John McLean, in his *Notes of a Twenty-five Years' Service in the Hudson's Bay Territory*, when writing of the period between 1837 and 1842, gives a good description of this type of costume:

The winter dress of the Nascopie consists of a jacket of deer-skin [undoubtedly caribou is meant], close all round, worn with the hair next to the skin, and an over-coat of the same material reaching to his knees, the hair outside. The coat overlaps in front and is secured by a belt, from which depends his knife and smoking-bag.[17]

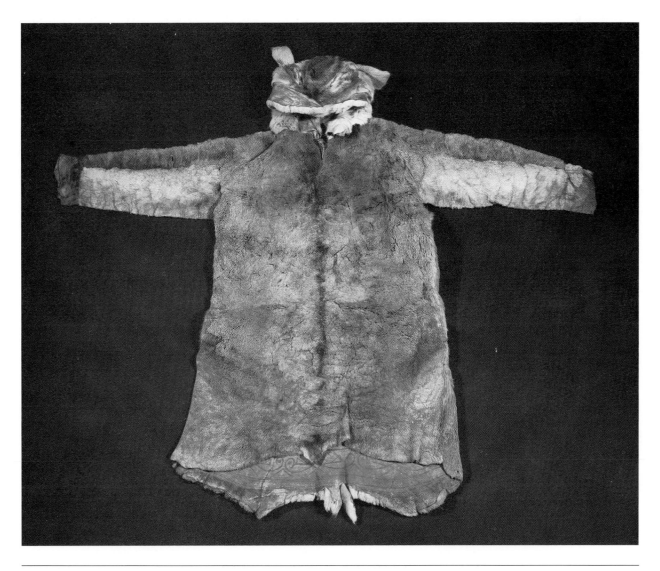

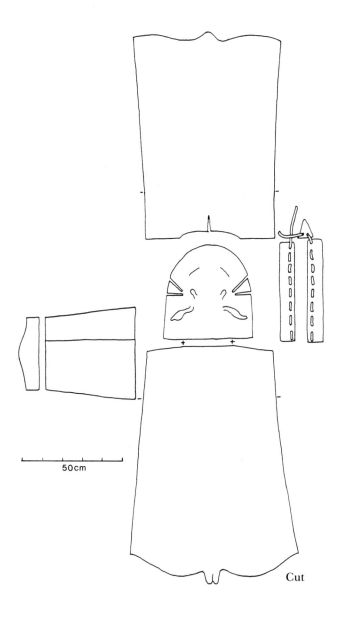

Cut

50cm

Quality: Good. Heavy skins, furred on outside; a simple painted border design on inside.

Condition: Good. Fur still thick; paint rather worn.

Cutting: Almost straight with a flare of only 1:1.15. The front is one skin and the back another, with no back gusset; both are used tail down with small tail-like extensions at centre bottom.

The hood is made from a caribou head, which appears to be part of the back skin but has been severed from it and then sewn back on. It is shaped to fit the wearer's head with small triangular darts cut out on either side. The cut-out triangles were left hanging loosely from their tips. The eyes have been sewn closed, the ears are open, and there are small horn projections. A band with fur on the inside has been attached to the face opening. It can be tightened around the face by a drawstring, which also runs through the small triangular gusset inserted in a slit at top centre front.

Size: Length, 108 cm. Back of neck to wrist, 85 cm.

Sewing: Irregular; some sinew and some cotton thread; loosely sewn on inside with about 18 stitches per 5 cm.

Colours: Yellow, now very faint, used for layout; red for drawing pattern; faint remnant of a blue line; brown for outer border.

Tools: A 3-prong, *A*, with yellow for layout. A narrow 2-prong, *B*, with blue. Single prongs, *C* with red, *D* with blue.

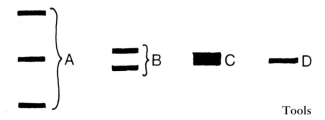

Tools

Bottom border: Double curves supported by diagonal crosses and surmounted by paired leaves; simple parallel lines above and below.

Outer borders: Brown and wide around bottom.

Markings: Shoulder seams roughly marked with red far up on inside of coat; applied after sewing.

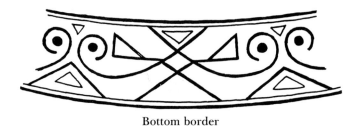

Bottom border

55. Canadian Ethnology Service, Canadian Museum of Civilization, Hull-Ottawa (III B 20)

Man's painted caribou-skin coat, furred on inside and sewn closed in front
Naskapi, northern Labrador, 1921–1922

See colour plate page 58

The history for this coat and No. 54 are the same. F. W. Waugh collected them in the interior of Labrador, back of Nain, while doing fieldwork for the National Museum of Man (now the Canadian Museum of Civilization).

The two coats were collected as a pair; No. 54 was supposedly worn over No. 55. Both coats have

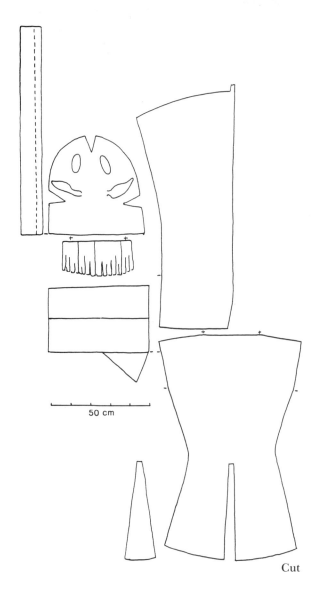

50 cm

Cut

hoods, however, and it seems most likely that each would have been worn with a hoodless coat.

The collars of the furred winter coats (Nos. 41, 49, 52–53, 55, 58), are all made of rather lightweight skin with fur on the outside, and they are pieced from narrow strips. According to Lucien Turner, the fur is from the cheek skins of the caribou; Turner mentions that the shape and size of these collars provided warmth and protection where it was most needed — across the back of the shoulders.[18]

Quality: Good. Excellent heavy skins, furred on inside; simple but good painting.

Condition: Skins and paint good; fur shedding.

Cutting: Flare of 1:1.6. The sleeves are very straight and narrow; the necessary width at the shoulder is provided by a triangular gusset at the back. At bottom centre front there are short pointed extensions (see Cutting section for comment).

The hood is made of a caribou head, fur side out, with short darts taken in the sides and down the nose to shape it. If the cut-out triangles were left hanging, they are now gone. The eyeholes are closed with cloth patches, and the ears are open. A wide band, furred on the inside, around the face, is folded back and threaded with a drawstring.

Size: Length, 112 cm. Back of neck to wrist, 86 cm.

Sewing: Entirely with sinew, with an irregular count of 15 stitches per 5 cm. The sewing was done on the inside, even though it is the fur side. The fronts were sewn together again after painting.

Colours: Yellow for layout; red for drawing motifs; laundry blue for details; brown for borders.

Tools: A 3-prong, *A*, with yellow for layout. A 2-prong, *B*, with red on sleeves. Four single prongs, *C* and *D* with red, *E* and *F* with blue.

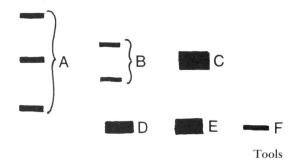

Tools

Bottom border: Two interlocking lines of scallops that form pointed ovals and lozenges alternately, with stemmed triangles at all junctures; parallel lines and double track above and below.

Central gore form: Three single horizontal lines. The single-line surrounds follow the edge of the inserted back gusset, coming to a slightly open blunt point where the gusset ends at the waist.

Collar: Furred on outside; slashed into a coarse fringe.

Gore forms 1 and 3: Similar to central gore form, with three single horizontal lines and single-line surrounds that come together in a sharp point at waist.

Front borders: Parallel lines enclosing long, simple, shallow scallops, turning below neck and extending partway to armholes.

Sleeves: Paired lines on outer face above and below elbow; no cuffs; skin drawstring threaded through wrist edge.

Outer borders: Brown; narrow down fronts, wider around bottom.

Markings: Red, rough; applied after sewing to shoulder seams, tops of armhole seams, and tops of sleeve seams.

Bottom border

56.   Royal Ontario Museum, Toronto
(958.131.630)

Man's painted caribou-skin coat
Naskapi, northern Labrador, probably about 1930

See colour plate page 58

This coat and Nos. 57–59 were bought by the Royal Ontario Museum from the estate of the noted ethnographer Frank G. Speck. There was no information concerning the source of the coats, but it seems likely that they were collected for Speck by Richard White in the Nain–Davis Inlet area.[19]

This late but very handsome example was made near the close of the period of the use of these coats.[20]

Quality: Good. Heavy skins with few fly marks; painting quite coarse but bottom border beautifully designed and strongly and skilfully painted.

Condition: Good. Skins somewhat soiled, slightly warped.

Cutting: A very slight flare of 1:1.4. The rounding of the neck is a late feature; the coat is quite short in length. There are points at the centre bottom of the fronts (see Cutting section for comment).

Size: Length, 93 cm. Back of neck to wrist, 75 cm.

Sewing: Entirely with sinew, 20 stitches per 5 cm.

Colours: Yellow for layout and background crosshatching; red for drawing pattern; laundry blue; brown.

Tools: A 2-prong, *A*, with yellow for layout. Three single prongs, *B* with red, *C* with blue, *D* with blue or yellow, for hatching and crosshatching. Two stamps for dots, *E* with blue, *F* with red.

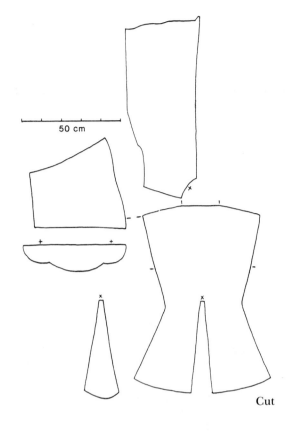

Cut

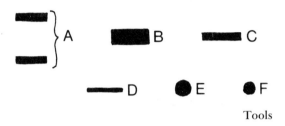

Tools

Bottom border: A very bold repeated double curve whose lines are doubled and enclose a row of dots; lines of scallops and half-scallops above and below.

Bottom border

Central gore form: Three horizontal lines of simple lozenges. The surrounds are bands of doubled half-scallops. The inner part of the form coincides fairly accurately with the back gusset.

Centre-back extension: A full wide triangle spreading out from waist towards shoulders, crossed by a line of scallop variation. The surrounds are a continuation of those in central gore form. The whole is topped by a line of single track.

Shoulders: A line of single track.

Collar: Bordered with single track.

Gore forms 1 and 5: Two horizontal bands with triangles. The surrounds of zigzags converge at the waist and then spread out again, stopping unfinished halfway to the shoulder.

Gore forms 2 and 4: Two horizontal lozenge bands. The surrounds of lozenge bands converge at the waist and then spread out again, stopping unfinished on either side of the underarm.

Front borders: A band of half-scallop variation, turning below neck and extending partway to armholes.

Sleeves: Two bands of single track, one above and one below elbow; no cuffs.

Outer borders: Brown around coat; red and narrow around collar.

Markings: Red, rough; applied after sewing to shoulder seams, tops of armhole seams, and tops of sleeve seams.

57. Royal Ontario Museum, Toronto (958.131.631)

Man's painted caribou-skin coat, sewn closed in front
Naskapi, northern Labrador, probably about 1930

Nos. 56–59 were bought by the Royal Ontario Museum from the estate of Frank G. Speck. There was no information concerning their source, but it seems likely that they were collected for Speck by Richard White in the Nain–Davis Inlet area.

Over the years the outline of the coats changed subtly, from a long elegant flaring shape to this almost windbreaker-like form. All except No. 59 have a piece cut out of the centre back with a triangular back gusset set into the gap. Usually this adds fullness, but sometimes, as with these late examples, it does not and it may even take away from the width.

But the tradition of that triangular back gusset is adhered to whether it is useful or not. The importance is not the centimetres of width it adds but the power that it gives to the wearer of the coat.

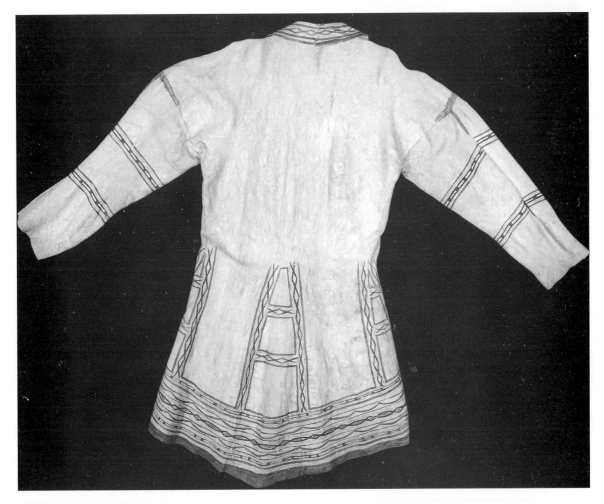

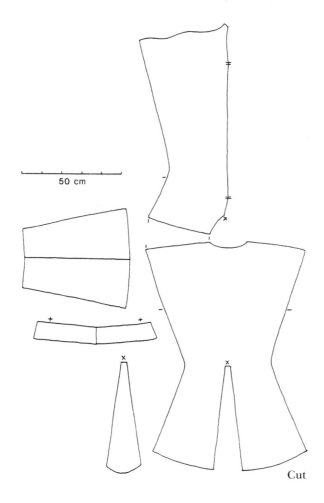

50 cm

Cut

Quality: Good for its period. Heavy skins with many fly marks; painting simple.

Condition: Excellent.

Cutting: Flare of 1:1.6. The neck opening is shaped, which is a late feature. There are slight projections at bottom of centre fronts (see Cutting section for comment).

Size: Length, 108 cm. Back of neck to wrist, 95 cm.

Sewing: Entirely with sinew, 16 stitches per 5 cm. The fronts have been sewn closed again after painting, a most unusual practice with a summer-weight coat.

Colours: Very strong. Yellow for layout and background crosshatching; red and laundry blue for drawing pattern; brown for outer bands. Blue and brown appear to be held in a medium more colourless than fish roe.

Tools: A 3-prong, A, and a 2-prong, B, both with yellow for layout. Three single prongs, C with red, D with blue, E with yellow for crosshatching.

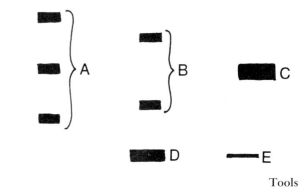

Tools

Bottom border: Two interlocking lines of scallops that alternately form pointed ovals and lozenges; a line of scallops and one of double track above and below.

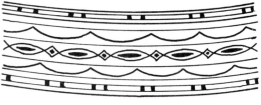

Bottom border

Central gore form: Two horizontal lozenge bands with surrounds of similar patterning. The inner part of the design fits exactly with the inserted back gusset; the surrounds terminate in an unfinished way on either side of the blunt point of the gusset.

Collar: A band of lozenges and, near neck edge, a band of double track.

Gore forms 1 and 3: Similar to central gore form.

Front borders: Lines of double track, turning below neck and extending a short distance towards armholes.

Sleeves: Two bands of single track, one just above and one just below elbow; no cuffs.

Outer borders: Brown; narrow on collar and down fronts; wider around bottom.

Markings: Red; applied after sewing to shoulder seams, tops of armholes seams, and tops of sleeve seams. A short line crosses shoulder seams at a right angle.

Collar

58. Royal Ontario Museum, Toronto (958.131.618)

Man's painted caribou-skin coat, furred on inside and sewn closed in front
Naskapi, northern Labrador, probably about 1930

Nos. 56–59 were bought by the Royal Ontario Museum from the estate of Frank G. Speck. There was no information concerning their source, but it seems likely that they were collected for Speck by Richard White in the Nain–Davis Inlet area.

This coat is similar to other furred coats but has the unusual addition of a beaded fringe, possibly evidence of Inuit influence.

Quality: Fair. Good, medium-weight skins; simple painting; beaded fringe.

Condition: Poor. Fur shedding badly; small tears at underarm and neck; paint very much worn.

Cutting: A minimal flare of 1:1.25. A small triangular gusset inserted at the top of the front seam enables the coat to fit over the wearer's head. At centre bottom on the right front there is a ragged bit of fur, which may be a remnant of the points that are found in this position on many winter coats (see Cutting section for comment).

The hood is made from a caribou head, fur side out, with the eye, ear, and horn openings sewn closed. In order to shape the hood, a small triangular cut was made in each side. The seams were sewn closed with the cut triangles left hanging above the little seam. One of these triangles is now missing. Around the face opening are two added bands that can be tightened with a drawstring. One has the fur side in; the other has the fur side out.

Size: Length, 110 cm. Back of neck to wrist, 95 cm.

Sewing: Sinew; some cotton thread; very irregular with between 15 and 20 stitches per 5 cm. The sewing was done on the inside, even though it is the furred side.

Colours: Yellow for layout; red for basic drawing; dark laundry blue for details.

Tools: A 3-prong, *A*, with yellow for layout and red in gore forms. Two single prongs, *B* with red, *C* with blue.

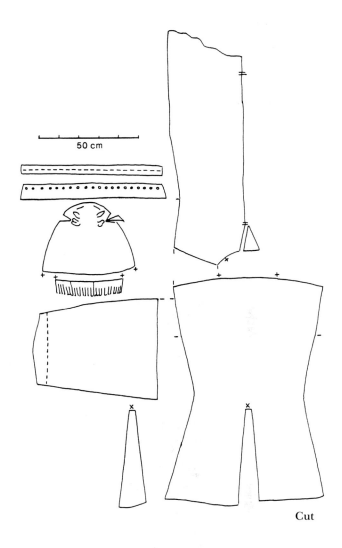

Cut

Tools

Bottom border: A repeated pattern of two wedge-shaped triangles with a stemmed triangle between them. It seems probable that this combination of motifs, which occurs quite often at this period, may represent a stylized flower between leaves. Above and below are parallel lines and a single track.

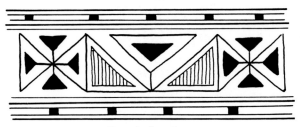

Bottom border

Central gore form: Crossed by triple lines. The surrounds, also triple lines, follow but do not quite coincide with the edge of the inserted back gusset.

Shoulders: No painted decoration; across back, a line of sparse beaded fringe consisting of glass beads strung on cotton thread with each string doubled back to form a loop at end.

Collar: Furred on outside; slashed into a coarse fringe.

Gore forms 1 and 3: Similar to central gore form but terminating in a sharp point at waist.

Front borders: A line of single track, turning below neck and extending partway to armholes.

Sleeves: A triple line repeated twice across front face only.

Cuffs: Simple turn-backs showing fur side of skin.

Outer borders: Dark blue around coat, a most unusual colour for this purpose.

Markings: Red, narrow, applied after sewing across tops of sleeve and armhole seams and on part of shoulder seams.

59. Royal Ontario Museum, Toronto (958.131.693)

Man's painted caribou-skin coat, furred on inside and sewn closed in front
Naskapi, northern Labrador, probably about 1930

Nos. 56–59 were bought by the Royal Ontario Museum from the estate of Frank G. Speck. There was no information concerning their source, but it seems likely that they were collected for Speck by Richard White in the Nain–Davis Inlet area.

It is an extraordinary chance that a coat so plain and of such poor quality as this one should have been kept and collected. It is important to this study because it underlines strongly the incredibly enduring traditions that were adhered to in the making of these caribou-skin hunting coats. The minimal decoration is in the usual places: bottom border, central gore form terminating in a blunt point at the waist, two side gore forms terminating in sharp points, and bandings on the sleeves. Although all the other coats in this catalogue have a back gusset inserted into a cut-out in the centre back, it was apparently not considered necessary with this very utilitarian garment. But the painted gore form simulates exactly the usual shape of a back gusset. There are no double- or triple-prong tools used, but the decoration is based on the use of parallel lines.

Another traditional practice, that of cutting the front skin in two and attaching the fronts to the back to make a single piece for ease of painting, has been adhered to even though it created the quite unnecessary work of cutting apart the fronts and then sewing them together again.

This coat may be a rather depressing end to a great line, but it is also fascinating.

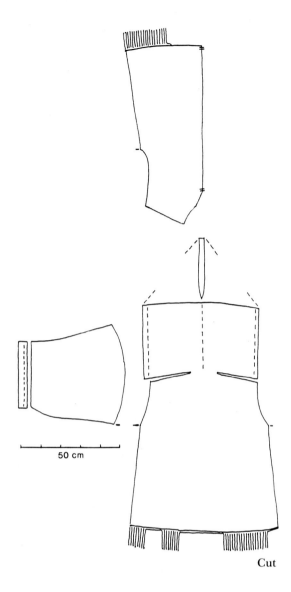

Cut

50 cm

Quality: Very poor. Skins much pieced; only token painted decoration.

Condition: Very poor. Skins torn and soiled; fur almost gone.

Cutting: Only the slightest flare of 1:1.2; no inserted back gusset. The hood is very simple, cut in one with the back, and has a band to lengthen it set in across the top of the head. An unusual feature is an added band of skin, slashed vertically to form a fringe, around the bottom of the coat.

Size: Length, 76 cm. Back of neck to wrist, 76 cm.

Sewing: Sinew except for front seam, which was sewn with heavy black cotton thread. Most of the sewing is on the skin side, the outside of the garment, and is rather uneven with 18 to 20 stitches per 5 cm.

Colours: Of very late type and not fast. Red for layout, now almost worn off; purple, which appears to have been made with something like an indelible pencil.

Tools: One single prong, *A*, with red. Probably a heavy pencil for purple line, *B*.

Tools

Bottom border: Sparse parallel lines in red and purple.

Central gore form: Two single horizontal purple lines with single-line surrounds that meet in a blunt point at waist, giving the appearance of a back gusset where none exists.

Gore forms 1 and 3: Similar to central gore form but terminating in sharp points.

Sleeves: Double lines above and below elbow on front face only.

Cuffs: Simple undecorated bands.

60. National Museum of Denmark, Copenhagen (1928. No. HI 1)

Man's painted caribou-skin coat
Naskapi, northern Quebec, Fort Chimo area, probably about 1926

See colour plate page 58

This coat was collected by Kaj Birket-Smith on the Fifth Thule Expedition. It was given to him by Captain G. Berthie, who was employed by Revillon Frères. The history is that Berthie bought the coat at Fort Chimo and was given the very interesting information that it had been made to wear at a special "mokoshan" feast.

The previous coat, No. 59, would have been a sad ending to our series. The thought to do honour to the caribou was still behind the making of the painted hunting coat, but little care was taken in carrying out that thought. This coat, made just about the same time, has the same thought behind it, and infinite care was taken to carry out that thought, but the use of the coat had changed. Men still dreamed about the hunt and how best to make it a successful one, and they still abided by the direction received in the dream. On this occasion the dream apparently resulted in a special "mokoshan" feast to be given before the hunt, with the hunter dressed in the best

possible coat that could be made to honour the caribou, which he hoped would give themselves to him. The coat was made only for the feast, not for the hunt.

Memory of the making of such an elaborate coat must have been almost gone by the time this hunter's wife produced her masterpiece. The double curves in the bottom border are traditional, as are the line decorations. Both were still being used on the simpler coats made for active hunting, such as Nos. 56–58, and on many smaller articles. It is in the patterning of the gore forms that tradition has been embellished on this coat. Very probably the maker had never seen a coat with seven fully developed gore forms of patterning—she knew only that they had existed and were filled with graduated motifs. Traditionally, those motifs in each area of patterning would have related to each other, whereas here the motifs are as various as the painter's imagination could make them. Traditionally, the horizontal divisions in a gore form are the same; here they are not. Traditionally, the gore forms are in pairs with similar motifs on each side of the coat; here they do not match. With all these departures from tradition it is fascinating that the shoulders have vertical bands similar to those used on the much, much earlier coats, Nos. 12–21. Memory is long, and this artist has dredged deep. This coat comes at the end of an era and provides a worthy ending for a great tradition.

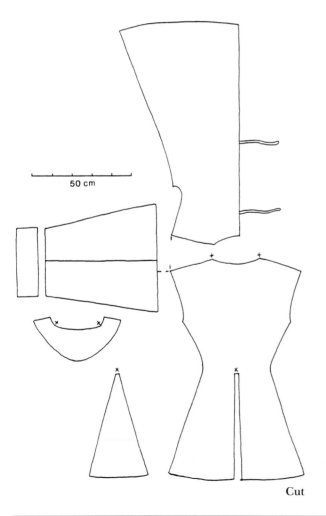

50 cm

Cut

Quality: Good. Skins excellent; painting elaborate but rather coarse.

Condition: Good. Skins supple and only slightly soiled. The appearance of the coat supports the probability that it was worn only once, on the occasion of the feast.

Cutting: Flare of almost 1:2. The neck opening and armholes have been shaped; otherwise the cutting is traditional. Two pairs of thong ties are attached to the fronts.

Size: Length, 100 cm. Back of neck to wrist, 88 cm.

Sewing: Entirely with sinew, 23 stitches per 5 cm.

Colours: Yellow for layout and for background filling of centre-back section; very bright orange and strong laundry blue both used for drawing motifs; brown for borders.

Tools: One 3-prong, *A,* and two 2-prongs, *B* and *C,* all with yellow for layout. Three single prongs, *D, E,* and *F,* with orange and blue.

Tools

Bottom border: Double curves above scallops with zigzags; parallel lines and narrow bands of simple motifs above and below.

Central gore form: Graduated compartments each with a different non-traditional floral motif; horizontal divides varied with combinations of zigzags and scallops; zigzag surrounds.

Bottom border

Central gore form

Centre-back extension: Graduated compartments with a variety of non-traditional motifs of same type as those in central gore form.

Shoulders: Both front and back crossed by a band with a single track and a line of zigzags; above, four vertical lines of single track running up to shoulder seams. This decoration is apparently a survival of the type of shoulder treatment used on much earlier coats, Nos. 12–21.

Collar: An eight-pointed rosette in the centre with a leaf spray and a four-pointed star on either side.

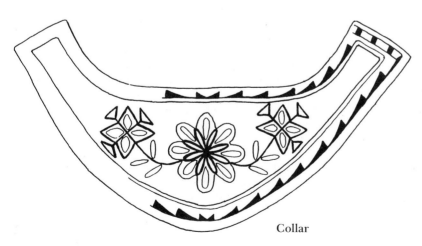

Collar

Gore forms 1 and 7

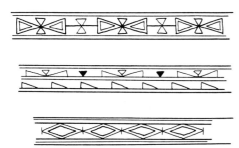

Sleeve bands

Gore forms 1 and 7: Do not match. Both have graduated compartments with different motifs of similar type to those in the central gore form, but double-curve variations are worked in with the floral designs. The surrounds, doubled half-scallops, converge at the waist and then spread out again in a fully patterned extension to shoulder.

Gore forms 2 and 6: Compartments with motifs of the same floral type as in central gore form; surrounds of lozenge bands and fully patterned extension to shoulder. As with gore forms 1 and 7, the motifs of the two sides do not match.

Gore forms 3 and 5: Matching; patterning similar to other gore forms; full extension to shoulder.

Front borders: Simple parallel lines.

Sleeves: Three bands of geometric motifs.

Cuffs: A small stemmed triangle between leaves, above paired wedge-shaped triangles.

Cuffs

Outer borders: Dark brown around coat, collar, and cuffs.

Markings: Orange, very light and narrow; applied after sewing to shoulder seams, with one small crossbar.

NOTES

Introduction

1. For background information on the area and its flora, fauna, climate, and history, and on the life of its native peoples, the following publications are interesting and useful.

Helm, ed. Various articles in this compendium describe the area.

Low, pp. 7L–19L. Low, in his report to the Geological Survey of Canada, gives an excellent listing of explorations done in the area before his travels of 1892–1895. In the pages following those cited, he comments on the climate, the botany, and the inhabitants of the area.

Tanner, Vaino. Tanner reports in a similar general way at a much later date (the 1930s).

Turner, Lucien M. Turner gives an excellent account of the geography and climate and of the material culture of the Naskapi in the Fort Chimo area during the early 1880s.

Hind; Hubbard. Travel journals such as those of Hind (1863) and Hubbard (1908), although they contain little information about the native people, provide a valuable picture of both the beauty and the ruggedness of the area in which the painted caribou-skin coats were made and worn.

Cabot 1909, 1912. These works provide general information and photographs of the country and its inhabitants during the early years of the 20th century. See Loring 1985 and 1987 for information about Cabot himself, an incredible and seemingly untiring traveller.

Speck 1977. The results of Frank G. Speck's many years of work in the area can be found in this very important book and also in his many articles.

See particularly Rogers 1963, 1969b, 1972; Rogers and Rogers. Although written after the painted coats went out of use, the papers of Edward S. Rogers, based on his fieldwork among the Mistassini Cree in 1953 and 1954, describe the surroundings and the traditional hunting lifestyle in which the coats would have been worn.

Tanner, Adrian. This book documents Tanner's fieldwork in the same Mistassini Cree area at a later date (1969–1970).

Henriksen. This is an account of Henriksen's life and travels with the Naskapi between 1966 and 1968 in an area north of that inhabited by the Mistassini Cree.

Fitzhugh, pp. 180–184. This work provides an interesting combination of archaeological, geological, ecological, and anthropological information.

2. Gardner.

3. See Tanner, Adrian, p. 141. Concerning his work among the Mistassini Cree in 1969–1970, Tanner says:

"the special coat or parka made of the skin of an animal . . . gives the wearer the animal's power. Today hunters no longer wear such garments." This statement is significant, for it indicates that even at that late date there was some memory in the area of a special coat worn for hunting. In the Catalogue of the present book there are four unusual coats collected by Lucien Turner in the early 1880s (Nos. 43–46) and two collected by Robert Flaherty about 1910 (Nos. 50–51), all of which probably originated in an area towards the east side of Hudson Bay.

4. Peterson, p. 332.

5. Banfield 1961, p. 73.

6. See Rogers and Leacock for Montagnais-Naskapi; see Preston for East Main Cree; see Mailhot for a fascinating discussion of the historic use of the names.

7. Turner, Lucien M., p. 103. Dr. Marguerite Mackenzie, Department of Linguistics, Memorial University, St. John's, Newfoundland, has kindly supplied the following commentary concerning the name Turner suggests: "Turner's 'Nenenot' is a local pronunciation of the term used by all speakers of Cree-Montagnais-Naskapi dialects to refer to themselves. The pronunciation varies slightly in accordance with phonetic rules, in different communities. Thus, in modern transcription, the same word appears as *iyiyu* for the coastal speakers of East Cree and present-day speakers of Naskapi at Kawawachikamach (formerly Schefferville), as *iyiynu* for inland East Cree, as *ilinu* or *ilnu* for speakers of western Montagnais (Betsiamites and Pointe Bleue), and as *ininu* or *innu* for all remaining Montagnais and Naskapi communities. A feature of Naskapi pronunciation includes replacement of *y* with *n* and of *n* with *y* in certain words. This phonological rule, along with an unsophisticated transcription system, accounts for Turner's rendering of *ininut*. The final *t* is the plural marker."

8. Speck 1977, p. 72.

9. Ibid, p. 80ff., gives one of the many versions of the story of the man who married a caribou and became "Lord of the Caribou." See also Speck 1985, pp. 61–67, for a very simple version of the same story.

10. Speck 1977 is basic for anyone desiring an understanding of the spiritual concepts of the area. See also Podolinsky Webber 1987, 1988a. I do not agree with Podolinsky Webber's very strong argument that the coats are of indigenous cut, showing no outside influence, but her papers are filled with an enormous amount of valuable information and insights concerning the important use of the coats. See also Henriksen, who postdates the use of the coats, but provides much understanding of the magic and taboos connected with the caribou hunt. See also

Tanner, Adrian, pp. 140–143, who says that decorative charms were worn to give power to the hunter and to show respect for the animal to be killed. He also mentions that special coats, no longer worn, gave the wearer the animal's power.

11. Henriksen, p. 51; Burnham 1981, p. 2.

12. Podolinsky Webber 1984, p. 116.

13. Financial assistance provided under the Cultural Property Export and Import Act of the Department of Communications, Canada, has made it possible for Canadian public cultural institutions to acquire many items of historical importance to the country. Some pieces have been brought back from abroad and some have been prevented from leaving the country. It is with this government help that coats Nos. 9–10, 23, and 28 are now safely in the collections of Canadian museums.

14. Podolinsky Webber 1988a. This work contains an introductory essay and a listing of 150 painted caribou-skin coats from the Quebec-Labrador area, with brief catalogue descriptions supplied by the various owning institutions.

15. During the early stages of this research, Harold Burnham worked closely with me. At that time we had not had access to any of the early coats with their extreme cut. We both felt that the more modified cuts of the later coats, although rather strange for a native garment, might well be indigenous. In 1968 Harold Burnham was asked to update the Denver Art Museum's *A Naskapi Painted Skin Shirt*, Material Culture Notes, Reports from the Ethnographic Laboratory no. 10, written by F. H. Douglas in 1939. He agreed to do so, and, on the strength of our research up to that time, he added considerable information to the original Douglas notes, including the statement that he felt that the Naskapi painted coat was an indigenous garment. Had Harold Burnham lived to see the further research that has been done since then, I am quite sure that he would agree with me that the Montagnais-Naskapi coat is not an indigenous form but that it is strongly influenced by contemporary European fashions.

16. Bradfield; Brooke and Laver; Yarwood. There are many excellent publications documenting European men's styles from the late 17th century on, but the changing silhouette can be followed easily in the works cited, which are illustrated with drawings.

History

1. See Burnham 1973 for enlargement on this idea.

2. See Duncan, see also Thompson, for Athapaskan costume. See Issenman and Rankin for illustrations of many types of Inuit garments.

3. See Brasser, catalogue entry 98, colour plate p. 54, for description and illustration of this coat.

4. An interesting comparison to this cut is presented by the earliest surviving North American garment, which is a shirt made of caribou skin that was in the Tradescant Collection in England by 1656; it is now in the Ashmolean Museum, Oxford. See Turner, Geoffrey, for diagram and description; see also Whitehead 1987, E 109, p. 36.

5. Champlain, vol. 1, p. 308.

6. The use of separate sleeves survived in women's caribou-skin garments well into the 20th century in northern Labrador. Two robes to be worn with separate sleeves collected by Robert Flaherty about 1910 are now in the collections of the Royal Ontario Museum, Toronto (965.1.13, HC 1917). The robes consist simply of two skins joined to make a tube, with ties at the shoulders. There are two similar women's robes and pairs of separate sleeves to go with them collected by Frank G. Speck at the Museum of the American Indian, Heye Foundation, New York (17/6570, 16/6752).

7. Champlain, vol. 3, p. 131ff.

8. Ibid. The glue mentioned would be the fish-roe painting medium that was used. It has a yellow colour and a hard shiny surface (see Colours section).

9. Thwaites, ed., vol. 3, p. 75. The reference to "elk" means "moose."

10. Ibid. In the English translation of this passage, the word *capot* is given as "cape," but a sleeved garment was probably intended.

11. See Gervers-Molnár for illustrations of the cuts of various types of simple warm garments of coat shape. See Burnham 1973, no. 15, for cut of a simple blanket-cloth capot. See Back; Beaudoin-Ross, for illustrations and discussion of the use of *capots* in Quebec.

12. Thwaites, ed., vol. 7, p. 9.

13. Ibid, vol. 7, p. 15.

14. Ibid, vol. 14, pp. 265–267.

15. Ibid, vol. 15, p. 223.

16. See Brasser, pp. 180–199, for illustrations of later presentation coats.

17. See Chartrand 1984, p. 37; Vachon, p. 310, for further information about this picture.

18. Surviving examples of early everyday clothing are very scarce. I am most grateful to Anne Buck, curator of the Gallery of English Costume, Platt Hall, Manchester, whose kindness, many years ago, made it possible for me to take out the measured diagram of the cut of this plain, but rare, woollen cloth coat.

19. Some twenty-five years ago Alika Podolinsky Webber uncovered this explanation while doing fieldwork among the Naskapi. She shared this information with Harold Burnham and me, and I have kept it in mind during the whole of this research. All the practical details of the coats reinforce the thought. She has now published this information in several of her papers; the reader is referred particularly to Podolinsky Webber 1987.

20. Cartwright, p. 251.

Caribou

1. See Peterson, pp. 330–334; Banfield 1974, pp. 383–388, for general information concerning the caribou.

2. The coin was designed by the Canadian sculptor

Emmanuel Hahn in 1937; he used the collections of the Royal Ontario Museum, Toronto, as a source of information.

3. I am grateful to the late Dr. Randolph Peterson, former curator of the Department of Mammalogy, Royal Ontario Museum, Toronto, and author of *The Mammals of Eastern Canada*, for providing clarification concerning the confused subject of whether the name woodland caribou (*Rangifer tarandus caribou*) should apply only to the more southern population or to all the caribou in the Quebec-Labrador peninsula. In a letter to me Dr. Peterson said: "In the last major systematic revision of the genus *Rangifer*, which includes both the Old World Reindeer and the New World Caribou, all taxa were shown to belong to a single species, *Rangifer tarandus* (Banfield 1961). In this revision he [Banfield] regarded the northern Labrador-Ungava population as . . . no different from the more southern Quebec and westward population of *Rangifer tarandus caribou*. Harper (1961) and others have pointed out that the northern Ungava population, living on the tundra and edge of the forest, have behaviour patterns quite similar to that of the Barrenland Caribou (*Rangifer tarandus groenlandicus*). In skull and antler size and shape as well as body size, it is a true 'Woodland' type although tends to be greyer in colour. If this population proves to be distinct from its more southern relatives, its name should be *Rangifer tarandus caboti*, see Harper (1961), Peterson (1966) and Hall (1981)." Further, Dr. Peterson suggested that in this study the northern caribou could be referred to as the "Ungava Caribou."

4. See Hubbard, pp. 160–165. Mrs. Hubbard gives a moving description of her excitement and delight when, in 1905, her party came upon a large herd of caribou and was able to observe the animals at close range. For those who are curious about Mrs. Hubbard's amazing journey, see the excellent article by Cooke.

5. See Turner, Lucien M., pp. 112–115; Low, p. 318ff., for descriptions of the hunt. See Cabot 1912, p. 239, for a description of some three to five hundred skinned carcasses of caribou drying on a beach in the sun, to produce meat for later use.

6. Turner, Lucien M., pp. 129–132; see also Speck 1937a.

7. See McLean, p. 262. Speaking of caribou skin, which he calls "rein-deer" skin, McLean says: "They have a particular art, too, of dressing this skin, so as to render it soft and pliable as chamois, in which state it becomes a valuable item of trade."

8. See Calef, p. 96, for a good description from farther west.

Cut of the Coats

1. See Conn, p. 81, for an excellent comment concerning the use of the word "tailored."

2. See Hatt; see Levin and Potapov. The many types of skin clothing covered by Gudmund Hatt provide no parallels for the shape of the Naskapi coats, nor do the garments illustrated in Levin and Potapov.

3. I am grateful to René Chartrand for suggesting the general influence that *capots* had on the development of the Montagnais-Naskapi painted coats, and also for pointing out just how close the appearance of the collar is to that of a *capot* hood thrown back over the shoulders. See Chartrand 1988 for information about the use of *capots* by the military in Canada well back into the 17th century.

4. Jane Sproull Thomson of the Newfoundland Museum, St. John's, proposed this possibility, with the additional suggestion that the projections may be a phallic symbol adding to the maleness of the coat.

Sewing

1. Turner, Lucien M., p. 87.

2. Harmon, pp. 202–203.

3. Currelly, p. 21.

4. Howley, p. 180; the same passage is quoted by Winter, p. 98.

5. See Such, p. 17, for mention of very fine needles of the Maritime Archaic period excavated at Port au Choix, Newfoundland.

6. The late Dr. Edward S. Rogers thought that a change to a smaller style of housing might be the answer. Valerie Grant, also of the Department of Ethnology, Royal Ontario Museum, Toronto, who has worked on the Labrador coast, suggested that the space restrictions might be due to the fact that the unfurred coats were made at a time when the winter snows were melting and dry working space was very limited.

Quill Wrapping and Beading

1. See Orchard, p. 106; Burnham 1981, p. 30, for illustration of the technique of bead weaving.

Layout of the Design

1. As stated earlier, Alika Podolinsky Webber has proposed, based on her extensive fieldwork in the area, that the triangle of the back gusset covered by the central gore form represented the Mythical Mountain where the Lord of the Caribou lived. The practical evidence of the cut of the coats bears out this thought. In her publication *The Naskapi Shaman* (1987) she adds to this interpretation of the meaning of the coat that the triangular shape of the central gore form represents the bottom half of a shaman's body, and the extension, with its inverted triangular shape up the back of the shoulders, represents the top half. When the shaman put the coat on, his own head completed the figure. This may well be, for the interpretation parallels those for other ritual types of clothing, such as Chinese court costumes (see, for example, Vollmer, p. 19). Undoubtedly these very special coats are a link in the circumpolar connection of such ideas, but it is beyond the scope of this publication to do more than suggest the fact.

Colours

1. Turner, Lucien M., p. 133.
2. Valerie Grant of the Department of Ethnology, Royal Ontario Museum, Toronto, by some magic means obtained the frozen sucker roe for the experiment.
3. For some years the Canadian Conservation Institute (CCI) in Ottawa has been carrying out research concerning the pigments, both native and imported, used on native artifacts made in Canada. In 1984 paint samples from four of the Royal Ontario Museum's Naskapi coats were sent to the CCI for analysis, and about the same time similar samples were sent from a number of coats in the Canadian Museum of Civilization, Hull-Ottawa. The results obtained from these tests have been used for information given in this section of the book. Paint from Naskapi coats provided only a small part of the CCI project, which involved over 1300 paint samples from native material originating in many parts of Canada. The CCI has now brought out a general final report and has sent individual reports to each of the museums that contributed samples to be tested concerning their material (Miller, Moffatt, and Sirois 1990a, 1990b, 1990c).
4. Low, pp. 64, 270.
5. This letter was received at the Royal Ontario Museum, Toronto, in April 1964, in response to an enquiry made by Harold Burnham. The letter came from J. E. McLaughlin, then sales manager of Reckitt and Colman (Canada) Limited, 2275 52nd Avenue, Lachine, P.Q.

Painting Tools

1. Information provided by Kevin Seymour, Department of Vertebrate Palaeontology, Royal Ontario Museum, Toronto.
2. Turner, Lucien M., p. 133.
3. LeClercq, p. 301: "[The corpse] is placed in the grave and covered with bark and the finest skins. . . . If it was a woman, her collar for use in dragging the sled, or in carrying wood, her axe, knife, blanket, necklaces of wampum and of beads, and her tools used for ornamenting and painting the clothes, as well as the needles for sewing the canoes and for lacing the snowshoes [were also placed in the grave]."
4. Podolinsky Webber 1968.
5. With the help of Peta Daniels, Department of New World Archaeology, Royal Ontario Museum, Toronto.
6. Gagné.

Design Motifs

1. Speck 1977, p. 198.
2. Podolinsky Webber 1988b, p. 30.
3. (Quadrates) These birch-bark bites are contemporary. They were made by a Cree woman from Beaver Lake, Manitoba, whose work was the subject of a special exhibition at the Thunder Bay National Exhibition Centre and Centre for Indian Art in 1983 and a catalogue: *Wigwas:*

Birchbark Biting by Angélique Merasty (Thunder Bay: Thunder Bay National Exhibition Centre and Centre for Indian Art, with assistance from the Ontario Ministry of Northern Affairs, 1983).
4. Davidson, p. 149ff. Winter, p. 100, quotes an early 19th-century description of Shananditti, the last surviving Beothuk woman, making a birch-bark bite: "She would take a piece of birchbark, double it up and bite with her teeth into a variety of figures of animals or other designs, that is to say when the bark was again unfolded the impressions thereon would be such."
5. Speck 1937b, p. 79.
6. A "Union Jack" motif similar to the one in the bottom border of coat No. 1 (see also the shoulders of No. 4) appears much later on the bottom border of a woman's painted caribou-skin robe collected by Robert Flaherty in northern Quebec between 1910 and 1912 and now in the Royal Ontario Museum, Toronto (965.1.13). The photograph below shows a detail of the border. Probably about two hundred years separate the painting of these two startlingly similar motifs.

7. (Double Curves) Speck 1914, 1937b, suggests nothing more than a floral connection for the double-curve design.

Podolinsky Webber, on the other hand, makes many references to the double curve and its meaning as male, both man and caribou. "These Indians traditionally painted a distinctive double-curve motif only on clothing and utensils that belonged to the males" (1982, p. 1). "For example, the double-curve motif is closely related to the sexual potency of man and of caribou" (1984, p. 102). "The Davis Inlet Naskapi very definitely interpret the double-curve motif to represent caribou, the animal important above all others to them" (1986, p. 16). "The double curve is a means for the Naskapi hunter to unite with his brother caribou. . . . [It] is not a static form the meaning of which is fixed . . . it is, rather, a dynamic symbol ever responsive to changing perceptions and to evolving interpretations" (1986, p. 20).
8. (Crosses) See Reid and Vastokas. On the cover of their exhibition catalogue, *From the Four Quarters*, an even-

armed cross with short crossbars similar to the small crosses on the collar of coat No. 1 is used as a logo for the exhibition.

See also Brasser, p. 23. Speaking about the large even-armed cross that spans the entire field of the magnificent Naskapi painted ceremonial blanket (Canadian Ethnology Service, Canadian Museum of Civilization, Hull-Ottawa, III B 588), Brasser says "Although it was the symbol of the Soul-Spirit, the Four World-Directions, and several other regional interpretations, the cross essentially symbolized the Omnipresent God — the Great Spirit — not in his remote and inactive position at the top of the cosmological pantheon, but as the Earthmaker. His representative, the Sun, is indicated by the circle at the centre of the cross; good weather was required for the caribou hunt."

See also Speck 1977, p. 115. Concerning crosses similar to the tiny one on the collar of coat No. 1, Speck says: "Besides this are seen the five orientated red dots so frequently repeated in the decorations of far northern North America, from the Cree to the Naskapi. These are generally admitted to be signatures of *mite'win,* or shamans."

9. (Crosshatching and Hatching) Podolinsky Webber 1984, p. 123, suggests that crosshatching may be protective nets "that catch illness."

10. (Diagonal Crosses) See Phillips 1984, p. 27, concerning the significance of this motif in the Great Lakes area: "Explicit images of Thunderbird families often depict the smaller figures as simple hourglass-shaped torsos. Although these forms would have been a recognizable shorthand for images of the manito to people within the culture, they are less easily read by the modern viewer." Brasser, p. 27, also mentions the hourglass form as being synonymous with the Thunderbird among the Sioux and Ojibwa. In those more westerly areas, the diagonal cross was shorthand for the Thunderbird; in the Naskapi area, it was shorthand for the double curve.

11. (Dots) See note 19.

12. (Growth Patterning) Dr. Edward S. Rogers, personal communication.

13. (Hearts) Speck 1977, pl. VI, shows a birch-bark food tray that has a series of "heart" motifs very similar to those on coat No. 43. Speck's caption states that the motif is "sun illumination," a revelation to the hunter, telling him where game may be found.

14. (Leaves) Deborah Metsger of the Department of Botany, Royal Ontario Museum, Toronto, checked many of the leaf motifs on the coats. Although most are too highly stylized to be recognizable, she suggested that the inspiration might be birch leaves for some; upland or small pussy willow leaves for leaves of broad rounded form like those on coat No. 16; small cranberry (*Vaccinium oxycoccus*), which characteristically has all its leaves protruding from one side of the stem, for the unfolding curves on the collar of coat No. 1; and sweet fern (*Comptonia*) for the leaves with serrated edges on Nos. 1, 5, and 50. She pointed out that the drawing of the small lanceolate leaves on coats Nos. 1–3 have surrounding borders that are very carefully drawn and suggest the inrolling of the leaves common to Ericaceous shrubs such as Labrador tea, sheep's laurel, blueberries, and cranberries.

15. (Ovals, Ovoids, and Pointed Ovals) Podolinsky Webber 1988b, fig. 16, illustrated a motif similar to that on coat No. 30, with information given in 1961 by Joe Rich, Davis Inlet, that the motif represents the eyes of the hunter "which look for game."

16. (Parallel Lines) See note 19.

17. (Stars) Speck 1977, p. 44, says: "A belief is evident that the souls of individuals become transformed into stars and rest in the firmament until they become reincarnated."

18. See Podolinsky Webber 1987 for pictures and descriptions of robes made for both shamans and boys.

19. (Tracks) Scattered through the literature are suggestions that the various types of line decorations, tracks, parallel lines, rows of dots, and other small motifs indicate either the tracks of hunters leading out from the camp and back with the game, or animal tracks, or even ways to reach the animals. The interpretations are all fairly vague, and, as is true for other motifs, probably only the owner of the coat and possibly the woman who painted the designs knew whether these small motifs had significance. Whether they did or not, they probably increased the power of the coat by the richness they added to the design.

20. (Zigzags) See note 19.

21. One of the coats collected by Lucien Turner at Fort Chimo between 1882 and 1884 (National Museum of Natural History, Smithsonian Institution, Washington, D.C., 90245) and not described in this series has an interesting later use of zigzags, with bands of plain small ones across the central gore form and wedge-shaped ones surrounding the side gore forms.

Catalogue of the Coats

1. (No. 1) See Brasser, fig. 103, p. 123, for illustration of trade shirt; see Burnham 1973, diagram 10, for use of small gussets to ease stress at neck edge.

2. (No. 2) I do not agree with Dr. Phillips's dating of this piece or with her statement that the painted designs were probably influenced by European textiles. I know of no contemporary European textiles, painted, printed, woven, or embroidered, that could have been used as models. The motifs used on this coat appear to me to be entirely of native origin.

3. (No. 3) I wish to express my deep appreciation for the help given by Dr. Hans Läng, curator of the Indianer-Museum der Stadt Zürich. Because of changes made in the gallery after the case containing this very special piece had been set up, it was possible to swing the front glass of the case out only a very short distance. With considerable physical effort, Dr. Läng managed to turn the coat so that I could see and photograph all sides of it. It was that effort that made it possible to present this description.

4. See Davidson, fig. 10, p. 128.

5. (No. 5) Thwaites, ed., vol. 15, p. 237.

6. (No. 12) Shirlee Smith, Hudson's Bay Society, in reply to an enquiry from Jonathan King.

7. (No. 14) Lefroy, pp. 159–160.

8. (No. 17) A coat with similarly simple and rather clumsy painting dominated by parallel lines and dots is in the Museum für Völkerkunde, Freiburg im Breisgau, Germany. It, too, was acquired from the Speyer Collection and has no known history. As the museum case in which the coat is displayed could not be opened, it was impossible to record the piece for this publication. The coat is published in Benndorf and Speyer (cat. no. 41, pls. 18–19).

9. (No. 18) Another coat with strong line decoration on the shoulders and many elements of patterning relating closely to Nos. 12–21 is in the British Museum, London (1921-10.14.112). It has good precise painting and most probably dates from the early 19th century. For lack of space it was regrettably not included in this catalogue. The coat is illustrated with a black and white photograph in Podolinsky Webber 1988a, pl. 119.

10. (No. 23) See Olsen, pp. 31–32, for dating of similar buttons.

11. (No. 28) A lavish use of this unusual type of leaf spray occurs on a coat in the Museum of the American Indian, Heye Foundation, New York (15/3165). It probably has an early 19th-century date comparable to that of No. 28. Regrettably, it is not included in this catalogue. It is illustrated with black and white photographs in Podolinsky Webber 1988a, pls. 71–72.

12. See Orchard, p. 106; Burnham 1981, p. 30, for illustration of the technique of bead weaving.

13. (No. 36) In the collection of the City of Bristol Museum and Art Gallery there is a second Naskapi coat (Ea 10397), which is not included in this catalogue. It is of comparable date to No. 36 and is a very handsome coat. There is a rather unclear photograph of it in Podolinsky Webber 1988a, pl. 129. It is known that one of these coats came from the Goldwyer Collection and one from William Lee, but it is not known which is which.

14. (No. 47) Flaherty, p. 99.

15. (No. 49) Turner, Lucien M., p. 123.

16. (No. 54) See Podolinsky Webber 1988a, pls. 47, 49, and 53, for black and white photographs of similar examples collected by Lucien Turner and now in the National Museum of Natural History, Smithsonian Institution, Washington, D.C.

17. McLean, p. 262; see Brody, p. 39, for a modern description.

18. (No. 55) Turner, Lucien M., p. 123.

19. (No. 56) See Deschênes for a full and interesting account of the work and writings of Frank G. Speck. Scattered through museum collections in both North America and Europe are other comparatively modern Naskapi coats that are similar to Nos. 56–59, in the Royal Ontario Museum, Toronto. Many were collected by Speck. They have not been included in the catalogue, as they would add little to the story, but a number are illustrated with photographs in Podolinsky Webber 1988a.

20. See VanStone, pp. 25–27 and pp. 99–105, for descriptions, diagrams, and photographs of coats collected by William Duncan Strong in 1927–1928 for the Field Museum of Natural History, Chicago. They bear many similarities to Nos. 56–57, two coats in the Royal Ontario Museum, Toronto, collected by Frank G. Speck.

LITERATURE CITED

Adair 1775
    Adair, James. *The History of the American Indians: Particularly Those Nations Adjoining to the Mississippi, East and West Florida, Georgia, South and North Carolina, and Virginia.* London. Reprint, with new foreword by Robert F. Berkhofer, Jr. New York and London: Johnson Reprint Corporation, 1968.

Back 1988
    Back, Francis. "Le capot canadien: ses origines et son évolution aux XVIIème et XVIIIème siècles." *Canadian Folklore Canadien* 10 (1–2): 99–128.

Banfield 1961
    Banfield, A. W. F. *A Revision of the Reindeer and Caribou Genus* Rangifer. Biological Series no. 66. National Museum of Canada Bulletin no. 177. Ottawa: Department of Northern Affairs and National Resources.

Banfield 1974
    Banfield, A. W. F. *The Mammals of Canada.* Toronto: University of Toronto Press.

Beaudoin-Ross 1988
    Beaudoin-Ross, Jacqueline. "The Influence of Fashion on Folk Costume." *Canadian Folklore Canadien* 10 (1–2): 79–97.

Benndorf and Speyer 1968
    Benndorf, Helga, and Arthur Speyer. *Indianer Nordamerikas, 1760–1860, aus der Sammlung Speyer.* Offenbach am Main: Deutsches Ledermuseum.

Bradfield 1959
    Bradfield, Nancy. *Historical Costumes of England, from the Eleventh to the Twentieth Century.* 2nd edition. London: George G. Harrup and Company.

Brasser 1976
    Brasser, Ted J. *"Bo'jou Nejee!": Profiles of Canadian Indian Art.* Exhibition catalogue. Ottawa: National Museum of Man.

Brody 1987
    Brody, Hugh. *Living Arctic: Hunters of the Canadian North.* London: Faber and Faber.

Brooke and Laver 1937
    Brooke, Iris, and James Laver. *English Costume from the Fourteenth through the Nineteenth Century.* New York: The Macmillan Company.

Burnham 1973
    Burnham, Dorothy K. *Cut My Cote.* Toronto: Royal Ontario Museum.

Burnham 1981
    Burnham, Dorothy K. *The Comfortable Arts: Traditional Spinning and Weaving in Canada.* Ottawa: National Gallery of Canada.

Cabot 1909
    Cabot, William B. Chapter 7: "The Indians." In *Labrador: The Country and the People,* by Wilfred T. Grenfell and others, pp. 184–225. Reprint. New York: The Macmillan Company, 1922.

Cabot 1912
    Cabot, William B. *In Northern Labrador.* London: John Murray.

Calef 1981
    Calef, George. *Caribou and the Barren-Lands.* Ottawa/Toronto: Canadian Arctic Resources Committee/Firefly Books Limited.

Cartwright 1911
    Cartwright, George. *Captain Cartwright and His Labrador Journal.* Edited by Charles Wendell Townsend. Boston: Dana Estes and Company. Originally published in 1792.

Champlain 1922–1936
    Champlain, Samuel de. *The Works of Samuel de Champlain, 1567–1635.* Edited by H. P. Biggar. Reprinted (from the French) and annotated by H. P. Biggar and others. 6 vols. Toronto: The Champlain Society.

Chartrand 1984
    Chartrand, René. *The French Soldier in Colonial America.* Historical Arms Series no. 18. Bloomfield, Ontario: Museum Restoration Service.

Chartrand 1988
    Chartrand, René. "The Winter Costume of Soldiers in Canada." *Canadian Folklore Canadien* 10 (1–2): 155–180.

Coe 1976
    Coe, Ralph T. *Sacred Circles: Two Thousand Years of North American Indian Art.* Exhibition catalogue. London: Arts Council of Great Britain.

Conn 1974
    Conn, Richard. *Robes of White Shell and Sunrise: Personal Decorative Arts of the Native American.* Denver: Denver Art Museum.

Cooke 1960
    Cooke, Alan. "A Woman's Way." *The Beaver* (summer 1960): 40.

Currelly 1956
    Currelly, Charles T. *I Brought the Ages Home.* Toronto. Reprint. Toronto: Royal Ontario Museum, 1976.

Davidson 1928
    Davidson, Daniel S. *Decorative Art of the Têtes de Boule of Quebec.* Indian Notes and Monographs vol. 10, no. 9. New York: Museum of the American Indian, Heye Foundation.

Deschênes 1981
    Deschênes, Jean-Guy. "La contribution de Frank G. Speck à l'anthropologie des Amérindiens de Québec." *Recherches amérindiennes au Québec* 11 (3): 205–220.
Deutsches Ledermuseum 1976
    Deutsches Ledermuseum. *Indianer Nordamerikas: Zirkumpolare Völker*. Katalog Heft 4. Würtzburg: Universitätsdruckerei, H. Stürtz AG.
Dickason 1972
    Dickason, Olive Patricia. *Indian Arts in Canada*. Ottawa: Department of Indian Affairs and Northern Development.
Douglas 1939
    Douglas, F. H. *A Naskapi Painted Skin Shirt*. Material Culture Notes, Reports from the Ethnographic Laboratory 10:38–43. Denver: Denver Art Museum.
Douglas 1969
    Douglas, F. H. "A Naskapi Painted Skin Shirt." Completely revised by Harold B. Burnham. In *Material Culture Notes*. Denver: Denver Art Museum.
Duncan 1989
    Duncan, Kate C. *Northern Athapaskan Art: A Beadwork Tradition*. Seattle: University of Washington Press.

Feest 1968
    Feest, Christian F. *Indianer Nordamerikas*. Vienna: Museum für Völkerkunde.
Fitzhugh 1972
    Fitzhugh, William W. *Environmental Archeology and Cultural Systems in Hamilton Inlet, Labrador: A Survey of the Central Labrador Coast from 3000 B.C. to the Present*. Smithsonian Contributions to Anthropology, no. 16. Washington, D.C.: Smithsonian Institution Press.
Flaherty 1924
    Flaherty, Robert J., in collaboration with Frances Hubbard Flaherty. *My Eskimo Friends: Nanook of the North*. Garden City, N.Y.: Doubleday, Page and Company.

Gagné 1986
    Gagné, Gérard. "Un pechahigan chez les Algonquiens de Sillery." *Recherches amérindiennes au Québec* 14 (2–3): 85–93.
Gardner 1981
    Gardner, James S. "General Environment." In *Subarctic*, edited by June Helm, pp. 5–14. Vol. 6, *Handbook of North American Indians*, edited by William C. Sturtevant. Washington, D.C.: Smithsonian Institution Press.
Gervers-Molnár 1973
    Gervers-Molnár, Veronika. *The Hungarian Szür: An Archaic Mantle of Eurasian Origin*. History, Technology, and Art Monograph 1. Toronto: Royal Ontario Museum.

Hall 1981
    Hall, E. Raymond. *The Mammals of North America*. Vol. 2. 2nd edition. New York: John Wiley and Sons.
Harmon 1957
    Harmon, Daniel Williams. *Sixteen Years in the Indian Country: The Journal of Daniel Williams Harmon, 1800–1816*. Edited by W. Kaye Lamb. Toronto: Macmillan Company of Canada Limited.
Harper 1961
    Harper, Francis. *Land and Fresh-Water Mammals of the Ungava Peninsula*. University of Kansas Museum of Natural History Miscellaneous Publication no. 27. Lawrence: University of Kansas.
Hatt 1969
    Hatt, Gudmund. "Arctic Skin Clothing in Eurasia and America: An Ethnographic Study." *Arctic Anthropology* 5 (2): 3–132.
Helm, ed., 1981
    Helm, June, ed. *Subarctic*. Vol. 6, *Handbook of North American Indians*, edited by William C. Sturtevant. Washington, D.C.: Smithsonian Institution Press.
Henriksen 1973
    Henricksen, Georg. *Hunters in the Barrens: The Naskapi on the Edge of the White Man's World*. Newfoundland Social and Economic Studies, no. 12. St. John's: Institute of Social and Economic Research, Memorial University of Newfoundland.
Hind 1863
    Hind, Henry Youle. *Explorations in the Interior of the Labrador Peninsula: The Country of the Montagnais and Nasquapee Indians*. 2 vols. London. Reprint. Millwood, N.Y.: Kraus Reprint Company, 1973.
Howley 1915
    Howley, James P. *The Beothucks or Red Indians: The Aboriginal Inhabitants of Newfoundland*. Cambridge. Facsimile edition. Toronto: Coles Publishing Company, 1980.
Hubbard 1908
    Hubbard, Mina Benson. *A Woman's Way through Unknown Labrador: An Account of the Exploration of the Nascaupee and George Rivers*. London. Reprint. St. John's: Breakwater Press, 1983.

Issenman and Rankin 1988
    Issenman, Betty, and Catherine Rankin. *Ivalu: Traditions of Inuit Clothing*. Montreal: McCord Museum of Canadian History.

Jesuit Relations: See Thwaites, ed.

King 1982
    King, J. C. H. *Thunderbird and Lightning: Indian Life in Northeastern North America, 1600–1900*. London: British Museum Publications.

Läng 1975
Läng, Hans. *Indianer Nordamerikas: Katalog zür Sammlung Hotz der Stadt Zürich.* Zürich: Schulamt der Stadt.

LeClercq 1691
LeClercq, Chrestien. *New Relations of Gaspesia.* Reprint. Toronto: The Champlain Society, 1910.

Lefroy 1955
Lefroy, John Henry. *In Search of the Magnetic North: A Soldier-Surveyor's Letters from the North-West 1843–1844.* Edited by F. G. Stanley. Toronto: Macmillan Company of Canada.

Levin and Potapov 1961
Levin, M. G., and L. P. Potapov. *Istoriko-etnograficheskii atlas Sibiri.* Moscow and Leningrad: ANSSSR.

Loring 1985
Loring, Stephen. *O Darkly Bright: The Labrador Journeys of William Brooks Cabot, 1899–1910.* Exhibition catalogue. Middlebury, Vt.: Middlebury College Press.

Loring 1987
Loring, Stephen. "William Brooks Cabot (1858–1949)." *Arctic: Journal of the Arctic Institute of North America* 40 (2): 168–169.

Low 1896
Low, A. P. *Report on Explorations in the Labrador Peninsula along the East Main, Koksoak, Hamilton, Manicuagan and Portions of Other Rivers in 1892–93–94–95.* Ottawa: Geological Survey of Canada.

McLean 1932
McLean, John. *John McLean's Notes of a Twenty-five Years' Service in the Hudson's Bay Territory.* Champlain Society Publication 19. Toronto: The Champlain Society. Facsimile edition. New York: Greenwood Press, 1968.

Mailhot 1986
Mailhot, José. "Beyond Everyone's Horizon Stand the Naskapi." *Ethnohistory* 33 (4): 384–418.

Miller, Moffatt, and Sirois 1990a
Miller, Judi, Elizabeth Moffatt, and Jane Sirois. "Native Materials Project: Canadian Museum of Civilization: Naskapi Artifacts, October 1990." Ottawa: Canadian Conservation Institute.

Miller, Moffatt, and Sirois 1990b
Miller, Judi, Elizabeth Moffatt, and Jane Sirois. "Native Materials Project: Royal Ontario Museum, October 1990." Ottawa: Canadian Conservation Institute.

Miller, Moffatt, and Sirois 1990c
Miller, Judi, Elizabeth Moffatt, and Jane Sirois. "Native Materials Project: Final Report, November 1990." Ottawa: Canadian Conservation Institute.

Musée de l'Homme/National Gallery of Canada 1969
Musée de l'Homme, Paris; National Gallery of Canada, Ottawa. *Chefs-d'oeuvre des arts indiens et esquimaux du Canada/Masterpieces of Indian and Eskimo Art from Canada.* Paris: Société des Amis du Musée de l'Homme.

Olsen 1965
Olsen, Stanley J. "Dating Early Plain Buttons by Their Form." In *Indian Trade Goods,* by Arthur Woodward, pp. 31–33. Oregon Archaeological Society Publication no. 2. Portland: Oregon Museum of Science and Industry.

Orchard 1975
Orchard, William G. *Beads and Beadwork of the American Indians: A Study Based on Specimens in the Museum of the American Indian.* 2nd edition. New York: Museum of the American Indian, Heye Foundation.

Patterson 1973
Patterson, Nancy-Lou. *Canadian Native Art: Arts and Crafts of Canadian Indians and Eskimos.* Toronto: Collier-Macmillan.

Peterson 1966
Peterson, Randolph L. *The Mammals of Eastern Canada.* Toronto: Oxford University Press.

Phillips 1984
Phillips, Ruth B. *Patterns of Power: The Jasper Grant Collection and Great Lakes Indian Art of the Early Nineteenth Century.* Exhibition catalogue. Kleinburg, Ontario: The McMichael Canadian Collection.

Phillips 1987a
Phillips, Ruth B. "Like a Star I Shine: Northern Woodlands Artistic Traditions." In *The Spirit Sings: Artistic Traditions of Canada's First Peoples,* by The Glenbow Museum, pp. 51–92. Toronto/Calgary: McClelland and Stewart/The Glenbow Museum.

Phillips 1987b
Phillips, Ruth B. "Eastern Subarctic." In *The Spirit Sings: Artistic Traditions of Canada's First Peoples,* by The Glenbow Museum, pp. 37–44. Exhibition catalogue. Toronto/Calgary: McClelland and Stewart/The Glenbow Museum.

Podolinsky Webber 1968
Podolinsky Webber, Alika. "A Painting Tool." *The Beaver* (autumn 1968): 24–26.

Podolinsky Webber 1982
Podolinsky Webber, Alika. *The Woman's Rolled-up Sewing Kit.* Victoria, B.C.: Private publication.

Podolinsky Webber 1984
Podolinsky Webber, Alika. *The Rod and the Circle.* Victoria, B.C.: Private publication.

Podolinsky Webber 1986
Podolinsky Webber, Alika. *Symbols of Breath.* Victoria, B.C.: Private publication.

Podolinsky Webber 1987
Podolinsky Webber, Alika. *The Naskapi Shaman.* Victoria, B.C.: Private publication.

Podolinsky Webber 1988a
Podolinsky Webber, Alika. *Naskapi Coats.* 2 vols. Victoria, B.C.: Private publication.

Podolinsky Webber 1988b
Podolinsky Webber, Alika. *The Sun and Its Containers.* Victoria, B.C.: Private publication.

Preston 1981
Preston, Richard J. "East Main Cree." In *Subarctic,* edited by June Helm, pp. 196–207. Vol. 6, *Handbook of North American Indians,* edited by William C. Sturtevant. Washington, D.C.: Smithsonian Institution Press.

Reid and Vastokas 1984
Reid, Dennis, and Joan Vastokas. *From the Four Quarters: Native and European Art in Ontario 5000 B.C. to 1867 A.D.* Exhibition catalogue. Toronto: Art Gallery of Ontario.

Rogers 1963
Rogers, Edward S. *The Hunting Group: Hunting Territory Complex among the Mistassini Indians.* Anthropological Series no. 63. National Museum of Canada Bulletin no. 195. Ottawa: Department of Northern Affairs and National Resources.

Rogers [1969a]
Rogers, Edward S. *The Naskapi Indians.* Chart. Toronto: Royal Ontario Museum, in cooperation with the Department of Indian Affairs and Northern Development, Ottawa.

Rogers 1969b
Rogers, Edward S. "The Naskapi." *The Beaver* (winter 1969): 40–43.

Rogers 1972
Rogers, Edward S. "The Mistassini Cree." In *Hunters and Gatherers Today,* edited by M. G. Bicchieri, pp. 90–137. New York: Holt, Rinehart and Winston.

Rogers 1985
Rogers, Edward S. Introduction to *A Northern Algonquian Source Book: Papers by Frank G. Speck,* edited by Edward S. Rogers, pp. ix–xii. New York: Garland Publishing.

Rogers and Rogers 1960
Rogers, Edward S., and Jean H. Rogers. "The Individual in Mistassini Society from Birth to Death." Contributions to Anthropology, Part 2, pp. 14–36. National Museum of Canada Bulletin no. 190. Ottawa: Department of Northern Affairs and National Resources.

Rogers and Leacock 1981
Rogers, Edward S., and Eleanor Leacock. "Montagnais-Naskapi." In *Subarctic,* edited by June Helm, pp. 169–189. Vol. 6, *Handbook of North American Indians,* edited by William C. Sturtevant. Washington, D.C.: Smithsonian Institution Press.

Speck 1914
Speck, Frank G. *The Double-Curve Motive in Northeastern Algonkian Art.* Anthropological Series no. 1. Geological Survey of Canada Memoir 42. Ottawa: Department of Mines.

Speck 1937a
Speck, Frank G. "Analysis of Eskimo and Indian Skin-dressing Methods in Labrador." *Ethnos* 2 (6): 345–353.

Speck 1937b
Speck, Frank G. *Montagnais Art in Birch-Bark, A Circumpolar Trait.* Indian Notes and Monographs vol. 11, no. 2. New York: Museum of the American Indian, Heye Foundation.

Speck 1977
Speck, Frank G. *Naskapi: The Savage Hunters of the Labrador Peninsula.* Foreword by J. E. Michael Kew. The Civilization of the American Indian Series vol. 10. Norman: University of Oklahoma Press. Originally published in 1935.

Speck 1985
Speck, Frank G. *A Northern Algonquian Source Book: Papers by Frank G. Speck.* Edited and with an introduction by Edward S. Rogers. New York: Garland Publishing.

Such 1978
Such, Peter. *Vanished Peoples: The Archaic Dorset and Beothuk People of Newfoundland.* Toronto: NC Press.

Tanner, Adrian, 1979
Tanner, Adrian. *Bringing Home Animals: Religious Ideology and Mode of Production of the Mistassini Cree Hunters.* Social and Economic Studies no. 23. St. John's: Institute of Social and Economic Research, Memorial University of Newfoundland.

Tanner, Vaino, 1944
Tanner, Vaino. "Outlines of the Geography, Life and Customs of Newfoundland-Labrador." *Acta Geographica* 8 (1): 1–907.

Thompson 1972
Thompson, Judy. *Preliminary Study of Traditional Kutchin Clothing in Museums.* Mercury Series, Ethnology Service, Paper no. 1. Ottawa: National Museum of Man.

Thwaites, ed., 1896–1901
Thwaites, Reuben Gold, ed. *The Jesuit Relations and Allied Documents: Travels and Explorations of the Jesuit Missionaries in New France, 1610–1791; The Original French, Latin, and Italian Texts with English Translations and Notes.* 73 vols. Cleveland: Burrows Brothers. Reprint. New York: Pageant, 1959.

Turner, Geoffrey, 1983
Turner, Geoffrey. "Skin Shirt." In *Tradescant's Rarities: Essays on the Foundation of the Ashmolean Museum, 1683, with a Catalogue of the Surviving Early Collections,* edited by Arthur Macgregor, p. 123. Oxford: Clarendon Press.

Turner, Lucien M., 1894
Turner, Lucien M. "Ethnology of the Ungava District. Hudson Bay Territory." In *Eleventh Annual Report of the Bureau of Ethnology, 1889–90*. Washington: Government Printing Office. Reprinted as *Indians and Eskimos in the Quebec-Labrador Peninsula: Ethnology of the Ungava District, Hudson Bay Territory*. Québec: Presses Comeditex, 1979.

Vachon 1982
Vachon, André. *Dreams of Empire: Canada before 1700: Records of Our History*. Ottawa: Public Archives of Canada.

VanStone 1985
VanStone, James W. *Material Culture of the Davis Inlet and Barren Ground Naskapi: The William Duncan Strong Collection*. Fieldiana: Anthropology, new series, no. 7. Chicago: Field Museum of Natural History.

Vollmer 1981
Vollmer, John E. *Five Colours of the Universe: Symbolism in Clothes and Fabrics of the Ch'ing Dynasty, 1644–1911*. Edmonton: The Edmonton Art Gallery.

Whitehead 1987
Whitehead, Ruth Holmes. "East Coast." In *The Spirit Sings: Artistic Traditions of Canada's First Peoples*, by The Glenbow Museum, pp. 11–36. Exhibition catalogue. Toronto/Calgary: McClelland and Stewart/The Glenbow Museum.

Winter 1975
Winter, Keith. *Shananditti: The Last of the Beothuks*. Vancouver: J. J. Douglas.

Yarwood 1967
Yarwood, Doreen. *English Costume: From the Second Century B.C. to 1967*. Revised edition. London: B. T. Batsford.

ILLUSTRATION CREDITS

We are grateful to the following for permission to publish their photographs. All the drawings and photographs not otherwise credited are the author's.

Erroll Bedford, p. 43 (centre and bottom)

Trustees of the British Museum, London: pp. 122, 123 (top), 145, 174, 204, 238

Canadian Museum of Civilization, Hull-Ottawa: pp. 6 (bottom), 17 (bottom), 18 (top)

Courtesy of the City of Bristol Museum and Art Gallery: p. 228

Deutsches Ledermuseum/Schuhmuseum, Offenbach am Main: p. 194

Glasgow Art Gallery and Museum: p. 207

Hunterian Museum, Glasgow: p. 104 (left)

Indianer-Museum der Stadt Zürich: p. 112

Metropolitan Toronto Public Library, Baldwin Room: p. 14 (right)

Courtesy of the McCord Museum of Canadian History, Montreal: p. 15

Musée de la civilisation, Québec: pp. 149, 190

Collection Musée de l'Homme, Paris: p. 120 (left)

Museum für Völkerkunde, Berlin: pp. 165, 197

Museum für Völkerkunde, Frankfurt am Main (Photo: Maria Obermaier): p. 171 (left)

Museum für Völkerkunde, Wien: p. 177 (left)

Museum für Völkerkunde und Schweizerisches Museum für Volkskunde, Basel: p. 168

National Archives of Canada, Ottawa
National Archives Library: pp. 7, 10, 12
National Map Collectiona: pp. 8, 11, 14 (left)
Reference and Reader Service Division: pp. 9, 16, 17 (top), 24

National Museum of Denmark, Department of Ethnography, Copenhagen: p. 297

National Museum of Natural History, Smithsonian Institution, Washington, D.C.: pp. 241, 244, 247, 249, 252, 255, 258

Trustees of the National Museums of Scotland: pp. 158, 224, 225 (top left), 231, 234

Newfoundland Museum, St. John's: pp. 184, 218

Estate of Randolph L. Peterson, Elizabeth Peterson, executrix: p. 21

Pitt Rivers Museum, Oxford: pp. 108, 116, 180

Collection Rijksmuseum voor Volkenkunde, Leiden, Netherlands: p. 142

Royal Ontario Museum, Toronto: pp. ii–iii, 2, 19 (top left and right), 31, 39, 40, 41, 45, 46, 47, 48, 50, 55, 60, 91 (right; top and bottom) 95, 103, 126, 129, 130, 134, 138, 162, 200, 203, 210, 214, 216 (top; left and right), 221, 260, 262, 266, 269, 272, 275, 278, 281, 283, 286, 289, 292, 295

INDEX OF THE COATS